YOUR MOST COMPREHENSIVE
AND REVEALING INDIVIDUAL FORECAST

AQUARIUS
1987
SUPER HOROSCOPE
JAN. 20—FEB. 18

CHARTER BOOKS, NEW YORK

CONTENTS

NOTE TO THE CUSP-BORN	iii
HISTORY AND USES OF ASTROLOGY	1
HOW TO USE THESE PREDICTIONS	20
THE MOON	21
MOON TABLES, 1987	
Time Conversions	28
Moon Tables	29
Planting Guide, 1987	33
Fishing Guide, 1987	34
Influence Over Daily Affairs	34
Influence Over Health and Plants	35
THE SIGNS OF THE ZODIAC	
Dominant Characteristics	37
Key Words	62
The Elements and the Qualities	63
How to Approximate Your Rising Sign	71
THE PLANETS OF THE SOLAR SYSTEM	76
FAMOUS PERSONALITIES	86
AQUARIUS: 1987	
Character Analysis	89
Love and Marriage	96
Yearly Forecast	125
Daily Forecast	129
November and December, 1986	228

THE PUBLISHERS REGRET THAT THEY CANNOT ANSWER INDIVIDUAL LETTERS REQUESTING PERSONAL HOROSCOPE INFORMATION

ALL RIGHTS RESERVED

COPYRIGHT © 1974, 1978, 1979, 1980, 1981, 1982 BY GROSSET & DUNLAP, INC.
COPYRIGHT © 1983, 1984 BY CHARTER COMMUNICATIONS, INC.
COPYRIGHT © 1985, 1986 BY THE BERKLEY PUBLISHING GROUP

ISBN: 0-441-79322-3

CHARTER BOOKS ARE PUBLISHED BY THE BERKLEY PUBLISHING GROUP,
200 MADISON AVENUE,
NEW YORK, NEW YORK 10016.

PRINTED IN THE UNITED STATES OF AMERICA

NOTE TO THE CUSP-BORN

First find the year of your birth, and then find the sign under which you were born according to your day of birth. Thus, you can determine if you are a true Aquarius (or Capricorn or Pisces), according to the variations of the dates of the Zodiac. (See also page 7.)

Are you *really* an Aquarius? If your birthday falls during the fourth week of January, at the beginning of Aquarius, will you still retain the traits of Capricorn, the sign of the Zodiac before Aquarius? And what if you were born later, in February—are you more Pisces than Aquarius? Many people born at the edge, or cusp, of a sign, have difficulty determining exactly what sign they are. If you are one of these people, here's how you can figure it out, once and for all.

Consult the following table. It will tell you the precise days on which the Sun entered and left your sign for the year of your birth. If you were born at the beginning or end of Aquarius, yours is a lifetime reflecting a process of subtle transformation. Your life on Earth will symbolize a significant change in consciousness, because you are either about to enter a whole new way of living or are leaving one behind.

If you were born around the last two weeks of January, you want to be free. You're committed somewhere because you want to be, not because some heavy figure stands behind you pulling the strings. You may want to read the horoscope book for Capricorn as well as Aquarius, for Capricorn holds the keys of many of your hidden uncertainties, secret guilts, subtle motivations and all your cosmic unfoldment from an occult point of view.

You are a person who will always break free from limitations or obstacles or break your leg trying.

When it comes to discipline you are ambiguous and complex. You need discipline to survive and succeed, but you openly reject it. Inwardly you find it hard to escape from the old problems of total freedom vs. strict routine and structure.

You have a grain of the conservative in you, a bit of the authority

CUSP-BORN

figure and a thirst for power you can't seem to shake. Yet peace is your mission and friendliness your purpose.

If you were born the third week of February you are either a mad genius or are just avoiding jail by the skin of your teeth. You may want to read the horoscope book for Pisces as well as Aquarius, for through Pisces you tap your talents and convert your assets into profit for others as well as yourself.

Your great love is ad-libbing, for there is no thrill like pulling something off at the last minute and *succeeding*. Your great successes come from last-minute reversals, unexpected turns of fate and the famous cavalry coming charging over the hill. You have the touch of the prophet—utopia with a touch of doomsday thrown in. When you are at your best you are being a friend.

DATES SUN ENTERS AQUARIUS (LEAVES CAPRICORN)

January 20 every year from 1900 to 2000, except for the following:

January 21:			January 19:	
1903	1920	1932	1977	1989
04	24	36	81	93
08	28	44	85	97
12				

DATES SUN LEAVES AQUARIUS (ENTERS PISCES)

February 19 every year from 1900 to 2000, except for the following:

February 18:				February 20:
1900	1954	1973	1989	1917
21	57	74	90	
25	58	77	91	
29	61	78	93	
33	62	81	94	
37	65	82	95	
41	66	85	97	
45	69	86	98	
49	70	87	99	
53				

HISTORY AND USES OF ASTROLOGY

Does astrology have a place in the fast-moving, ultra-scientific world we live in today? Can it be justified in a sophisticated society whose outriders are already preparing to step off the moon into the deep space of the planets themselves? Or is it just a hangover of ancient superstition, a psychological dummy for neurotics and dreamers of every historical age?

These are the kind of questions that any inquiring person can be expected to ask when they approach a subject like astrology which goes beyond, but never excludes, the materialistic side of life.

The simple, single answer is that astrology works. It works for tens of millions of people in the western world alone. In the United States there are 10 million followers and in Europe, an estimated 25 million. America has more than 4000 practicing astrologers, Europe nearly three times as many. Even down-under Australia has its hundreds of thousands of adherents. The importance of such vast numbers of people from diverse backgrounds and cultures is recognized by the world's biggest newspapers and magazines who probably devote more of their space to this subject in a year than to any other. In the eastern countries, astrology has enormous followings, again, because it has been proved to work. In countries like India, brides and grooms for centuries have been chosen on the basis of astrological compatibility. The low divorce rate there, despite today's heavy westernizing influence, is attributed largely to this practice.

In the western world, astrology today is more vital than ever before; more practicable because it needs a sophisticated society like ours to understand and develop its contribution to the full; more valid because science itself is confirming the precepts of astrological knowledge with every new exciting step. The ordinary person who daily applies astrology intelligently does not have to wonder whether it is true nor believe in it blindly. He can see it working for himself. And, if he can use it—and this book is designed to help the reader to do just that—he can make living a far richer experience, and become a more developed personality and a better person.

Astrology is the science of relationships. It is not just a study of planetary influences on man and his environment. It is the study of man himself.

We are at the center of our personal universe, of all our relationships. And our happiness or sadness depends on how we act, how we relate to the people and things that surround us. The emotions that we generate have a distinct affect—for better or worse—on the world around us. Our friends and our enemies will confirm this. Just look in the mirror the next time you are angry. In other words, each of us is a kind of sun or planet or star and our influence on our personal universe, whether loving, helpful or destructive, varies with our changing moods, expressed through our individual character.

And to an extent that includes the entire galaxy, this is true of the planetary bodies. Their radiations affect each other, including the earth and all the things on it. And in comparatively recent years, giant constellations called "quasars" have been discovered. These exist far beyond the night stars that we can observe, and science says these quasars are emitting radiating influences more powerful and different than ever recorded on earth. Their effect on man from an astrological point of view is under deep study. Compared with these inter-stellar forces, our personal "radiations" are negligible on the planetary scale. But ours are just as potent in the way they affect our moods, and our ability to control them. To this extent they determine much of the happiness and satisfaction in our lives. For instance, if we were bound and gagged and had to hold some strong emotion within us without being able to move, we would soon start to feel very uncomfortable. We are obviously pretty powerful radiators inside, in our own way. But usually, we are able to throw off our emotion in some sort of action—we have a good cry, walk it off, or tell someone our troubles—before it can build up too far and make us physically ill. Astrology helps us to understand the universal forces working on us, and through this understanding, we can become more properly adjusted to our surroundings and find ourselves coping where others may flounder.

Closely related to our emotions is the "other side" of our personal universe, our physical welfare. Our body, of course, is largely influenced by things around us over which we have very little control. The phone rings, we hear it. The train runs late. We snag our stocking or cut our face shaving. Our body is under a constant bombardment of events that influence our lives to varying degrees.

The question that arises from all this is, what makes each of us act so that we have to involve other people and keep the ball of activity and evolution rolling? This is the question that both science and astrology are involved with. The scientists have attacked it from different angles: anthropology, the study of human evolution as body, mind and response to environment; anatomy, the study of bodily structure; psychology, the science of the human mind; and so on. These studies have produced very impressive classifications and valuable information, but because the approach to the problem is fragmented, so is the result. They remain "branches" of science. Science generally studies effects. It keeps turning up wonderful answers but no lasting solutions. Astrology, on the other hand approaches the question from the broader viewpoint. Astrology began its inquiry with the totality of human experience and saw it as an effect. It then looked to find the cause, or at least the prime movers, and during thousands of years of observation of man and his *universal* environment, came up with the extraordinary principle of planetary influence—or astrology, which, from the Greek, means the science of the stars.

Modern science, as we shall see, has confirmed much of astrology's foundations—most of it unintentionally, some of it reluctantly, but still, indisputably.

It is not difficult to imagine that there must be a connection between outer space and the earth. Even today, scientists are not too sure how our earth was created, but it is generally agreed that it is only a tiny part of the universe. And as a part of the universe, people on earth see and feel the influence of heavenly bodies in almost every aspect of our existence. There is no doubt that the sun has the greatest influence on life on this planet. Without it there would be no life, for without it there would be no warmth, no division into day and night, no cycles of time or season at all. This is clear and easy to see. The influence of the moon, on the other hand, is more subtle, though no less definite.

There are many ways in which the influence of the moon manifests itself here on earth, both on human and animal life. It is a well-known fact, for instance, that the large movements of water on our planet—that is the ebb and flow of the tides—are caused by the moon's gravitational pull. Since this is so, it follows that these water movements do not occur only in the oceans, but that all bodies of water are affected, even down to the tiniest puddle.

The human body, too, which consists of about 70 percent water, falls within the scope of this lunar influence. For example the menstrual cycle of most women corresponds to the lunar month; the period of pregnancy in humans is 273 days, or equal to nine lunar months. Similarly, many illnesses reach a crisis at the change of the moon, and statistics in many countries have shown that the crime rate is highest at the time of the full moon. Even human sexual desire has been associated with the phases of the moon. But, it is in the movement of the tides that we get the clearest demonstration of planetary influence, and the irresistible correspondence between the so-called metaphysical and the physical.

Tide tables are prepared years in advance by calculating the future positions of the moon. Science has known for a long time that the moon is the main cause of tidal action. But only in the last few years has it begun to realize the possible extent of this influence on mankind. To begin with, the ocean tides do not rise and fall as we might imagine from our personal observations of them. The moon as it orbits around the earth, sets up a circular wave of attraction which pulls the oceans of the world after it, broadly in an east to west direction. This influence is like a phantom wave crest, a loop of power stretching from pole to pole which passes over and around the earth like an invisible shadow. It travels with equal effect across the land masses and, as scientists were recently amazed to observe, caused oysters placed in the dark in the middle of the United States where there is no sea, to open their shells to receive the non-existent tide. If the land-locked oysters react to this invisible signal, what effect does it have on us who not so long ago in evolutionary time, came out of the sea and still have its salt in our blood and sweat?

Less well known is the fact that the moon is also the primary force behind the circulation of blood in human beings and animals, and the movement of sap in trees and plants. Agriculturists have established that the moon has a distinct influence on crops, which explains why for centuries people have planted according to moon cycles. The habits of many animals, too, are directed by the movement of the moon. Migratory birds, for instance, depart only at or near the time of the full moon. Just as certain fish, eels in particular, move only in accordance with certain phases of the moon.

Know Thyself—Why?

In today's fast-changing world, everyone still longs to know what the future holds. It is the one thing that everyone has in common: rich and poor, famous and infamous, all are deeply concerned about tomorrow.

But the key to the future, as every historian knows, lies in the past. This is as true of individual people as it is of nations. You cannot understand your future without first understanding your past, which is simply another way of saying that you must first of all know yourself.

The motto "know thyself" seems obvious enough nowadays, but it was originally put forward as the foundation of wisdom by the ancient Greek philosophers. It was then adopted by the "mystery religions" of the ancient Middle East, Greece and Rome, and is still used in all genuine schools of mind training or mystical discipline, both in those of the East, based on yoga, and those of the West. So it is universally accepted now, and has been through the ages.

But how do you go about discovering what sort of person you are? The first step is usually classification into some sort of system of types. Astrology did this long before the birth of Christ. Psychology has also done it. So has modern medicine, in its way.

One system classifies men according to the source of the impulses they respond to most readily: the muscles, leading to direct bodily action; the digestive organs, resulting in emotion, or the brain and nerves. Another such system says that character is determined by the endocrine glands, and gives us labels like "pituitary," "thyroid" and "hyperthyroid" types. These different systems are neither contradictory nor mutually exclusive. In fact, they are very often different ways of saying the same thing.

Very popular and useful classifications were devised by Dr. C. G. Jung, the eminent disciple of Freud. Jung observed among the different faculties of the mind, four which have a predominant influence on character. These four faculties exist in all of us without exception, but not in perfect balance. So when we say, for instance, that a man is a "thinking type," it means that in any situation he tries to be rational. It follows that emotion, which some say is the opposite of thinking, will be his weakest function. This type can be sensible and reasonable, or calculating and unsympathetic. The emotional type, on the other hand, can often be recognized by exaggerated language—everything is either marvelous or terrible—and in extreme cases they even invent dramas and quarrels out of nothing just to make life more interesting.

The other two faculties are intuition and physical sensation. The sensation type does not only care for food and drink, nice clothes and furniture; he is also interested in all forms of physical experience. Many scientists are sensation types as are athletes and nature-lovers. Like sensation, intuition is a form of perception and we all possess it. But it works through that part of the mind which is not under conscious control—consequently it sees meanings and connections which are not obvious to thought or emotion. Inventors and original thinkers are always intuitive, but so, too, are superstitious people who see meanings where none exist.

Thus, sensation tells us what is going on in the world, feeling (that is, emotion) tells us how important it is to ourselves, thinking enables us to interpret it and work out what we should do about it, and intuition tells us what it means to ourselves and others. All four faculties are essential, and all are present in every one of us. But some people are guided chiefly by one, others by another.

Besides these four types, Jung observed a division into extrovert and introvert, which cuts across them. By and large, the introvert is one who finds truth inside himself rather than outside. He is not, therefore, ideally suited to a religion or a political party which tells him what to believe. Original thinkers are almost necessarily introverts. The extrovert, on the other hand, finds truth coming to him from outside. He believes in experts and authorities, and wants to think that nature and the laws of nature really exists, that they are what they appear to be and not just generalities made by men.

A disadvantage of all these systems of classification, is that one cannot tell very easily where to place oneself. Some people are reluctant to admit that they act to please their emotions. So they deceive themselves for years by trying to belong to whichever type they think is the "best." Of course, there is no best; each has its faults and each has its good points.

The advantage of the signs of the Zodiac is that they simplify classification. Not only that, but your date of birth is personal—it is unarguably yours. What better way to know yourself than by going back as far as possible to the very moment of your birth? And this is precisely what your horoscope is all about.

What Is a Horoscope?

If you had been able to take a picture of the heavens at the moment of your birth, that photograph would be your horoscope. Lacking such a snapshot, it is still possible to recreate the picture—and this is at the basis of the astrologer's art. In other words, your horoscope is a representation of the skies with the planets in the exact positions they occupied at the time you were born.

This information, of course, is not enough for the astrologer. He has to have a background of significance to put the photograph on. You will get the idea if you imagine two balls—one inside the other. The inner one is transparent. In the center of both is the astrologer, able to look up, down and around in all directions. The outer sphere is the Zodiac which is divided into twelve approximately equal segments, like the segments of an orange. The inner ball is our photograph. It is transparent except for the images of the planets. Looking out from the center, the astrologer sees the planets in various segments of the Zodiac. These twelve segments are known as the signs or houses.

The position of the planets when each of us is born is always different. So the photograph is always different. But the Zodiac and its signs are fixed.

Now, where in all this are you, the subject of the horoscope?

HISTORY / 7

You, or your character, is largely determined by the sign the sun is in. So that is where the astrologer looks first in your horoscope.

There are twelve signs in the Zodiac and the sun spends approximately one month in each. As the sun's motion is almost perfectly regular, the astrologers have been able to fix the dates governing each sign. There are not many people who do not know which sign of the Zodiac they were born under or who have not been amazed at some time or other at the accuracy of the description of their own character. Here are the twelve signs, the ancient zodiacal symbol, and their dates for the year 1987.*

ARIES	Ram	March 20–April 20
TAURUS	Bull	April 20–May 21
GEMINI	Twins	May 21–June 21
CANCER	Crab	June 21–July 23
LEO	Lion	July 23–August 23
VIRGO	Virgin	August 23–September 23
LIBRA	Scales	September 23–October 23
SCORPIO	Scorpion	October 23–November 22
SAGITTARIUS	Archer	November 22–December 22
CAPRICORN	Sea-Goat	December 22–January 20
AQUARIUS	Water-Bearer	January 20–February 18
PISCES	Fish	February 18–March 20

The time of birth—apart from the date—is important in advanced astrology because the planets travel at such great speed that the patterns they form change from minute to minute. For this reason, each person's horoscope is his and his alone. Further on we will see that the practicing astrologer has ways of determining and reading these minute time changes which dictate the finger character differences in us all.

However, it is still possible to draw significant conclusions and make meaningful predictions based simply on the sign of the Zodiac a person is born under. In a horoscope, the signs do not necessarily correspond with the divisions of the houses. It could be that a house begins half way across a sign. It is the interpretation of such combinations of different influences that distinguishes the professional astrologer from the student and the follower.

However, to gain a workable understanding of astrology, it is not necessary to go into great detail. In fact, the beginner is likely to find himself confused if he attempts to absorb too much too quickly. It should be remembered that this is a science and to become proficient at it, and especially to grasp the tremendous scope of possibilities in man and his affairs and direct them into a worthwhile reading, takes a great deal of study and experience.

*These dates are fluid and change with the motion of the Earth from year to year.

If you do intend to pursue it seriously you will have to learn to figure the exact moment of birth against the degrees of longitude and latitude of the planets at that precise time. This involves adapting local time to Greenwich Mean Time (G.M.T.), reference to tables of houses to establish the Ascendant, as well as making calculations from Ephemeris—the tables of the planets' positions.

After reading this introduction, try drawing up a rough horoscope to get the "feel" of reading some elementary characteristics and natal influences.

Draw a circle with twelve equal segments. Write in counterclockwise the names of the signs—Aries, Taurus, Gemini etc.— one for each segment. Look up an ephemeris for the year of the person's birth and note down the sign each planet was in on the birthday. Do not worry about the number of degrees (although if a planet is on the edge of a sign its position obviously should be considered). Write the name of the planet in the segment/sign on your chart. Write the number 1 in the sign where the sun is. This is the first house. Number the rest of the houses, counterclockwise till you finish at 12. Now you can investigate the probable basic expectation of experience of the person concerned. This is done first of all by seeing what planet or planets is/are in what sign and house. (See also page 72.)

The 12 houses control these functions:

1st.	Individuality, body appearance, general outlook on life	(Personality house)
2nd.	Finance, business	(Money house)
3rd.	Relatives, education, correspondence	(Relatives house)
4th.	Family, neighbors	(Home house)
5th.	Pleasure, children, attempts, entertainment	(Pleasure house)
6th.	Health, employees	(Health house)
7th.	Marriage, partnerships	(Marriage house)
8th.	Death, secret deals, difficulties	(Death house)
9th.	Travel, intellectual affairs	(Travel house)
10th.	Ambition, social standing	(Business and Honor house)
11th.	Friendship, social life, luck	(Friends house)
12th.	Troubles, illness, loss	(Trouble house)

The characteristics of the planets modify the influence of the Sun according to their natures and strengths.

Sun: Source of life. Basic temperament according to sun sign. The will.
Moon: Superficial nature. Moods. Changeable. Adaptive. Mother.
Mercury: Communication. Intellect. Reasoning power. Curiosity. Short travels.
Venus: Love. Delight. Art. Beautiful possessions.
Mars: Energy. Initiative. War. Anger. Destruction. Impulse.
Jupiter: Good. Generous. Expansive. Opportunities. Protection.
Saturn: Jupiter's opposite. Contraction. Servant. Delay. Hardwork. Cold. Privation. Research. Lasting rewards after long struggle.
Uranus: Fashion. Electricity. Revolution. Sudden changes. Modern science.
Neptune: Sensationalism. Mass emotion. Devastation. Delusion.
Pluto: Creates and destroys. Lust for power. Strong obsessions.

Superimpose the characteristics of the planets on the functions of the house in which they appear. Express the result through the character of the birth (sun) sign, and you will get the basic idea of how astrology works.

Of course, many other considerations have been taken into account in producing the carefully worked out predictions in this book: The aspects of the planets to each other; their strength according to position and sign; whether they are in a house of exaltation or decline; whether they are natural enemies or not; whether a planet occupies his own sign; the position of a planet in relation to its own house or sign; whether the planet is male, female or neuter; whether the sign is a fire, earth, water or air sign. These are only a few of the colors on the astrologer's pallet which he must mix with the inspiration of the artist and the accuracy of the mathematician.

The Problem of Love

Love, of course, is never a problem. The problem lies in recognizing the difference between infatuation, emotion, sex and, sometimes, the downright deceit of the other person. Mankind, with its record of broken marriages, despair and disillusionment, is obviously not very good at making these distinctions.

Can astrology help?

Yes. In the same way that advance knowledge can usually help in any human situation. And there is probably no situation as human, as poignant, as pathetic and universal, as the failure of man's love.

Love, of course, is not just between man and woman. It involves love of children, parents, home and so on. But the big problems usually involve the choice of partner.

Astrology has established degrees of compatibility that exist between people born under the various signs of the Zodiac. Because people are individuals, there are numerous variations and modifications and the astrologer, when approached on mate and marriage matters makes allowances for them. But the fact remains that some groups of people are suited for each other and some are not and astrology has expressed this in terms of characteristics which all can study and use as a personal guide.

No matter how much enjoyment and pleasure we find in the different aspects of each other's character, if it is not an overall compatibility, the chances of our finding fulfillment or enduring happiness in each other are pretty hopeless. And astrology can help us to find someone compatible.

History of Astrology

The origins of astrology have been lost far back in history, but we do know that reference is made to it as far back as the first written records of the human race. It is not hard to see why. Even in primitive times, people must have looked for an explanation for the various happenings in their lives. They must have wanted to know why people were different from one to another. And in their search they turned to the regular movements of the sun, moon and stars to see if they could provide an answer.

It is interesting to note that as soon as man learned to use his tools in any type of design, or his mind in any kind of calculation, he turned his attention to the heavens. Ancient cave dwellings reveal dim crescents and circles representative of the sun and moon, rulers of day and night. Mesopotamia and the civilization of Chaldea, in itself the foundation of those of Babylonia and Assyria, show a complete picture of astronomical observation and well-developed astrological interpretation.

Humanity has a natural instinct for order. The study of anthropology reveals that primitive people—even as far back as prehistoric times—were striving to achieve a certain order in their lives. They tried to organize the apparent chaos of the universe. They had the desire to attach meaning to things. This demand for order has persisted throughout the history of man. So that observing the regularity of the heavenly bodies made it logical that primitive peoples should turn heavenwards in their search for an understanding of the world in which they found themselves so random and alone.

And they did find a significance in the movements of the stars. Shepherds tending their flocks, for instance, observed that when the cluster of stars now known as the constellation Aries was in sight, it was the time of fertility and they associated it with the Ram. And they noticed that the growth of plants and plant life corresponded with different phases of the moon, so that certain times were favorable for the planting of crops, and other times were not. In this way, there grew up a tradition of seasons and causes connected with the passage of the sun through the twelve signs of the Zodiac.

Astrology was valued so highly that the king was kept informed of the daily and monthly changes in the heavenly bodies, and the results of astrological studies regarding events of the future. Head astrologers were clearly men of great rank and position, and the office was said to be a hereditary one.

Omens were taken, not only from eclipses and conjunctions of the moon or sun with one of the planets, but also from storms and earthquakes. In the eastern civilizations, particularly, the reverence inspired by astrology appears to have remained unbroken since the very earliest days. In ancient China, astrology, astronomy and religion went hand in hand. The astrologer, who was also an astronomer, was part of the official government service and had his own corner in the Imperial Palace. The duties of the Imperial astrologer, whose office was one of the most important in the land, were clearly defined, as this extract from early records shows:

"This exalted gentleman must concern himself with the stars in the heavens, keeping a record of the changes and movements of the Planets, the Sun and the Moon, in order to examine the movements of the terrestial world with the object of prognosticating good and bad fortune. He divides the territories of the nine regions of the empire in accordance with their dependence on particular celestial bodies. All the fiefs and principalities are connected with the stars and from this their prosperity or misfortune should be ascertained. He makes prognostications according to the twelve years of the Jupiter cycle of good and evil of the terrestial world. From the colors of the five kinds of clouds, he determines the coming of floods or droughts, abundance or famine. From the twelve winds, he draws conclusions about the state of harmony of heaven and earth, and takes note of good and bad signs that result from their accord or disaccord. In general, he concerns himself with five kinds of phenomena so as to warn the Emperor to come to the aid of the government and to allow for variations in the ceremonies according to their circumstances."

The Chinese were also keen observers of the fixed stars, giving them such unusual names as Ghost Vehicle, Sun of Imperial Concubine, Imperial Prince, Pivot of Heaven, Twinkling Brilliance or Weaving Girl. But, great astrologers though they may have been, the Chinese lacked one aspect of mathematics that the Greeks applied to astrology—deductive geometry. Deductive geometry was the basis of much classical astrology in and after the time of the Greeks, and this explains the different methods of prognostication used in the East and West.

Down through the ages the astrologer's art has depended, not so much on the uncovering of new facts, though this is important, as on the interpretation of the facts already known. This is the essence of his skill. Obviously one cannot always tell how people will react (and this underlines the very important difference between astrology and predestination which will be discussed later on) but one can be prepared, be forewarned, to know what to expect.

But why should the signs of the zodiac have any effect at all on the formation of human character? It is easy to see why people thought they did, and even now we constantly use astrological expressions in our everyday speech. The thoughts of "lucky star," "ill-fated," "star-crossed," "mooning around," are interwoven into the very structure of our language.

In the same way that the earth has been created by influences from outside, there remains an indisputable togetherness in the working of the universe. The world, after all, is a coherent structure, for if it were not, it would be quite without order and we would never know what to expect. A dog could turn into an apple, or an elephant sprout wings and fly at any moment without so much as a by your leave. But nature, as we know, functions according to laws, not whims, and the laws of nature are certainly not subject to capricious exceptions.

This means that no part of the universe is ever arbitrarily cut off from any other part. Everything is therefore to some extent linked with everything else. The moon draws an imperceptible tide on every puddle; tiny and trivial events can be effected by outside forces (such as the fall of a feather by the faintest puff of wind). And so it is fair to think that the local events at any moment reflect to a very small extent the evolution of the world as a whole.

From this principle follows the possibility of divination, and also knowledge of events at a distance, provided one's mind were always as perfectly undisturbed, as ideally smooth, as a mirror or unruffled lake. Provided, in other words, that one did not confuse the picture with hopes, guesses, and expectations. When people try to foretell the future by cards or crystal ball gazing they find it much easier to confuse the picture with expectations than to reflect it clearly.

But the present does contain a good deal of the future to which it leads—not all, but a good deal. The diver halfway between bridge and water is going to make a splash; the train whizzing towards the station will pass through it unless interfered with; the burglar breaking a pane of glass has exposed himself to the possibility of a prison sentence. Yet this is not a doctrine of determinism, as was emphasized earlier. Clearly, there are forces already at work in the present, and any one of them could alter the situation in some way. Equally, a change of decision could alter the whole situation as well. So the future depends, not on an irresistible force, but on a small act of free will.

An individual's age, physique, and position on the earth's surface are remote consequences of his birth. Birth counts as the original cause for all that happens subsequently. The horoscope, in this case, means "this person represents the further evolution of the state of the universe pictured in this chart." Such a chart can apply equally to man or woman, dog, ship or even limited company.

If the evolution of an idea, or of a person, is to be understood as a totality, it must continue to evolve from its own beginnings, which is to say, in the terms in which it began. The brown-eyed person will be faithful to brown eyes all his life; the traitor is being faithful to some complex of ideas which has long been evolving in him; and the person born at sunset will always express, as he evolves, the psychological implications or analogies of the moment when the sun sinks out of sight.

This is the doctrine that an idea must continue to evolve in terms of its origin. It is a completely non-materialist doctrine, though it never fails to apply to material objects. And it implies, too, that the individual will continue to evolve in terms of his moment of origin, and therefore possibly of the sign of the Zodiac rising on the eastern horizon at his birth. It also implies that the signs of the Zodiac themselves will evolve in the collective mind of the human race in the same terms that they were first devised and not in the terms in which modern astrologers consciously think they ought to work.

For the human race, like every other kind of animal, has a collective mind, as Professor Jung discovered in his investigation of dreams. If no such collective mind existed, no infant could ever learn anything, for communication would be impossible. Furthermore, it is absurd to suggest that the conscious mind could be older than the "unconscious," for an infant's nervous system functions correctly before it has discovered the difference between "myself" and "something else" or discovered what eyes and hands are for. Indeed, the involuntary muscles function correctly even before birth, and will never be under conscious control. They are part of what we call the "unconscious" which is not really "unconscious" at all. To the contrary, it is totally aware of itself and everything else; it is merely that part of the mind that cannot be controlled by conscious effort.

And human experience, though it varies in detail with every individual, is basically the same for each one of us, consisting of sky and earth, day and night, waking and sleeping, man and woman, birth and death. So there is bound to be in the mind of the human race a very large number of inescapable ideas, which are called our natural archetypes.

There are also, however, artificial or cultural archetypes which are not universal or applicable to everyone, but are nevertheless inescapable within the limits of a given culture. Examples of these are the cross in Christianity, and the notion of "escape from the wheel of rebirth" in India. There was a time when these ideas did not exist. And there was a time, too, when the scheme of the Zodiac did not exist. One would not expect the Zodiac to have any influence on remote and primitive peoples, for example, who have never heard of it. If the Zodiac is only an archetype, their horoscopes probably would not work and it would not matter which sign they were born under.

But where the Zodiac is known, and the idea of it has become worked into the collective mind, then there it could well appear to have an influence, even if it has no physical existence. For ideas do not have a physical existence, anyway. No physical basis has yet been discovered for the telepathy that controls an anthill; young swallows migrate before, not after, their parents; and the weaverbird builds its intricate nest without being taught. Materialists suppose, but cannot prove, that "instinct" (as it is called, for no one knows how it works) is controlled by nucleic acid in the chromosomes. This is not a genuine explanation, though, for it only pushes the mystery one stage further back.

Does this mean, then, that the human race, in whose civilization the idea of the twelve signs of the Zodiac has long been embedded, is divided into only twelve types? Can we honestly believe that it is really as simple as that? If so, there must be pretty wide ranges of variation within each type. And if, to explain the variation, we call in heredity and environment, experiences in early childhood, the thyroid and other glands, and also the four functions of the mind mentioned at the beginning of this introduction, and extroversion and introversion, then one begins to wonder if the original classification was worth making at all. No sensible person believes that his favorite system explains everything. But even so, he will not find it much use at all if it does not even save him the trouble of bothering with the others.

Under the Jungian system, everyone has not only a dominant or principal function, but also a secondary or subsidiary one, so that the four can be arranged in order of potency. In the intuitive type, sensation is always the most inefficient function, but the second most inefficient function can be either thinking (which tends to make original thinkers such as Jung himself) or else feeling (which tends to make artistic people). Therefore, allowing for introversion and extroversion, there are at least four kinds of intuitive types, and sixteen types in all. Furthermore, one can see how the sixteen types merge into each other, so that there are no unrealistic or unconvincingly rigid divisions.

In the same way, if we were to put every person under only one sign of the Zodiac, the system becomes too rigid and unlike life. Besides, it was never intended to be used like that. It may be convenient to have only twelve types, but we know that in practice there is every possible gradation between aggressiveness and timidity, or between conscientiousness and laziness. How, then, do we account for this?

The Tyrant and the Saint

Just as the thinking type of man is also influenced to some extent by sensation and intuition, but not very much by emotion, so a person born under Leo can be influenced to some extent by one or two (but not more) of the other signs. For instance, famous persons born under the sign of Gemini include Henry VIII, whom nothing and no-one could have induced to abdicate, and Edward VIII, who did just that. Obviously, then, the sign Gemini does not fully explain the complete character of either of them.

Again, under the opposite sign, Sagittarius, were both Stalin, who was totally consumed with the notion of power, and Charles V, who freely gave up an empire because he preferred to go into a monastery. And we find under Scorpio, many uncompromising characters such as Luther, de Gaulle, Indira Gandhi and Montgomery, but also Petain, a successful commander whose name later became synonymous with collaboration.

A single sign is therefore obviously inadequate to explain the differences between people; it can only explain resemblances, such as the combativeness of the Scorpio group, or the far-reaching devotion of Charles V and Stalin to their respective ideals—the Christian heaven and the Communist utopia.

But very few people are born under one sign only. As well as the month of birth, as was mentioned earlier, the day matters, and, even more, the hour, which ought, if possible, to be noted to the nearest minute. Without this, it is impossible to have an actual horoscope, for the word horoscope means literally, "a consideration of the hour."

The month of birth tells you only which sign of the Zodiac was occupied by the sun. The day and hour tell you what sign was occupied by the moon. And the minute tells you which sign was rising on the eastern horizon. This is called the Ascendant, and it is supposed to be the most important thing in the whole horoscope.

If you were born at midnight, the sun is then in an important position, although invisible. But at one o'clock in the morning the sun is not important, so the moment of birth will not matter much. The important thing then will be the Ascendant, and possibly one or two of the planets. At a given day and hour, say, dawn on January 1st, or 9:00 p.m. on the longest day, the Ascendant will always be the same at any given place. But the moon and planets alter from day to day, at different speeds and have to be looked up in an astronomical table.

The sun is said to signify one's heart, that is to say, one's deepest desires and inmost nature. This is quite different from the moon, which, as we have seen, signifies one's superficial way of behaving. When the ancient Romans referred to the Emperor Augustus as a Capricornian, they meant that he had the moon in Capricorn; they did not pay much attention to the sun, although he was born at sunrise. Or, to take another example, a modern astrologer would call Disraeli a Scorpion because he had Scorpio rising, but most people would call him Sagittarian because he had the sun there. The Romans would have called him Leo because his moon was in Leo.

The sun, as has already been pointed out, is important if one is born near sunrise, sunset, noon or midnight, but is otherwise not reckoned as the principal influence. So if one does not seem to fit one's birth month, it is always worthwhile reading the other signs, for one may have been born at a time when any of them were rising or occupied by the moon. It also seems to be the case that the influence of the sun develops as life goes on, so that the month of birth is easier to guess in people over the age of forty. The young are supposed to be influenced mainly by their Ascendant which characterizes the body and physical personality as a whole.

It should be clearly understood that it is nonsense to assume that all people born at a certain time will exhibit the same characteristics, or that they will even behave in the same manner. It is quite obvious that, from the very moment of its birth, a child is subject to the effects of its environment, and that this in turn will influence its character and heritage to a decisive extent. Also to be taken into account are education and economic conditions, which play a very important part in the formation of one's character as well.

However, it is clearly established that people born under one sign of the Zodiac do have certain basic traits in their character which are different from those born under other signs. It is obvious to every thinking person that certain events produce different reactions in various people. For instance, if a man slips on a banana skin and falls heavily on the pavement, one passer-by may laugh and find this extremely amusing, while another may just walk on, thinking: "What a fool falling down like that. He should look where he is going." A third might also walk away saying to himself: "It's none of my business—I'm glad it wasn't me." A fourth might walk past and think: "I'm sorry for that man, but I haven't the time to be bothered with helping him." And a fifth might stop to help the fallen man to his feet, comfort him and take him home. Here is just one event which could produce entirely different reactions in different people. And, obviously, there are many more. One that comes to mind immediately is the violently opposed views to events such as wars, industrial strikes, and so on. The fact that people have different attitudes to the same event is simply another way of saying that they have different characters. And this is not something that can be put down to background, for people of the same race, religion, or class, very often express quite different reactions to happenings or events. Similarly, it is often the case that members of the same family, where there is clearly uniform background of economic and social standing, education, race and religion, often argue bitterly among themselves over political and social issues.

People have, in general, certain character traits and qualities which, according to their environment, develop in either a positive or a negative manner. Therefore, selfishness (inherent selfishness, that is) might emerge as unselfishness; kindness and consideration as cruelty and lack of consideration towards others. In the same way, a naturally constructive person, may, through frustration, become destructive, and so on. The latent characteristics with which people are born can, therefore, through environment and good or bad training, become something that would appear to be its opposite, and so give the lie to the astrologer's description of their character. But this is not the case. The true character is still there, but it is buried deep beneath these external superficialities.

Careful study of the character traits of different signs can be immeasurable help, and can render beneficial service to the intelligent person. Undoubtedly, the reader will already have discovered that, while he is able to get on very well with some people, he just "cannot stand" others. The causes sometimes seem inexplicable. At times there is intense dislike, at other times immediate sympathy. And there is, too, the phenomenon of love at first sight, which is also apparently inexplicable. People appear to be either sympathetic or unsympathetic towards each other for no apparent reason.

Now if we look at this in the light of the Zodiac, we find that people born under different signs are either compatible or incompatible with each other. In other words, there are good and bad interrelating factors among the various signs. This does not, of course, mean that humanity can be divided into groups of hostile camps. It would be quite wrong to be hostile or indifferent toward people who happen to be born under an incompatible sign. There is no reason why everybody should not, or cannot, learn to control and adjust their feelings and actions, especially after they are aware of the positive qualities of other people by studying their character analyses, among other things.

Every person born under a certain sign has both positive and negative qualities, which are developed more or less according to his free will. Nobody is entirely good or entirely bad, and it is up to each one of us to learn to control himself on the one hand, and at the same time to endeavor to learn about himself and others.

It cannot be repeated often enough that, though the intrinsic nature of man and his basic character traits are born in him, nevertheless it is his own free will that determines whether he will make really good use of his talents and abilities—whether, in other words, he will overcome his vices or allow them to rule him. Most of us are born with at least a streak of laziness, irritability, or some other fault in our nature, and it is up to each one of us to see that we exert sufficient willpower to control our failings so that they do not harm ourselves or others.

Astrology can reveal our inclinations and tendencies. Our weaknesses should not be viewed as shortcomings that are impossible to change. The horoscope of a man may show him to have criminal leanings, for instance, but this does not mean he will definitely become a criminal.

The ordinary man usually finds it difficult to know himself. He is often bewildered. Astrology can frequently tell him more about himself than the different schools of psychology are able to do. Knowing his failings and shortcomings, he will do his best to overcome them, and make himself a better and more useful member of society and a helpmate to his family and friends. It can also save him a great deal of unhappiness and remorse.

And yet it may seem absurd that an ancient philosophy, something that is known as a "pseudo-science," could be a prop to the men and women of the twentieth century. But below the materialistic surface of modern life, there are hidden streams of feeling and thought. Symbology is reappearing as a study worthy of the scholar; the psychosomatic factor in illness has passed from the writings of the crank to those of the specialist; spiritual healing in all its forms is no longer a pious hope but an accepted phenomenon. And it is into this context that we consider astrology, in the sense that it is an analysis of human types.

Astrology and medicine had a long journey together, and only parted company a couple of centuries ago. There still remain in medical language such astrological terms as "saturnine," "choleric," and "mercurial," used in the diagnosis of physical tendencies. The herbalist, for long the handyman of the medical profession, has been dominated by astrology since the days of the Greeks. Certain herbs traditionally respond to certain planetary influences, and diseases must therefore be treated to ensure harmony between the medicine and the disease.

No one expects the most eccentric of modern doctors to go back to the practices of his predecessors. We have come a long way since the time when phases of the moon were studied in illness. Those days were a medical nightmare, with epidemics that were beyond control, and an explanation of the Black Death sought in conjunction with the planets. Nowadays, astrological diagnosis of disease has literally no parallel in modern life. And yet, age-old symbols of types and of the vulnerability of, say, the Saturnian to chronic diseases or the choleric to apoplexy and blood pressure and so on, are still applicable.

But the stars are expected to foretell and not only to diagnose. The astrological forecaster has a counterpart on a highly conventional level in the shape of the weather prophet, racing tipster and stock market forecaster, to name just three examples. All in their own way are aiming at the same result. They attempt to look a little further into the pattern of life and also try to determine future patterns accurately.

Astrological forecasting has been remarkably accurate, but often it is wide of the mark. The brave man who cares to predict world events takes dangerous chances. Individual forecasting is less clear cut; it can be a help or a disillusionment. Then welcome to the nagging question: if it is possible to foreknow, is it right to foretell? A complex point of ethics on which it is hard to pronounce judgment. The doctor faces the same dilemma if he finds that symptoms of a mortal disease are present in his patient and that he can only prognosticate a steady decline. How much to tell an individual in a crisis is a problem that has perplexed many distinguished scholars. Honest and conscientious astrologers in this modern world, where so many people are seeking guidance, face the same problem.

The ancient cults, the symbols of old religions, are eclipsed for the moment. They may return with their old force within a decade or two. But at present the outlook is dark. Human beings badly need assurance, as they did in the past, that all is not chaos. Somewhere, somehow, there is a pattern that must be worked out. As to the why and wherefore, the astrologer is not expected to give judgment. He is just someone who, by dint of talent and training, can gaze into the future.

Five hundred years ago it was customary to call in a learned man who was an astrologer who was probably also a doctor and a philosopher. By his knowledge of astrology, his study of planetary influences, he felt himself qualified to guide those in distress. The world has moved forward at a fantastic rate since then, and in this twentieth century speed has been the keyword everywhere. Tensions have increased, the spur of ambition has been applied indiscriminately. People are uncertain of themselves. At first sight it seems fantastic in the light of modern thinking that they turn to the most ancient of all studies, and get someone to calculate a horoscope for them. But is it *really* so fantastic if you take a second look? For astrology is concerned with tomorrow, with survival. And in a world such as ours, those two things are the keywords of the time in which we live.

HOW TO USE THESE PREDICTIONS

A person reading the predictions in this book should understand that they are produced from the daily position of the planets for a group of people and are not, of course, individually specialized. To get the full benefit of them he should relate the predictions to his own character and circumstances, co-ordinate them, and draw his own conclusions from them.

If he is a serious observer of his own life he should find a definite pattern emerge that will be a helpful and reliable guide.

The point is that we always retain our free will. The stars indicate certain directional tendencies but we are not compelled to follow. We can do or not do, and wisdom must make the choice.

We all have our good and bad days. Sometimes they extend into cycles of weeks. It is therefore advisable to study daily predictions in a span ranging from the day before to several days ahead; also to re-read the monthly predictions for similar cycles.

Daily predictions should be taken very generally. The word "difficult" does not necessarily indicate a whole day of obstruction or inconvenience. It is a warning to you to be cautious. Your caution will often see you around the difficulty before you are involved. This is the correct use of astrology.

In another section, detailed information is given about the influence of the moon as it passes through the various signs of the Zodiac. It includes instructions on how to use the Moon Tables. This information should be used in conjunction with the daily forecasts to give a fuller picture of the astrological trends.

THE MOON

Moon is the nearest planet to the earth. It exerts more observable influence on us from day to day than any other planet. The effect is very personal, very intimate, and if we are not aware of how it works it can make us quite unstable in our ideas. And the annoying thing is that at these times we often see our own instability but can do nothing about it. A knowledge of what can be expected may help considerably. We can then be prepared to stand strong against the moon's negative influences and use its positive ones to help us to get ahead. Who has not heard of going with the tide?

Moon reflects, has no light of its own. It reflects the sun—the life giver—in the form of vital movement. Moon controls the tides, the blood rhythm, the movement of sap in trees and plants. Its nature is inconstancy and change so it signifies our moods, our superficial behavior—walking, talking and especially thinking. Being a true reflector of other forces, moon is cold, watery like the surface of a still lake, brilliant and scintillating at times, but easily ruffled and disturbed by the winds of change.

The moon takes 28½ days to circle the earth and the Zodiac. It spends just over 2¼ days in each sign. During that time it reflects the qualities, energies and characteristics of the sign and, to a degree, the planet which rules the sign. While the moon in its transit occupies a sign incompatible with our own birth sign, we can expect to feel a vague uneasiness, perhaps a touch of irritableness. We should not be discouraged nor let the feeling get us down, or, worse still, allow ourselves to take the discomfort out on others. Try to remember that the moon has to change signs within 55 hours and, provided you are not physically ill, your mood will probably change with it. It is amazing how frequently depression lifts with the shift in the moon's position. And, of course, when the moon is transiting a sign compatible or sympathetic to yours you will probably feel some sort of stimulation or just plain happy to be alive.

In the horoscope, the moon is such a powerful indicator that competent astrologers often use the sign it occupied at birth as the birth sign of the person. This is done particularly when the sun is on the cusp, or edge, of two signs. Most experienced astrologers, however, coordinate both sun and moon signs by reading and confirming from one to the other and secure a far more accurate and personalized analysis.

For these reasons, the moon tables which follow this section (see pages 28-35) are of great importance to the individual. They show the days and the exact times the moon will enter each sign of the Zodiac for the year. Remember, you have to adjust the indicated times to local time. The corrections, already calculated for most of the main cities, are at the beginning of the tables. What follows now is a guide to the influences that will be reflected to the earth by the moon while it transits each of the twelve signs. The influence is at its peak about 26 hours after the moon enters a sign.

MOON IN ARIES

This is a time for action, for reaching out beyond the usual self-imposed limitations and faint-hearted cautions. If you have plans in your head or on your desk, put them into practice. New ventures, applications, new jobs, new starts of any kind—all have a good chance of success. This is the period when original and dynamic impulses are being reflected onto the earth. The energies are extremely vital and favor the pursuit of pleasure and adventure in practically every form. Sick people should feel an improvement. Those who are well will probably find themselves exuding confidence and optimism. People fond of physical exercise should find their bodies growing with tone and well-being. Boldness, strength, determination should characterize most of your activities with a readiness to face up to old challenges. Yesterday's problems may seem petty and exaggerated—so deal with them. Strike out alone. Self-reliance will attract others to you. This is a good time for making friends. Business and marriage partners are more likely to be impressed with the man and woman of action. Opposition will be overcome or thrown aside with much less effort than usual. CAUTION: Be dominant but not domineering.

MOON IN TAURUS

The spontaneous, action-packed person of yesterday gives way to the cautious, diligent, hardworking "thinker." In this period ideas will probably be concentrated on ways of improving finances. A great deal of time may be spent figuring out and going over schemes and plans. It is the right time to be careful with detail. People will find themselves working longer than usual at their desks. Or devoting more time to serious thought about the future. A strong desire to put order into business and financial arrangements may cause extra work. Loved ones may complain of being neglected and may fail to appreciate that your efforts are for their ultimate benefit. Your desire for system may extend to criticism of arrangements in the home and lead to minor upsets. Health may be affected through overwork. Try to secure a reasonable amount of rest and relaxation, although the tendency will be to "keep going" despite good advice. Work done conscientiously in this period should result in a solid contribution to your future security. CAUTION: Try not to be as serious with people as the work you are engaged in.

MOON IN GEMINI

The humdrum of routine and too much work should suddenly end. You are likely to find yourself in an expansive, quicksilver world of change and self-expression. Urges to write, to paint, to experience the freedom of some sort of artistic outpouring, may be very strong. Take full advantage of them. You may find yourself finishing something you began and put aside long ago. Or embarking on something new which could easily be prompted by a chance meeting, a new acquaintance, or even an advertisement. There may be a yearning for a change of scenery, the feeling to visit another country (not too far away), or at least to get away for a few days. This may result in short, quick journeys. Or, if you are planning a single visit, there may be some unexpected changes or detours on the way. Familiar activities will seem to give little satisfaction unless they contain a fresh element of excitement or expectation. The inclination will be towards untried pursuits, particularly those that allow you to express your inner nature. The accent is on new faces, new places. CAUTION: Do not be too quick to commit yourself emotionally.

MOON IN CANCER

Feelings of uncertainty and vague insecurity are likely to cause problems while the moon is in Cancer. Thoughts may turn frequently to the warmth of the home and the comfort of loved ones. Nostalgic impulses could cause you to bring out old photographs and letters and reflect on the days when your life seemed to be much more rewarding and less demanding. The love and understanding of parents and family may be important, and, if it is not forthcoming you may have to fight against a bit of self-pity. The cordiality of friends and the thought of good times with them that are sure to be repeated will help to restore you to a happier frame of mind. The feeling to be alone may follow minor setbacks or rebuffs at this time, but solitude is unlikely to help. Better to get on the telephone or visit someone. This period often causes peculiar dreams and upsurges of imaginative thinking which can be very helpful to authors of occult and mystical works. Preoccupation with the more personal world of simple human needs should overshadow any material strivings. CAUTION: Do not spend too much time thinking—seek the company of loved ones or close friends.

MOON IN LEO

New horizons of exciting and rather extravagant activity open up. This is the time for exhilarating entertainment, glamorous and lavish parties, and expensive shopping sprees. Any merrymaking that relies upon your generosity as a host has every chance of being a spectacular success. You should find yourself right in the center of the fun, either as the life of the party or simply as a person whom happy people like to be with. Romance thrives in this heady atmosphere and friendships are likely to explode unexpectedly into serious attachments. Children and younger people should be attracted to you and you may find yourself organizing a picnic or a visit to a fun-fair, the cinema or the seaside. The sunny company and vitality of youthful companions should help you to find some unsuspected energy. In career, you could find an opening for promotion or advancement. This should be the time to make a direct approach. The period favors those engaged in original research. CAUTION: Bask in popularity but not in flattery.

MOON IN VIRGO

Off comes the party cap and out steps the busy, practical worker. He wants to get his personal affairs straight, to rearrange them, if necessary, for more efficiency, so he will have more time for more work. He clears up his correspondence, pays outstanding bills, makes numerous phone calls. He is likely to make inquiries, or sign up for some new insurance and put money into gilt-edged investment. Thoughts probably revolve around the need for future security—to tie up loose ends and clear the decks. There may be a tendency to be "finicky," to interfere in the routine of others, particularly friends and family members. The motive may be a genuine desire to help with suggestions for updating or streamlining their affairs, but these will probably not be welcomed. Sympathy may be felt for less fortunate sections of the community and a flurry of some sort of voluntary service is likely. This may be accompanied by strong feelings of responsibility on several fronts and health may suffer from extra efforts made. CAUTION: Everyone may not want your help or advice.

MOON IN LIBRA

These are days of harmony and agreement and you should find yourself at peace with most others. Relationships tend to be smooth and sweet-flowing. Friends may become closer and bonds deepen in mutual understanding. Hopes will be shared. Progress by cooperation could be the secret of success in every sphere. In business, established partnerships may flourish and new ones get off to a good start. Acquaintances could discover similar interests that lead to congenial discussions and rewarding exchanges of some sort. Love, as a unifying force, reaches its optimum. Marriage partners should find accord. Those who wed at this time face the prospect of a happy union. Cooperation and tolerance are felt to be stronger than dissension and impatience. The argumentative are not quite so loud in their bellowings, nor as inflexible in their attitudes. In the home, there should be a greater recognition of the other point of view and a readiness to put the wishes of the group before selfish insistence. This is a favorable time to join an art group. CAUTION: Do not be too independent—let others help you if they want to.

MOON IN SCORPIO

Driving impulses to make money and to economize are likely to cause upsets all round. No area of expenditure is likely to be spared the axe, including the household budget. This is a time when the desire to cut down on extravagance can become near fanatical. Care must be exercised to try to keep the aim in reasonable perspective. Others may not feel the same urgent need to save and may retaliate. There is a danger that possessions of sentimental value will be sold to realize cash for investment. Buying and selling of stock for quick profit is also likely. The attention may turn to having a good clean up round the home and at the office. Neglected jobs could suddenly be done with great bursts of energy. The desire for solitude may intervene. Self-searching thoughts could disturb. The sense of invisible and mysterious energies at work could cause some excitability. The reassurance of loves ones may help. CAUTION: Be kind to the people you love.

MOON IN SAGITTARIUS

These are days when you are likely to be stirred and elevated by discussions and reflections of a religious and philosophical nature. Ideas of far-away places may cause unusual response and excitement. A decision may be made to visit someone overseas, perhaps a person whose influence was important to your earlier character development. There could be a strong resolution to get away from present intellectual patterns, to learn new subjects and to meet more interesting people. The superficial may be rejected in all its forms. An impatience with old ideas and unimaginative contacts could lead to a change of companions and interests. There may be an upsurge of religious feeling and metaphysical inquiry. Even a new insight into the significance of astrology and other occult studies is likely under the curious stimulus of the moon in Sagittarius. Physically, you may express this need for fundamental change by spending more time outdoors: sports, gardening or going for long walks. CAUTION: Try to channel any restlessness into worthwhile study.

MOON IN CAPRICORN

Life in these hours may seem to pivot around the importance of gaining prestige and honor in the career, as well as maintaining a spotless reputation. Ambitious urges may be excessive and could be accompanied by quite acquisitive drives for money. Effort should be directed along strictly ethical lines where there is no possibility of reproach or scandal. All endeavors are likely to be characterized by great earnestness, and an air of authority and purpose which should impress those who are looking for leadership or reliability. The desire to conform to accepted standards may extend to sharp criticism of family members. Frivolity and unconventional actions are unlikely to amuse while the moon is in Capricorn. Moderation and seriousness are the orders of the day. Achievement and recognition in this period could come through community work or organizing for the benefit of some amateur group. CAUTION: Dignity and esteem are not always self-awarded.

MOON IN AQUARIUS

Moon in Aquarius is in the second last sign of the Zodiac where ideas can become disturbingly fine and subtle. The result is often a mental "no-man's land" where imagination cannot be trusted with the same certitude as other times. The dangers for the individual are the extremes of optimism and pessimism. Unless the imgination is held in check, situations are likely to be misread, and rosy conclusions drawn where they do not exist. Consequences for the unwary can be costly in career and business. Best to think twice and not speak or act until you think again. Pessimism can be a cruel self-inflicted penalty for delusion at this time. Between the two extremes are strange areas of self-deception which, for example, can make the selfish person think he is actually being generous. Eerie dreams which resemble the reality and even seem to continue into the waking state are also possible. CAUTION: Look for the fact and not just for the image in your mind.

MOON IN PISCES

Everything seems to come to the surface now. Memory may be crystal clear, throwing up long-forgotten information which could be valuable in the career or business. Flashes of clairvoyance and intuition are possible along with sudden realizations of one's own nature, which may be used for self-improvement. A talent, never before suspected, may be discovered. Qualities not evident before in friends and marriage partners are likely to be noticed. As this is a period in which the truth seems to emerge, the discovery of false characteristics is likely to lead to disenchantment or a shift in attachments. However, where qualities are realized it should lead to happiness and deeper feeling. Surprise solutions could bob up for old problems. There may be a public announcement of the solving of a crime or mystery. People with secrets may find someone has "guessed" correctly. The secrets of the soul or the inner self also tend to reveal themselves. Religious and philosophical groups may make some interesting discoveries. CAUTION: Not a time for activities that depend on secrecy.

MOON TABLES

CORRECTION FOR NEW YORK TIME, FIVE HOURS WEST OF GREENWICH

Montreal, Ottawa, Quebec, Boston, Detroit,
Washington, Atlanta, Miami, Havana, Lima, Bogota...........Same time

Halifax, Bermuda, San Juan, LaPaz, Caracas, Santiago,
Barbados..Add 1 hour

St. John's, Brasilia, Rio de Janeiro, Buenos Aires,
Montevideo, Sao Paulo...Add 2 hours

Azores, Cape Verde Islands..Add 3 hours

Canary Islands, Madeira, Reykjavik......................................Add 4 hours

London, Paris, Amsterdam, Madrid, Lisbon.
Gibraltar, Belfast, Rabat, Rome...Add 5 hours

Oslo, Stockholm, Frankfurt, Belgrade
Rome, Prague..Add 6 hours

Bucharest, Beirut, Tel Aviv, Athens,
Istanbul, Cairo, Alexandria, Cape Town,
Johannesburg...Add 7 hours

Moscow, Leningrad, Baghdad, Dhahran, Addis
Ababa, Nairobi, Teheran, Zanzibar.....................................Add 8 hours

Bombay, Delhi, Calcutta, Sri Lanka.................................Add 10½ hours

Winnipeg, Churchill, Chicago, New Orleans,
Houston, Mexico City...Deduct 1 hour

Edmonton, Helena, Denver, Albuquerque,
Phoenix, El Paso..Deduct 2 hours

Vancouver, Seattle, Portland, Reno, San
Francisco, Los Angeles..Deduct 3 hours

Anchorage, Fairbanks, Honolulu, Kodiak.........................Deduct 5 hours

Nome, Samoa, Tonga, Midway...Deduct 6 hours

Auckland, Suva, Wake, Wellington...................................Deduct 7 hours

Sydney, Melbourne, Guam, Port Moresby........................Deduct 9 hours

Tokyo, Okinawa, Pusan, Darwin......................................Deduct 10 hours

Hong Kong, Shanghai, Manila, Perth, Peking.................Deduct 11 hours

1987 MOON TABLES—NEW YORK TIME

JANUARY
Day Moon Enters
1. Aquar. 7:29 am
2. Aquar.
3. Pisces 8:22 am
4. Pisces
5. Aries 0:17 pm
6. Aries
7. Taurus 8:31 pm
8. Taurus
9. Taurus
10. Gemini 7:49 am
11. Gemini
12. Cancer 8:30 pm
13. Cancer
14. Cancer
15. Leo 9:10 am
16. Leo
17. Virgo 8:35 pm
18. Virgo
19. Virgo
20. Libra 6:15 am
21. Libra
22. Scorpio 1:23 pm
23. Scorpio
24. Sagitt. 5:07 pm
25. Sagitt.
26. Capric. 6:22 pm
27. Capric.
28. Aquar. 6:26 pm
29. Aquar.
30. Pisces 6:40 pm
31. Pisces

FEBRUARY
Day Moon Enters
1. Aries 9:31 pm
2. Aries
3. Aries
4. Taurus 4:00 am
5. Taurus
6. Gemini 2:33 pm
7. Gemini
8. Gemini
9. Cancer 3:20 am
10. Cancer
11. Leo 3:48 pm
12. Leo
13. Leo
14. Virgo 2:55 am
15. Virgo
16. Libra 0:01 pm
17. Libra
18. Scorpio 7:05 pm
19. Scorpio
20. Scorpio
21. Sagitt. 0:03 am
22. Sagitt.
23. Capric. 1:42 am
24. Capric.
25. Aquar. 4:08 am
26. Aquar.
27. Pisces 5:13 am
28. Pisces

MARCH
Day Moon Enters
1. Aries 7:42 am
2. Aries
3. Taurus 1:16 pm
4. Taurus
5. Gemini 10:17 pm
6. Gemini
7. Gemini
8. Cancer 10:29 am
9. Cancer
10. Leo 11:20 pm
11. Leo
12. Leo
13. Virgo 10:15 am
14. Virgo
15. Libra 6:48 pm
16. Libra
17. Libra
18. Scorpio 0:58 am
19. Scorpio
20. Sagitt. 5:46 am
21. Sagitt.
22. Capric. 8:52 pm
23. Capric.
24. Aquar. 11:40 am
25. Aquar.
26. Pisces 1:59 pm
27. Pisces
28. Aries 5:26 pm
29. Aries
30. Taurus 10:38 pm
31. Taurus

Summer time to be considered where applicable.

1987 MOON TABLES—NEW YORK TIME

APRIL		MAY		JUNE	
Day Moon Enters		Day Moon Enters		Day Moon Enters	
1. Taurus		1. Gemini		1. Leo	
2. Gemini	7:00 am	2. Cancer	2:25 am	2. Leo	
3. Gemini		3. Cancer		3. Virgo	11:11 am
4. Cancer	6:30 pm	4. Leo	3:09 pm	4. Virgo	
5. Cancer		5. Leo		5. Libra	9:21 pm
6. Cancer		6. Leo		6. Libra	
7. Leo	7:36 am	7. Virgo	3:14 am	7. Libra	
8. Leo		8. Virgo		8. Scorpio	3:50 am
9. Virgo	6:41 am	9. Libra	2:19 pm	9. Scorpio	
10. Virgo		10. Libra		10. Sagitt.	6:41 am
11. Virgo		11. Scorpio	5:48 pm	11. Sagitt.	
12. Libra	3:11 am	12. Scorpio		12. Capric.	7:10 am
13. Libra		13. Sagitt.	8:14 pm	13. Capric.	
14. Scorpio	8:24 am	14. Sagitt.		14. Aquar.	6:50 am
15. Scorpio		15. Capric.	9:41 pm	15. Aquar.	
16. Sagitt.	11:56 am	16. Capric.		16. Pisces	8:31 am
17. Sagitt.		17. Aquar.	10:54 pm	17. Pisces	
18. Capric.	2:36 pm	18. Aquar.		18. Aries	0:15 pm
19. Capric.		19. Aquar.		19. Aries	
20. Aquar.	5:25 pm	20. Pisces	1:51 am	20. Taurus	7:22 pm
21. Aquar.		21. Pisces		21. Taurus	
22. Pisces	8:33 pm	22. Aries	6:49 am	22. Taurus	
23. Pisces		23. Aries		23. Gemini	5:14 am
24. Pisces		24. Taurus	1:56 pm	24. Gemini	
25. Aries	1:18 am	25. Taurus		25. Cancer	4:29 pm
26. Aries		26. Gemini	10:53 pm	26. Cancer	
27. Taurus	7:11 am	27. Gemini		27. Cancer	
28. Taurus		28. Gemini		28. Leo	5:00 am
29. Gemini	3:42 pm	29. Cancer	10:01 am	29. Leo	
30. Gemini		30. Cancer		30. Virgo	5:43 pm
		31. Leo	10:20 pm		

Summer time to be considered where applicable.

1987 MOON TABLES—NEW YORK TIME

JULY		AUGUST		SEPTEMBER	
Day Moon Enters		Day Moon Enters		Day Moon Enters	
1. Virgo		1. Scorpio	7:49 pm	1. Sagitt.	
2. Virgo		2. Scorpio		2. Capric.	0:03 pm
3. Libra	5:02 am	3. Scorpio		3. Capric.	
4. Libra		4. Sagitt.	1:35 am	4. Aquar.	1:39 pm
5. Scorpio	0:50 pm	5. Sagitt.		5. Aquar.	
6. Scorpio		6. Capric.	3:41 am	6. Pisces	1:59 pm
7. Sagitt.	4:46 pm	7. Capric.		7. Pisces	
8. Sagitt.		8. Aquar.	3:53 am	8. Aries	3:04 pm
9. Capric.	5:36 pm	9. Aquar.		9. Aries	
10. Capric.		10. Pisces	3:32 am	10. Taurus	6:11 pm
11. Aquar.	5:15 pm	11. Pisces		11. Taurus	
12. Aquar.		12. Aries	4:34 am	12. Taurus	
13. Pisces	5:03 pm	13. Aries		13. Gemini	0:49 am
14. Pisces		14. Taurus	8:39 am	14. Gemini	
15. Aries	7:21 pm	15. Taurus		15. Cancer	11:37 am
16. Aries		16. Gemini	4:52 pm	16. Cancer	
17. Aries		17. Gemini		17. Cancer	
18. Taurus	1:09 am	18. Gemini		18. Leo	0:18 am
19. Taurus		19. Cancer	4:25 am	19. Leo	
20. Gemini	10:35 am	20. Cancer		20. Virgo	0:40 pm
21. Gemini		21. Leo	5:24 pm	21. Virgo	
22. Cancer	10:29 pm	22. Leo		22. Libra	10:56 pm
23. Cancer		23. Leo		23. Libra	
24. Cancer		24. Virgo	5:37 am	24. Libra	
25. Leo	11:13 am	25. Virgo		25. Scorpio	7:22 am
26. Leo		26. Libra	4:22 pm	26. Scorpio	
27. Virgo	11:32 pm	27. Libra		27. Sagitt.	1:28 pm
28. Virgo		28. Libra		28. Sagitt.	
29. Virgo		29. Scorpio	1:34 am	29. Capric.	5:57 pm
30. Libra	10:55 am	30. Scorpio		30. Capric.	
31. Libra		31. Sagitt.	8:04 am		

Summer time to be considered where applicable.

1987 MOON TABLES—NEW YORK TIME

OCTOBER
Day Moon Enters
1. Aquar. 9:00 pm
2. Aquar.
3. Pisces 11:04 pm
4. Pisces
5. Pisces
6. Aries 0:48 am
7. Aries
8. Taurus 4:04 am
9. Taurus
10. Gemini 10:01 am
11. Gemini
12. Cancer 7:35 pm
13. Cancer
14. Cancer
15. Leo 8:00 am
16. Leo
17. Virgo 8:30 pm
18. Virgo
19. Virgo
20. Libra 7:11 am
21. Libra
22. Scorpio 2:31 pm
23. Scorpio
24. Sagitt. 7:47 pm
25. Sagitt.
26. Capric. 11:34 pm
27. Capric.
28. Capric.
29. Aquar. 2:35 am
30. Aquar.
31. Pisces 5:19 am

NOVEMBER
Day Moon Enters
1. Pisces
2. Aries 8:45 am
3. Aries
4. Taurus 1:02 pm
5. Taurus
6. Gemini 7:10 pm
7. Gemini
8. Gemini
9. Cancer 4:17 am
10. Cancer
11. Leo 3:52 pm
12. Leo
13. Leo
14. Virgo 4:48 am
15. Virgo
16. Libra 4:09 pm
17. Libra
18. Scorpio 11:44 pm
19. Scorpio
20. Scorpio
21. Sagitt. 4:14 am
22. Sagitt.
23. Capric. 6:50 am
24. Capric.
25. Aquar. 8:31 am
26. Aquar.
27. Pisces 10:51 am
28. Pisces
29. Aries 2:37 pm
30. Aries

DECEMBER
Day Moon Enters
1. Taurus 7:58 pm
2. Taurus
3. Taurus
4. Gemini 3:08 am
5. Gemini
6. Cancer 0:07 pm
7. Cancer
8. Leo 11:37 pm
9. Leo
10. Leo
11. Virgo 0:27 pm
12. Virgo
13. Virgo
14. Libra 0:19 am
15. Libra
16. Scorpio 9:34 am
17. Scorpio
18. Sagitt. 2:16 pm
19. Sagitt.
20. Capric. 4:18 pm
21. Capric.
22. Aquar. 4:45 pm
23. Aquar.
24. Pisces 5:48 pm
25. Pisces
26. Aries 8:17 pm
27. Aries
28. Aries
29. Taurus 1:38 am
30. Taurus
31. Gemini 9:29 am

Summer time to be considered where applicable.

1987 PHASES OF THE MOON—NEW YORK TIME

New Moon	First Quarter	Full Moon	Last Quarter
(1986)	Jan. 6	Jan. 14	Jan. 22
Jan. 29	Feb. 5	Feb. 13	Feb. 21
Feb. 27	March 7	March 15	March 22
March 29	April 6	April 13	April 20
April 27	May 5	May 13	May 19
May 27	June 4	June 11	June 18
June 26	July 4	July 10	July 17
July 25	Aug. 2	Aug. 9	Aug. 16
Aug. 24	Aug. 31	Sept. 7	Sept. 14
Sept. 22	Sept. 30	Oct. 6	Oct. 14
Oct. 22	Oct. 29	Nov. 5	Nov. 13
Nov. 20	Nov. 27	Dec. 5	Dec. 13
Dec. 20	Dec. 27	(1988)	(1988)

Summer time to be considered where applicable.

1987 PLANTING GUIDE

	Aboveground Crops	Root Crops	Pruning	Weeds Pests
January	4-8-9-13-14-31	21-22-23-24-27-28	23-24	16-17-18-19-25-26
February	1-4-5-9-10-28	17-18-19-20-23-24	19-20	14-15-21-22-25-26
March	4-5-9-10-31	16-17-18-19-23-27-28	18-19-27-28	21-25
April	1-5-6-12-13-28	14-15-19-20-23-24	15-23-24	17-21-22-25-26
May	2-3-10-11-12-30-31	16-17-20-21-25-26	20-21	14-15-18-19-23
June	6-7-8-9-26-27	13-17-21-22	17	15-19-20-24
July	4-5-6-10-31	11-14-15-18-19-23-24	14-15-23-24	12-13-16-17-21-22
August	1-2-3-6-7-27-28-29-30	10-11-15-19-20-21	10-11-19-20-21	12-13-17-18-22-23
September	3-23-24-25-26-30	11-12-16-17	16-17	9-10-13-14-18-19-20-21-22
October	1-4-5-23-24-27-28	8-9-13-14-21	13-14	7-11-12-16-17-18-19
November	1-24-28	6-9-10-17-18-19	9-10-19	7-8-12-13-14-15
December	2-3-21-25-26-29-30	7-8-14-15-16-17	7-8-17	5-9-10-11-12-13-19

1987 FISHING GUIDE

	Good	Best
January	6-12-15-16-17-18-29	13-14-22
February	11-12-13-14-15-16-21	5-10-28
March	7-12-13-14-15-22-29	16-17-18
April	11-16-17	6-12-13-14-15-20-28
May	6-14-15-27	10-11-12-13-16-20
June	4-10-11-12-14-18	8-9-13-26
July	8-9-12-13-17-25	4-10-11-14
August	8-9-12-16-24	2-6-7-10-11
September	1-4-5-6-8-9-10-14	7-23-30
October	6-7-10-29	4-5-8-9-14-22
November	2-3-4-7-8-13	5-6-20-28
December	4-5-6-13-20-27	2-3-7-8

MOON'S INFLUENCE OVER DAILY AFFAIRS

The Moon makes a complete transit of the Zodiac every 27 days 7 hours and 43 minutes. In making this transit the Moon forms different aspects with the planets and consequently has favorable or unfavorable bearings on affairs and events for persons according to the sign of the Zodiac under which they were born.

Whereas the Sun exclusively represents fire, the Moon rules water. The action of the Moon may be described as fluctuating, variable, absorbent and receptive. It is well known that the attraction to the Moon in combination with the movement of the Earth is responsible for the tides. The Moon has a similar effect on men. A clever navigator will make use of the tides to bring his ship to the intended destination. You also can reach your "destination" better by making use of your tides.

When the Moon is in conjunction with the Sun it is called a New Moon; when the Moon and Sun are in opposition it is called a Full Moon. From New Moon to Full Moon, first and second quarter—which takes about two weeks—the Moon is increasing or waxing. From Full Moon to New Moon, third and fourth quarter, the Moon is said to be decreasing or waning. The Moon Table indicates the New Moon and Full Moon and the quarters.

ACTIVITY	MOON IN
Business	
buying and selling	Sagittarius, Aries, Gemini, Virgo
new, requiring public support	1st and 2nd quarter
meant to be kept quiet	3rd and 4th quarter
Investigation	3rd and 4th quarter
Signing documents	1st & 2nd quarter, Cancer, Scorpio, Pisces
Advertising	2nd quarter, Sagittarius
Journeys and trips	1st & 2nd quarter, Gemini, Virgo
Renting offices, etc.	Taurus, Leo, Scorpio, Aquarius
Painting of house/apartment	3rd & 4th quarter, Taurus, Scorpio, Aquarius
Decorating	Gemini, Libra, Aquarius
Buying clothes and accessories	Taurus, Virgo
Beauty salon or barber shop visit	1st & 2nd quarter, Taurus, Leo, Libra, Scorpio, Aquarius
Weddings	1st & 2nd quarter

MOON'S INFLUENCE OVER YOUR HEALTH

ARIES	Head, brain, face, upper jaw
TAURUS	Throat, neck, lower jaw
GEMINI	Hands, arms, lungs, shoulders, nervous system
CANCER	Esophagus, stomach, breasts, womb, liver
LEO	Heart, spine
VIRGO	Intestines, liver
LIBRA	Kidneys, lower back
SCORPIO	Sex and eliminative organs
SAGITTARIUS	Hips, thighs, liver
CAPRICORN	Skin, bones, beeth, knees
AQUARIUS	Circulatory system, lower legs
PISCES	Feet, tone of being

Try to avoid work being done on that part of the body when the Moon is in the sign governing that part.

MOON'S INFLUENCE OVER PLANTS

Centuries ago it was established that seeds planted when the Moon is in certain signs and phases called "fruitful" will produce more than seeds planted when the Moon is in a Barren sign.

FRUITFUL SIGNS	BARREN SIGNS	DRY SIGNS
Taurus	Aries	Aries
Cancer	Gemini	Gemini
Libra	Leo	Sagittarius
Scorpio	Virgo	Aquarius
Capricorn	Sagittarius	
Pisces	Aquarius	

ACTIVITY	MOON IN
Mow lawn, trim plans	Fruitful sign, 1st & 2nd quarter
Plant flowers	Fruitful sign, 2nd quarter; best in Cancer and Libra
Prune	Fruitful sign, 3rd & 4th quarter
Destroy pests; spray	Barren sign, 4th quarter
Harvest potatoes, root crops	Dry sign, 3rd & 4th quarter; Taurus, Leo, and Aquarius

THE SIGNS: DOMINANT CHARACTERISTICS

March 21–April 20

The Positive Side of Aries

The Arien has many positive points to his character. People born under this first sign of the Zodiac are often quite strong and enthusiastic. On the whole, they are forward-looking people who are not easily discouraged by temporary setbacks. They know what they want out of life and they go out after it. Their personalities are strong. Others are usually quite impressed by the Arien's way of doing things. Quite often they are sources of inspiration for others traveling the same route. Aries men and women have a special zest for life that is often contagious; for others, they are often the example of how life should be lived.

The Aries person usually has a quick and active mind. He is imaginative and inventive. He enjoys keeping busy and active. He generally gets along well with all kinds of people. He is interested in mankind, as a whole. He likes to be challenged. Some would say he thrives on opposition, for it is when he is set against that he often does his best. Getting over or around obstacles is a challenge he generally enjoys. All in all, the Arien is quite positive and young-thinking. He likes to keep abreast of new things that are happening in the world. Ariens are often fond of speed. They like things to be done quickly and this sometimes aggravates their slower colleagues and associates.

The Aries man or woman always seems to remain young. Their whole approach to life is youthful and optimistic. They never say die, no matter what the odds. They may have an occasional setback, but it is not long before they are back on their feet again.

The Negative Side of Aries

Everybody has his less positive qualities—and Aries is no exception. Sometimes the Aries man or woman is not very tactful in communicating with others; in his hurry to get things done he is apt to

be a little callous or inconsiderate. Sensitive people are likely to find him somewhat sharp-tongued in some situations. Often in his eagerness to achieve his aims, he misses the mark altogether. At times the Arien is too impulsive. He can occasionally be stubborn and refuse to listen to reason. If things do not move quickly enough to suit the Aries man or woman, he or she is apt to become rather nervous or irritable. The uncultivated Arien is not unfamiliar with moments of doubt and fear. He is capable of being destructive if he does not get his way. He can overcome some of his emotional problems by steadily trying to express himself as he really is, but this requires effort.

April 21–May 20

The Positive Side of Taurus

The Taurus person is known for his ability to concentrate and for his tenacity. These are perhaps his strongest qualities. The Taurus man or woman generally has very little trouble in getting along with others; it's his nature to be helpful toward people in need. He can always be depended on by his friends, especially those in trouble.

The Taurean generally achieves what he wants through his ability to persevere. He never leaves anything unfinished but works on something until it has been completed. People can usually take him at his word; he is honest and forthright in most of his dealings. The Taurus person has a good chance to make a success of his life because of his many positive qualities. The Taurean who aims high seldom falls short of his mark. He learns well by experience. He is thorough and does not believe in short-cuts of any kind. The Taurean's thoroughness pays off in the end, for through his deliberateness he learns how to rely on himself and what he has learned. The Taurus person tries to get along with others, as a rule. He is not overly critical and likes people to be themselves. He is a tolerant person and enjoys peace and harmony—especially in his home life.

The Taurean is usually cautious in all that he does. He is not a person who believes in taking unnecessary risks. Before adopting any one line of action, he will weigh all of the pros and cons. The

Taurus person is steadfast. Once his mind is made up it seldom changes. The person born under this sign usually is a good family person—reliable and loving.

The Negative Side of Taurus

Sometimes the Taurus man or woman is a bit too stubborn. He won't listen to other points of view if his mind is set on something. To others, this can be quite annoying. The Taurean also does not like to be told what to do. He becomes rather angry if others think him not too bright. He does not like to be told he is wrong, even when he is. He dislikes being contradicted.

Some people who are born under this sign are very suspicious of others—even of those persons close to them. They find it difficult to trust people fully. They are often afraid of being deceived or taken advantage of. The Taurean often finds it difficult to forget or forgive. His love of material things sometimes makes him rather avaricious and petty.

May 21–June 20

The Positive Side of Gemini

The person born under this sign of the Heavenly Twins is usually quite bright and quick-witted. Some of them are capable of doing many different things. The Gemini person very often has many different interests. He keeps an open mind and is always anxious to learn new things.

The Geminian is often an analytical person. He is a person who enjoys making use of his intellect. He is governed more by his mind than by his emotions. He is a person who is not confined to one view; he can often understand both sides to a problem or question. He knows how to reason; how to make rapid decisions if need be.

He is an adaptable person and can make himself at home almost anywhere. There are all kinds of situations he can adapt to. He is a person who seldom doubts himself; he is sure of his talents and his

ability to think and reason. The Geminian is generally most satisfied when he is in a situation where he can make use of his intellect. Never short of imagination, he often has strong talents for invention. He is rather a modern person when it comes to life; the Geminian almost always moves along with the times—perhaps that is why he remains so youthful throughout most of his life.

Literature and art appeal to the person born under this sign. Creativity in almost any form will interest and intrigue the Gemini man or woman.

The Geminian is often quite charming. A good talker, he often is the center of attraction at any gathering. People find it easy to like a person born under this sign because he can appear easygoing and usually has a good sense of humor.

The Negative Side of Gemini

Sometimes the Gemini person tries to do too many things at one time—and as a result, winds up finishing nothing. Some Geminians are easily distracted and find it rather difficult to concentrate on one thing for too long a time. Sometimes they give in to trifling fancies and find it rather boring to become too serious about any one thing. Some of them are never dependable, no matter what they promise.

Although the Gemini man or woman often appears to be well-versed on many subjects, this is sometimes just a veneer. His knowledge may be only superficial, but because he speaks so well he gives people the impression of erudition. Some Geminians are sharp-tongued and inconsiderate; they think only of themselves and their own pleasure.

June 21–July 20

The Positive Side of Cancer

The Cancerians's most positive point is his understanding nature. On the whole, he is a loving and sympathetic person. He would never go out of his way to hurt anyone. The Cancer man or woman

is often very kind and tender; they give what they can to others. They hate to see others suffering and will do what they can to help someone in less fortunate circumstances than themselves. They are often very concerned about the world. Their interest in people generally goes beyond that of just their own families and close friends; they have a deep sense of brotherhood and respect humanitarian values. The Cancerian means what he says, as a rule; he is honest about his feelings.

The Cancer man or woman is a person who knows the art of patience. When something seems difficult, he is willing to wait until the situation becomes manageable again. He is a person who knows how to bide his time. The Cancerian knows how to concentrate on one thing at a time. When he has made his mind up he generally sticks with what he does, seeing it through to the end.

The Cancerian is a person who loves his home. He enjoys being surrounded by familiar things and the people he loves. Of all the signs, Cancer is the most maternal. Even the men born under this sign often have a motherly or protective quality about them. They like to take care of people in their family—to see that they are well loved and well provided for. They are usually loyal and faithful. Family ties mean a lot to the Cancer man or woman. Parents and in-laws are respected and loved. The Cancerian has a strong sense of tradition. He is very sensitive to the moods of others.

The Negative Side of Cancer

Sometimes the Cancerian finds it rather hard to face life. It becomes too much for him. He can be a little timid and retiring, when things don't go too well. When unfortunate things happen, he is apt to just shrug and say, "Whatever will be will be." He can be fatalistic to a fault. The uncultivated Cancerian is a bit lazy. He doesn't have very much ambition. Anything that seems a bit difficult he'll gladly leave to others. He may be lacking in initiative. Too sensitive, when he feels he's been injured, he'll crawl back into his shell and nurse his imaginary wounds. The Cancer woman often is given to crying when the smallest thing goes wrong.

Some Cancerians find it difficult to enjoy themselves in environments outside their homes. They make heavy demands on others, and need to be constantly reassured that they are loved.

July 21–August 21

The Positive Side of Leo

Often Leos make good leaders. They seem to be good organizers and administrators. Usually they are quite popular with others. Whatever group it is that he belongs to, the Leo man is almost sure to be or become the leader.

The Leo person is generous most of the time. It is his best characteristic. He or she likes to give gifts and presents. In making others happy, the Leo person becomes happy himself. He likes to splurge when spending money on others. In some instances it may seem that the Leo's generosity knows no boundaries. A hospitable person, the Leo man or woman is very fond of welcoming people to his house and entertaining them. He is never short of company.

The Leo person has plenty of energy and drive. He enjoys working toward some specific goal. When he applies himself correctly, he gets what he wants most often. The Leo person is almost never unsure of himself. He has plenty of confidence and aplomb. He is a person who is direct in almost everything he does. He has a quick mind and can make a decision in a very short time.

He usually sets a good example for others because of his ambitious manner and positive ways. He knows how to stick to something once he's started. Although the Leo person may be good at making a joke, he is not superficial or glib. He is a loving person, kind and thoughtful.

There is generally nothing small or petty about the Leo man or woman. He does what he can for those who are deserving. He is a person others can rely upon at all times. He means what he says. An honest person, generally speaking, he is a friend that others value.

The Negative Side of Leo

Leo, however, does have his faults. At times, he can be just a bit too arrogant. He thinks that no one deserves a leadership position except him. Only he is capable of doing things well. His opinion of himself is often much too high. Because of his conceit, he is sometimes rather unpopular with a good many people. Some Leos are too materialistic; they can only think in terms of money and profit.

Some Leos enjoy lording it over others—at home or at their place of business. What is more, they feel they have the right to. Egocentric to an impossible degree, this sort of Leo cares little about how others think or feel. He can be rude and cutting.

August 22–September 22

The Positive Side of Virgo

The person born under the sign of Virgo is generally a busy person. He knows how to arrange and organize things. He is a good planner. Above all, he is practical and is not afraid of hard work.

The person born under this sign, Virgo, knows how to attain what he desires. He sticks with something until it is finished. He never shirks his duties, and can always be depended upon. The Virgo person can be thoroughly trusted at all times.

The man or woman born under this sign tries to do everything to perfection. He doesn't believe in doing anything half-way. He always aims for the top. He is the sort of a person who is constantly striving to better himself—not because he wants more money or glory, but because it gives him a feeling of accomplishment.

The Virgo man or woman is a very observant person. He is sensitive to how others feel, and can see things below the surface of a situation. He usually puts this talent to constructive use.

It is not difficult for the Virgoan to be open and earnest. He believes in putting his cards on the table. He is never secretive or under-handed. He's as good as his word. The Virgo person is generally plain-spoken and down-to-earth. He has no trouble in expressing himself.

The Virgo person likes to keep up to date on new developments in his particular field. Well-informed, generally, he sometimes has a keen interest in the arts or literature. What he knows, he knows well. His ability to use his critical faculties is well-developed and sometimes startles others because of its accuracy.

The Virgoan adheres to a moderate way of life; he avoids excesses. He is a responsible person and enjoys being of service.

The Negative Side of Virgo

Sometimes a Virgo person is too critical. He thinks that only he can do something the way it should be done. Whatever anyone else does is inferior. He can be rather annoying in the way he quibbles over insignificant details. In telling others how things should be done, he can be rather tactless and mean.

Some Virgos seem rather emotionless and cool. They feel emo-

tional involvement is beneath them. They are sometimes too tidy, too neat. With money they can be rather miserly. Some try to force their opinions and ideas on others.

September 23–October 22

The Positive Side of Libra

Librans love harmony. It is one of their most outstanding character traits. They are interested in achieving balance; they admire beauty and grace in things as well as in people. Generally speaking, they are kind and considerate people. Librans are usually very sympathetic. They go out of their way not to hurt another person's feelings. They are outgoing and do what they can to help those in need.

People born under the sign of Libra almost always make good friends. They are loyal and amiable. They enjoy the company of others. Many of them are rather moderate in their views; they believe in keeping an open mind, however, and weighing both sides of an issue fairly before making a decision.

Alert and often intelligent, the Libran, always fair-minded, tries to put himself in the position of the other person. They are against injustice; quite often they take up for the underdog. In most of their social dealings, they try to be tactful and kind. They dislike discord and bickering, and most Libras strive for peace and harmony in all their relationships.

The Libra man or woman has a keen sense of beauty. They appreciate handsome furnishings and clothes. Many of them are artistically inclined. Their taste is usually impeccable. They know how to use color. Their homes are almost always attractively arranged and inviting. They enjoy entertaining people and see to it that their guests always feel at home and welcome.

The Libran gets along with almost everyone. He is well-liked and socially much in demand.

The Negative Side of Libra

Some people born under this sign tend to be rather insincere. So eager are they to achieve harmony in all relationships that they will even go so far as to lie. Many of them are escapists. They find facing

the truth an ordeal and prefer living in a world of make-believe.

In a serious argument, some Librans give in rather easily even when they know they are right. Arguing, even about something they believe in, is too unsettling for some of them.

Librans sometimes care too much for material things. They enjoy possessions and luxuries. Some are vain and tend to be jealous.

October 23–November 22

The Positive Side of Scorpio

The Scorpio man or woman generally knows what he or she wants out of life. He is a determined person. He sees something through to the end. The Scorpion is quite sincere, and seldom says anything he doesn't mean. When he sets a goal for himself he tries to go about achieving it in a very direct way.

The Scorpion is brave and courageous. They are not afraid of hard work. Obstacles do not frighten them. They forge ahead until they achieve what they set out for. The Scorpio man or woman has a strong will.

Although the Scorpion may seem rather fixed and determined, inside he is often quite tender and loving. He can care very much for others. He believes in sincerity in all relationships. His feelings about someone tend to last; they are profound and not superficial.

The Scorpio person is someone who adheres to his principles no matter what happens. He will not be deterred from a path he believes to be right.

Because of his many positive strengths, the Scorpion can often achieve happiness for himself and for those that he loves.

He is a constructive person by nature. He often has a deep understanding of people and of life, in general. He is perceptive and unafraid. Obstacles often seem to spur him on. He is a positive person who enjoys winning. He has many strengths and resources; challenge of any sort often brings out the best in him.

The Negative Side of Scorpio

The Scorpio person is sometimes hypersensitive. Often he imagines injury when there is none. He feels that others do not bother to

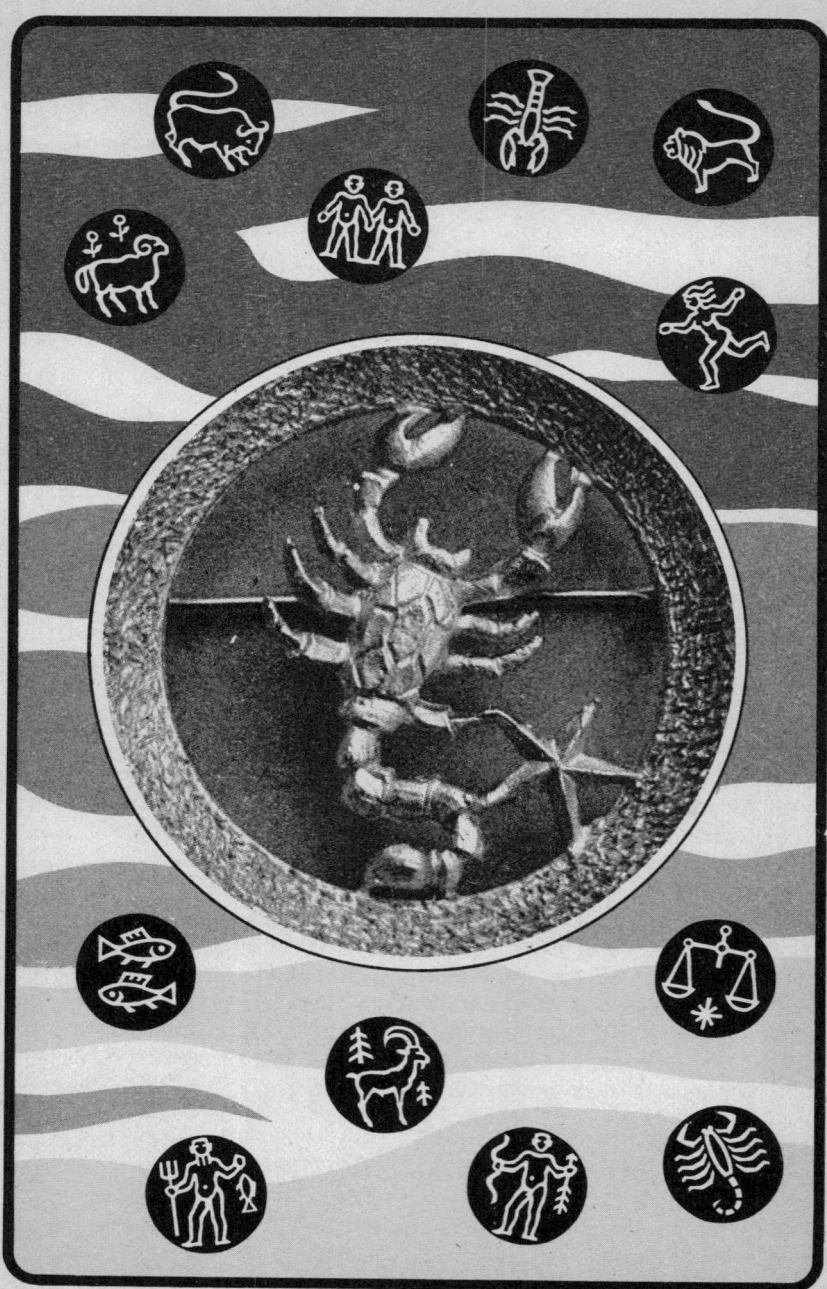

recognize him for his true worth. Sometimes he is given to excessive boasting in order to compensate for what he feels is neglect

The Scorpio person can be rather proud and arrogant. They can be rather sly when they put their minds to it and they enjoy outwitting persons or institutions noted for their cleverness.

Their tactics for getting what they want are sometimes devious and ruthless. They don't care too much about what others may think. If they feel others have done them an injustice, they will do their best to seek revenge. The Scorpion often has a sudden, violent temper; and this person's interest in sex is sometimes quite unbalanced or excessive.

November 23–December 20

The Positive Side of Sagittarius

People born under this sign are often honest and forthright. Their approach to life is earnest and open. The Sagittarian is often quite adult in his way of seeing things. They are broadminded and tolerant people. When dealing with others the person born under the sign of Sagittarius is almost always open and forthright. He doesn't believe in deceit or pretension. His standards are high. People who associate with the Sagittarian, generally admire and respect him.

The Sagittarian trusts others easily and expects them to trust him. He is never suspicious or envious and almost always thinks well of others. People always enjoy his company because he is so friendly and easy-going. The Sagittarius man or woman is often good-humored. He can always be depended upon by his friends, family, and co-workers.

The person born under this sign of the Zodiac likes a good joke every now and then; he is keen on fun and this makes him very popular with others.

A lively person, he enjoys sports and outdoor life. The Sagittarian is fond of animals. Intelligent and interesting, he can begin an animated conversation with ease. He likes exchanging ideas and discussing various views.

He is not selfish or proud. If someone proposes an idea or plan that is better than his, he will immediately adopt it. Imaginative yet practical, he knows how to put ideas into practice.

He enjoys sport and game, and it doesn't matter if he wins or loses. He is a forgiving person, and never sulks over something that has not worked out in his favor.

He is seldom critical, and is almost always generous.

The Negative Side of Sagittarius

Some Sagittarians are restless. They take foolish risks and seldom learn from the mistakes they make. They don't have heads for money and are often mismanaging their finances. Some of them devote much of their time to gambling.

Some are too outspoken and tactless, always putting their feet in their mouths. They hurt others carelessly by being honest at the wrong time. Sometimes they make promises which they don't keep. They don't stick close enough to their plans and go from one failure to another. They are undisciplined and waste a lot of energy.

December 21–January 19

The Positive Side of Capricorn

The person born under the sign of Capricorn is usually very stable and patient. He sticks to whatever tasks he has and sees them through. He can always be relied upon and he is not averse to work.

An honest person, the Capricornian is generally serious about whatever he does. He does not take his duties lightly. He is a practical person and believes in keeping his feet on the ground.

Quite often the person born under this sign is ambitious and knows how to get what he wants out of life. He forges ahead and never gives up his goal. When he is determined about something, he almost always wins. He is a good worker—a hard worker. Although things may not come easy to him, he will not complain, but continue working until his chores are finished.

He is usually good at business matters and knows the value of money. He is not a spendthrift and knows how to put something away for a rainy day; he dislikes waste and unnecessary loss.

The Capricornian knows how to make use of his self-control. He

can apply himself to almost anything once he puts his mind to it. His ability to concentrate sometimes astounds others. He is diligent and does well when involved in detail work.

The Capricorn man or woman is charitable, generally speaking, and will do what is possible to help others less fortunate. As a friend, he is loyal and trustworthy. He never shirks his duties or responsibilities. He is self-reliant and never expects too much of the other fellow. He does what he can on his own. If someone does him a good turn, then he will do his best to return the favor.

The Negative Side of Capricorn

Like everyone, the Capricornian, too, has his faults. At times, he can be over-critical of others. He expects others to live up to his own high standards. He thinks highly of himself and tends to look down on others.

His interest in material things may be exaggerated. The Capricorn man or woman thinks too much about getting on in the world and having something to show for it. He may even be a little greedy.

He sometimes thinks he knows what's best for everyone. He is too bossy. He is always trying to organize and correct others. He may be a little narrow in his thinking.

January 20–February 18

The Positive Side of Aquarius

The Aquarius man or woman is usually very honest and forthright. These are his two greatest qualities. His standards for himself are generally very high. He can always be relied upon by others. His word is his bond.

The Aquarian is perhaps the most tolerant of all the Zodiac personalities. He respects other people's beliefs and feels that everyone is entitled to his own approach to life.

He would never do anything to injure another's feelings. He is never unkind or cruel. Always considerate of others, the Aquarian is always willing to help a person in need. He feels a very strong tie between himself and all the other members of mankind.

The person born under this sign is almost always an individualist. He does not believe in teaming up with the masses, but prefers going his own way. His ideas about life and mankind are often quite advanced. There is a saying to the effect that the average Aquarian is fifty years ahead of his time.

He is broadminded. The problems of the world concern him greatly. He is interested in helping others no matter what part of the globe they live in. He is truly a humanitarian sort. He likes to be of service to others.

Giving, considerate, and without prejudice, Aquarians have no trouble getting along with others.

The Negative Side of Aquarius

The Aquarian may be too much of a dreamer. He makes plans but seldom carries them out. He is rather unrealistic. His imagination has a tendency to run away with him. Because many of his plans are impractical, he is always in some sort of a dither.

Others may not approve of him at all times because of his unconventional behavior. He may be a bit eccentric. Sometimes he is so busy with his own thoughts, that he loses touch with the realities of existence.

Some Aquarians feel they are more clever and intelligent than others. They seldom admit to their own faults, even when they are quite apparent. Some become rather fanatic in their views. Their criticism of others is sometimes destructive and negative.

February 19–March 20

The Positive Side of Pisces

The Piscean can often understand the problems of others quite easily. He has a sympathetic nature. Kindly, he is often dedicated in the way he goes about helping others. The sick and the troubled often turn to him for advice and assistance.

He is very broadminded and does not criticize others for their faults. He knows how to accept people for what they are. On the whole, he is a trustworthy and earnest person. He is loyal to his

ous and good-natured, he is a lover of peace; he is often willing to help others solve their differences. People who have taken a wrong turn in life often interest him and he will do what he can to persuade them to rehabilitate themselves.

He has a strong intuitive sense and most of the time he knows how to make it work for him; the Piscean is unusually perceptive and often knows what is bothering someone before that person, himself, is aware of it. The Pisces man or woman is an idealistic person, basically, and is interested in making the world a better place in which to live. The Piscean believes that everyone should help each other. He is willing to do more than his share in order to achieve cooperation with others.

The person born under this sign often is talented in music or art. He is a receptive person; he is able to take the ups and downs of life with philosophic calm.

The Negative Side of Pisces

Some Pisceans are often depressed; their outlook on life is rather glum. They may feel that they have been given a bad deal in life and that others are always taking unfair advantage of them. The Piscean sometimes feels that the world is a cold and cruel place. He is easily discouraged. He may even withdraw from the harshness of reality into a secret shell of his own where he dreams and idles away a good deal of his time.

The Piscean can be rather lazy. He lets things happen without giving the least bit of resistance. He drifts along, whether on the high road or on the low. He is rather short on willpower.

Some Pisces people seek escape through drugs or alcohol. When temptation comes along they find it hard to resist. In matters of sex, they can be rather permissive.

THE SIGNS AND THEIR KEY WORDS

		POSITIVE	NEGATIVE
ARIES	self	courage, initiative, pioneer instinct	brash rudeness, selfish impetuosity
TAURUS	money	endurance, loyalty, wealth	obstinacy, gluttony
GEMINI	mind	versatility	capriciousness, unreliability
CANCER	family	sympathy, homing instinct	clannishness, childishness
LEO	children	love, authority, integrity	egotism, force
VIRGO	work	purity, industry, analysis	fault-finding, cynicism
LIBRA	marriage	harmony, justice	vacillation, superficiality
SCORPIO	sex	survival, regeneration	vengeance, discord
SAGITTARIUS	travel	optimism, higher learning	lawlessness
CAPRICORN	career	depth	narrowness, gloom
AQUARIUS	friends	human fellowship, genius	perverse unpredictability
PISCES	confinement	spiritual love, universality	diffusion, escapism

THE ELEMENTS AND QUALITIES OF THE SIGNS

ELEMENT	SIGN	QUALITY	SIGN
FIRE	ARIES LEO SAGITTARIUS	CARDINAL	ARIES LIBRA CANCER CAPRICORN
EARTH	TAURUS VIRGO CAPRICORN	FIXED	TAURUS LEO SCORPIO AQUARIUS
AIR	GEMINI LIBRA AQUARIUS	MUTABLE	GEMINI VIRGO SAGITTARIUS PISCES
WATER	CANCER SCORPIO PISCES		

Every sign has both an element and a quality associated with it. The element indicates the basic makeup of the sign, and the quality describes the kind of activity associated with each.

Signs can be grouped together according to their *element* and *quality*. Signs of the same element share many basic traits in common. They tend to form stable configurations and ultimately harmonious relationships. Signs of the same quality are often less harmonious, but they share many dynamic potentials for growth as well as profound fulfillment.

THE FIRE SIGNS

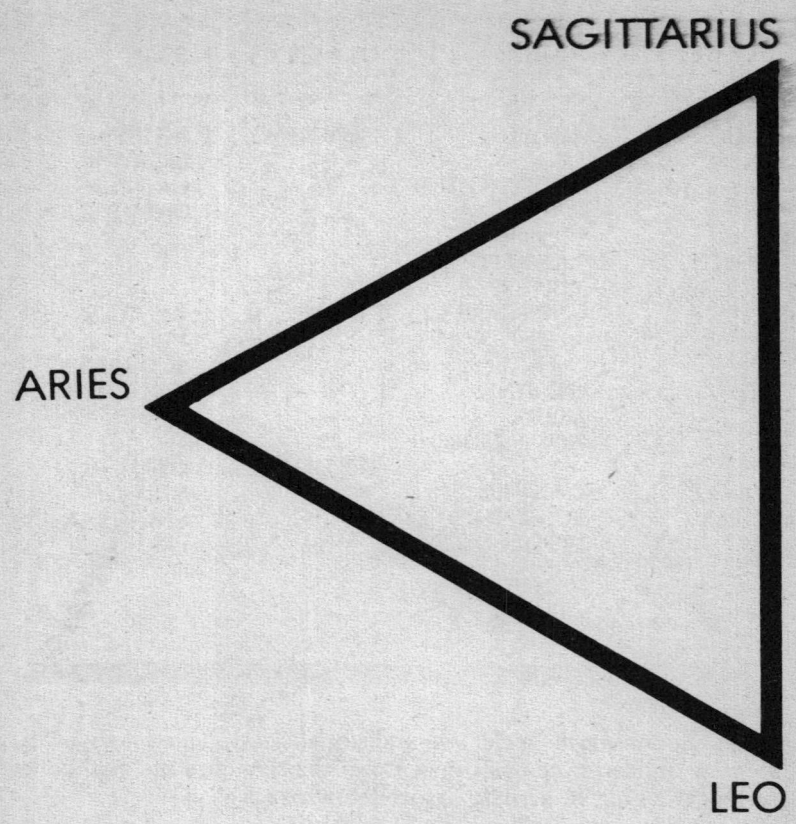

This is the fire group. On the whole these are emotional, volatile types, quick to anger, quick to forgive. They are adventurous, powerful people and act as a source of inspiration for everyone. They spark into action with immediate exuberant impulses. They are intelligent, self-involved, creative and idealistic. They all share a certain vibrancy and glow that outwardly reflects an inner flame and passion for living.

THE EARTH SIGNS

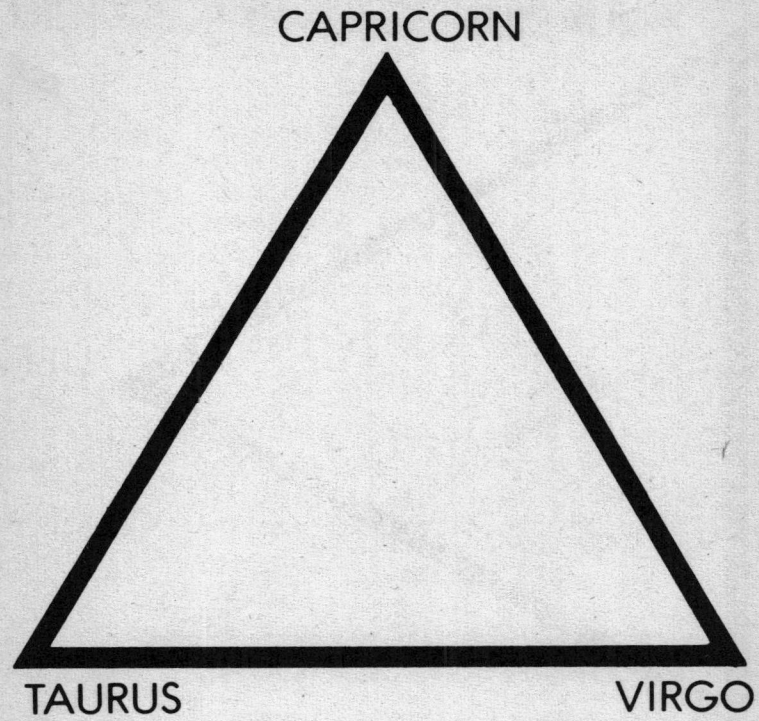

This is the earth group. They are in constant touch with the material world and tend to be conservative. Although they are all capable of spartan self-discipline, they are earthy, sensual people who are stimulated by the tangible, elegant and luxurious. The thread of their lives is always practical, but they do fantasize and are often attracted to dark, mysterious, emotional people. They are like great cliffs overhanging the sea, forever married to the ocean but always resisting erosion from the dark, emotional forces that thunder at their feet.

THE AIR SIGNS

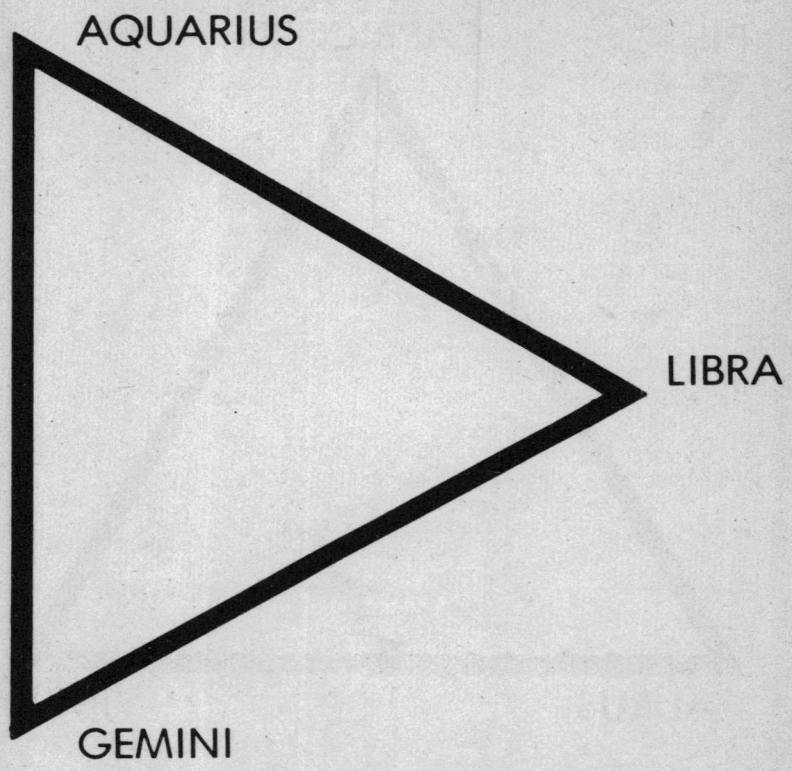

This is the air group. They are light, mental creatures desirous of contact, communication and relationship. They are involved with people and the forming of ties on many levels. Original thinkers, they are the bearers of human news. Their language is their sense of word, color, style and beauty. They provide an atmosphere suitable and pleasant for living. They add change and versatility to the scene, and it is through them that we can explore new territory of human intelligence and experience.

THE WATER SIGNS

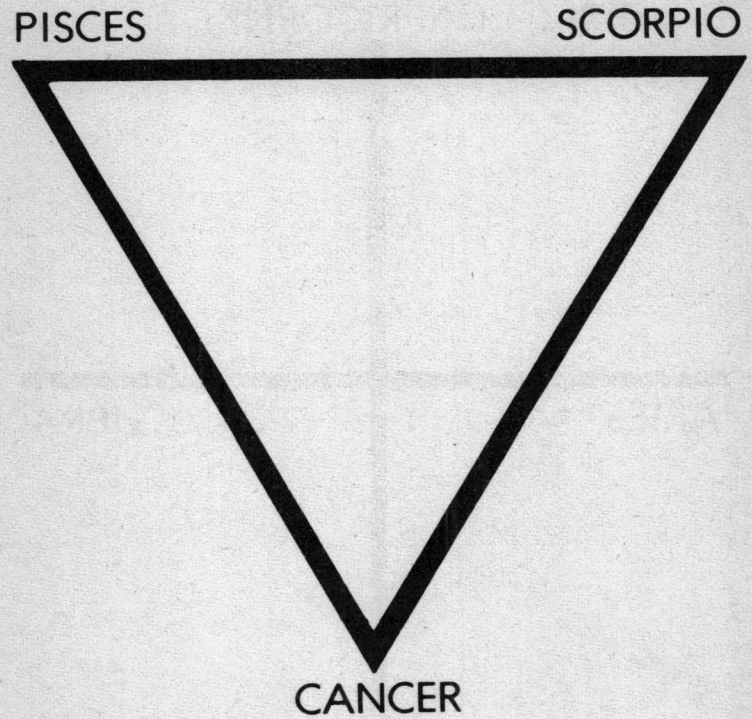

This is the water group. Through the water people, we are all joined together on emotional, non-verbal levels. They are silent, mysterious types whose magic hypnotizes even the most determined realist. They have uncanny perceptions about people and are as rich as the oceans when it comes to feeling, emotion or imagination. They are sensitive, mystical creatures with memories that go back beyond time. Through water, life is sustained. These people have the potential for the depths of darkness or the heights of mysticism and art.

THE CARDINAL SIGNS

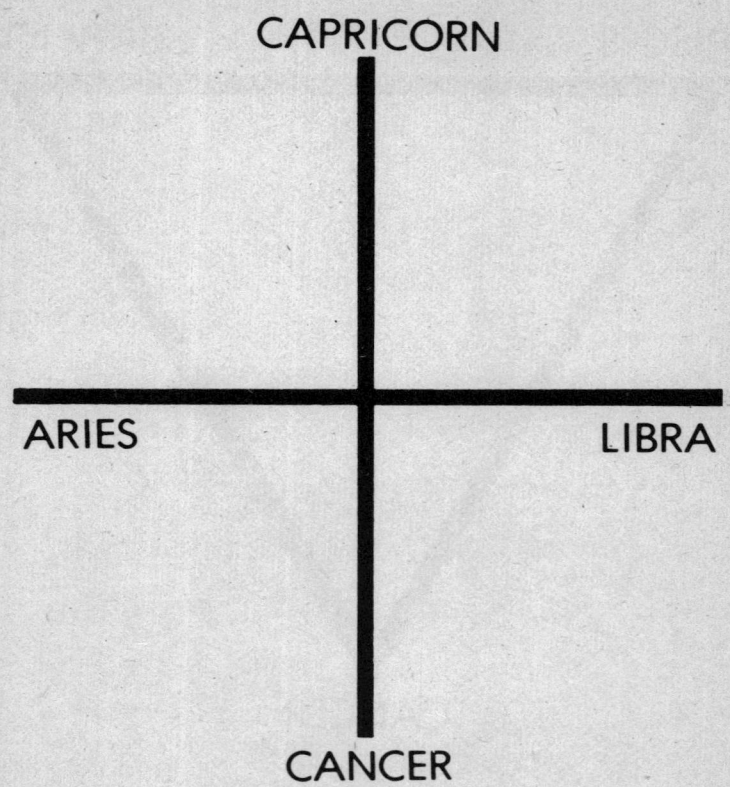

Put together, this is a clear-cut picture of dynamism, activity, tremendous stress and remarkable achievement. These people know the meaning of great change since their lives are often characterized by significant crises and major successes. This combination is like a simultaneous storm of summer, fall, winter and spring. The danger is chaotic diffusion of energy; the potential is irrepressible growth and victory.

THE FIXED SIGNS

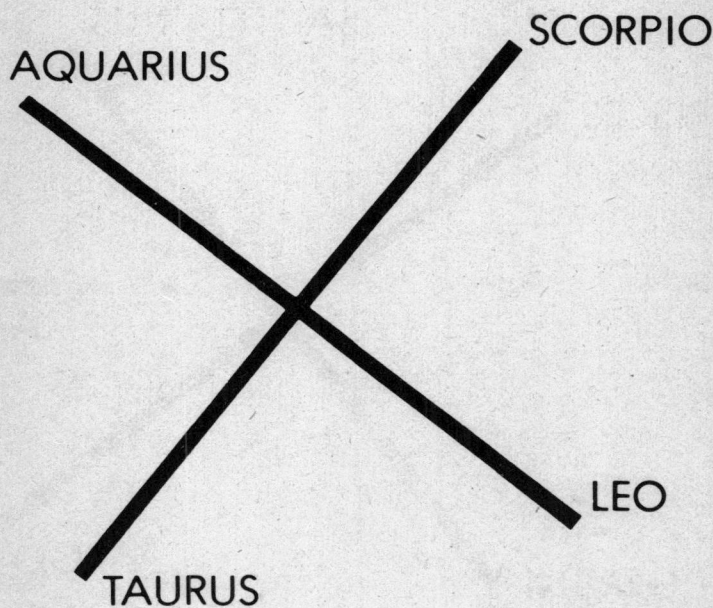

Fixed signs are always establishing themselves in a given place or area of experience. Like explorers who arrive and plant a flag, these people claim a position from which they do not enjoy being deposed. They are staunch, stalwart, upright, trusty, honorable people, although their obstinacy is well-known. Their contribution is fixity, and they are the angels who support our visible world.

THE MUTABLE SIGNS

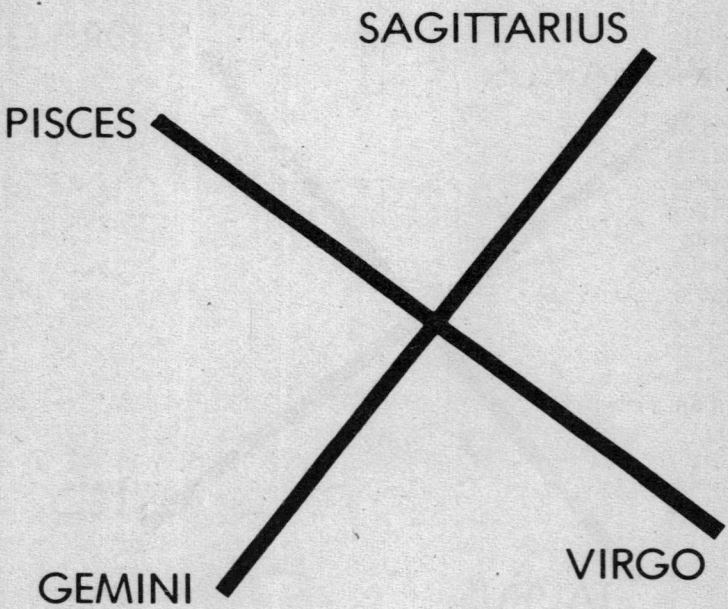

Mutable people are versatile, sensitive, intelligent, nervous and deeply curious about life. They are the translators of all energy. They often carry out or complete tasks initiated by others. Combinations of these signs have highly developed minds; they are imaginative and jumpy and think and talk a lot. At worst their lives are a Tower of Babel. At best they are adaptable and ready creatures who can assimilate one kind of experience and enjoy it while anticipating coming changes.

HOW TO APPROXIMATE YOUR RISING SIGN

Apart from the month and day of birth, the exact *time* of birth is another vital factor in the determination of an accurate horoscope. Not only do the planets move with great speed, but one must know how far the Earth has turned during the day. That way you can determine exactly where the planets are located with respect to the precise birthplace of an individual. This makes *your* horoscope *your* horoscope. In addition to these factors, another grid is laid upon that of the Zodiac and the planets: the houses. After all three have been considered, specific planetary relationships can be measured and analyzed in accordance with certain ordered procedures. It is the skillful translation of all this complex astrological language that a serious astrologer strives for in his attempt at coherent astrological synthesis. Keep this in mind.

The horoscope sets up a kind of framework around which the life of an individual grows like wild ivy, this way and that, weaving its way around the trellis of the natal positions of the planets. The year of birth tells us the positions of the distant, slow-moving planets like Jupiter, Saturn, Uranus and Pluto. The month of birth indicates the Sun sign, or birth sign as it is commonly called, as well as indicating the positions of the rapidly moving planets like Venus, Mercury and Mars. The day of birth locates the position of our Moon, and the moment of birth determines the houses through what is called the Ascendant, or Rising Sign.

As the Earth rotates on its axis once every 24 hours, each one of the twelve signs of the Zodiac appears to be "rising" on the horizon, with a new one appearing about every two hours. Actually it is the turning of the Earth that exposes each sign to view, but you will remember that in much of our astrological work we are discussing "apparent" motion. This *Rising Sign* marks the Ascendant and it colors the whole orientation of a horoscope. It indicates the sign governing the first house of the chart, and will thus determine which signs will govern all the other houses. The idea is a bit complicated at first, and we needn't dwell on complications in this introduction, but if you can imagine two color wheels with twelve divisions superimposed upon each other, one moving slowly and the other remaining still, you will have some idea of how the signs keep shifting the "color" of the houses as the Rising Sign continues to change every two hours.

The important point is that the birth chart, or horoscope, actually does define specific factors of a person's makeup. It contains a picture of being, much the way the nucleus of a tiny cell contains the potential for an entire elephant, or a packet of seeds contains a rosebush. If there were no order or continuity to the world, we could plant roses and get elephants. This same order that gives continuous flow to our lives often annoys people if it threatens to determine too much of their lives. We must grow from what we were planted, and there's no reason why we can't do that magnificently. It's all there in the horoscope. Where there is limitation, there is breakthrough; where there is crisis, there is transformation. Accurate analysis of a horoscope can help you find these points of breakthrough and transformation, and it requires knowledge of subtleties and distinctions that demand skillful judgment in order to solve even the simplest kind of personal question.

It is still quite possible, however, to draw some conclusions based upon the sign occupied by the Sun alone. In fact, if you're just being introduced to this vast subject, you're better off keeping it simple. Otherwise it seems like an impossible jumble, much like trying to read a novel in a foreign language without knowing the basic vocabulary. As with anything else, you can progress in your appreciation and understanding of astrology in direct proportion to your interest. To become really good at it requires study, experience, patience and above all—and maybe simplest of all—a fundamental understanding of what is actually going on right up there in the sky over your head. It is a vital living process you can observe, contemplate and ultimately understand. You can start by observing sunrise, or sunset, or even the full Moon.

In fact you can do a simple experiment after reading this introduction. You can erect a rough chart by following the simple procedure below:

1. Draw a circle with twelve equal segments.

2. Starting at what would be the nine o'clock position on a clock, number the segments, or houses, from 1 to 12 in a *counterclockwise direction*.

3. Label house number 1 in the following way: 4 A.M.-6 A.M.

4. In a counterclockwise direction, label the rest of the houses: 2 A.M.-4 A.M., MIDNIGHT-2 A.M., 10 P.M-MIDNIGHT, 8 P.M.-10 P.M., 6 P.M.-8 P.M., 4 P.M.-6 P.M., 2 P.M.-4 P.M., NOON-2 P.M., 10 A.M.-NOON, 8 A.M.-10 A.M., and 6 A.M.-8 A.M.

5. Now find out what time you were born and place the sun in the appropriate house.

6. Label the edge of that house with your Sun sign. You now have a description of your basic character and your fundamental drives. You can also see in what areas of life on Earth you will be most likely to focus your constant energy and center your activity.

7. If you are really feeling ambitious, label the rest of the houses with the signs, starting with your Sun sign, in order, still in a *counterclockwise direction*. When you get to Pisces, start over with Aries and keep going until you reach the house behind the Sun.

8. Look to house number 1. The sign that you have now labeled and attached to house number 1 is your Rising sign. It will color your self-image, outlook, physical constitution, early life and whole orientation to life. Of course this is a mere approximation, since there are many complicated calculations that must be made with respect to adjustments for birth time, but if you read descriptions of the sign preceding and the sign following the one you have calculated in the above manner, you may be able to identify yourself better. In any case, when you get through labeling all the houses, your drawing should look something like this:

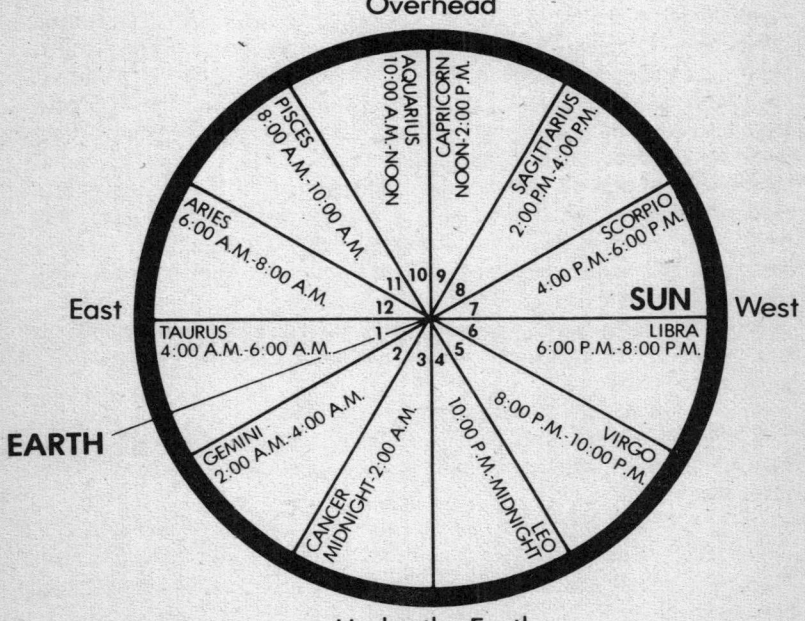

Basic chart illustrating the position of the Sun in Scorpio, with the Ascendant Taurus as the Rising Sign.

This individual was born at 5:15 P.M. on October 31 in New York City. The Sun is in Scorpio and is found in the 7th house. The Rising sign, or the sign governing house number 1, is Taurus, so this person is a blend of Scorpio and Taurus.

Any further calculation would necessitate that you look in an ephemeris, or table of planetary motion, for the positions of the rest of the planets for your particular birth year. But we will take the time to define briefly all the known planets of our Solar System and the Sun to acquaint you with some more of the astrological vocabulary that you will be meeting again and again. (See page 21 for a full explanation of the Moon in all the Signs.)

THE PLANETS AND SIGNS THEY RULE

The signs of the Zodiac are linked to the planets in the following way. Each sign is governed or ruled by one or more planets. No matter where the planets are located in the sky at any given moment, they still rule their respective signs, and when they travel through the signs they rule, they have special dignity and their effects are stronger.

Following is a list of the planets and the signs they rule. After looking at the list, go back over the definitions of the planets and see if you can determine how the planet ruling *your* Sun sign has affected your life.

SIGNS	RULING PLANETS
Aries	Mars, Pluto
Taurus	Venus
Gemini	Mercury
Cancer	Moon
Leo	Sun
Virgo	Mercury
Libra	Venus
Scorpio	Mars, Pluto
Sagittarius	Jupiter
Capricorn	Saturn
Aquarius	Saturn, Uranus
Pisces	Jupiter, Neptune

THE PLANETS OF THE SOLAR SYSTEM

Here are the planets of the Solar System. They all travel around the Sun at different speeds and different distances. Taken with the Sun, they all distribute individual intelligence and ability throughout the entire chart.

The planets modify the influence of the Sun in a chart according to their own particular natures, strengths and positions. Their positions must be calculated for each year and day, and their function and expression in a horoscope will change as they move from one area of the Zodiac to another.

Following, you will find brief statements of their pure meanings.

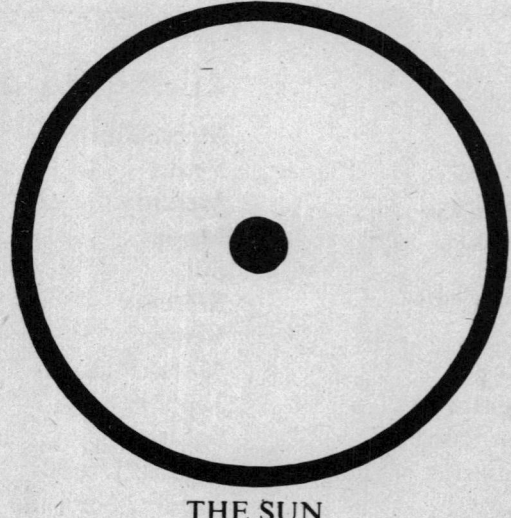

THE SUN

SUN

This is the center of existence. Around this flaming sphere all the planets revolve in endless orbits. Our star is constantly sending out its beams of light and energy without which no life on Earth would be possible. In astrology it symbolizes everything we are trying to become, the center around which all of our activity in life will always revolve. It is the symbol of our basic nature and describes the natural and constant thread that runs through everything that we do from birth to death on this planet.

To early astrologers, the sun seemed to be another planet because it crossed the heavens every day, just like the rest of the bodies in the sky.

It is the only star near enough to be seen well—it is, in fact, a dwarf star. Approximately 860,000 miles in diameter, it is about ten times as wide as the giant planet Jupiter. The next nearest star is nearly 300,000 times as far away, and if the Sun were located as far away as most of the bright stars, it would be too faint to be seen without a telescope.

Everything in the horoscope ultimately revolves around this singular body. Although other forces may be prominent in the charts of some individuals, still the Sun is the total nucleus of being and symbolizes the complete potential of every human being alive. It is vitality and the life force. Your whole essence comes from the position of the Sun.

You are always trying to express the Sun according to its position by house and sign. Possibility for all development is found in the Sun, and it marks the fundamental character of your personal radiations all around you.

It is the symbol of strength, vigor, wisdom, dignity, ardor and generosity, and the ability for a person to function as a mature individual. It is also a creative force in society. It is consciousness of the gift of life.

The underdeveloped solar nature is arrogant, pushy, undependable and proud, and is constantly using force.

MERCURY

Mercury is the planet closest to the Sun. It races around our star, gathering information and translating it to the rest of the system. Mercury represents your capacity to understand the desires of your own will and to translate those desires into action.

In other words it is the planet of Mind and the power of communication. Through Mercury we develop an ability to think, write, speak and observe—to become aware of the world around us. It colors our attitudes and vision of the world, as well as our capacity to communicate our inner responses to the outside world. Some people who have serious disabilities in their power of verbal communication have often wrongly been described as people lacking intelligence.

Although this planet (and its position in the horoscope) indicates your power to communicate your thoughts and perceptions to the world, intelligence is something deeper. Intelligence is distributed throughout all the planets. It is the relationship of the planets to each other that truly describes what we call intelligence. Mercury rules speaking, language, mathematics, draft and design, students, messengers, young people, offices, teachers and any pursuits where the mind of man has wings.

VENUS

Venus is beauty. It symbolizes the harmony and radiance of a rare and elusive quality: beauty itself. It is refinement and delicacy, softness and charm. In astrology it indicates grace, balance and the aesthetic sense. Where Venus is we see beauty, a gentle drawing in of energy and the need for satisfaction and completion. It is a special touch that finishes off rough edges. It is sensitivity, and affection, and it is always the place for that other elusive phenomenon: love. Venus describes our sense of what is beautiful and loving. Poorly developed, it is vulgar, tasteless and self-indulgent. But its ideal is the flame of spiritual love—Aphrodite, goddess of love, and the sweetness and power of personal beauty.

MARS

This is raw, crude energy. The planet next to Earth but outward from the Sun is a fiery red sphere that charges through the horoscope with force and fury. It represents the way you reach out for new adventure and new experience. It is energy and drive, initiative, courage and daring. The power to start something and see it through. It can be thoughtless, cruel and wild, angry and hostile, causing cuts, burns, scalds and wounds. It can stab its way through a chart, or it can be the symbol of healthy spirited adventure, well-channeled constructive power to begin and keep up the drive. If you have trouble starting things, if you lack the get-up-and-go to start the ball rolling, if you lack aggressiveness and self-confidence, chances are there's another planet influencing your Mars. Mars rules soldiers, butchers, surgeons, salesmen—any field that requires daring, bold skill, operational technique or self-promotion.

JUPITER

This is the largest planet of the Solar System. Scientists have recently learned that Jupiter reflects more light than it receives from the Sun. In a sense it is like a star itself. In astrology it rules good luck and good cheer, health, wealth, optimism, happiness, success and joy. It is the symbol of opportunity and always opens the way for new possibilities in your life. It rules exuberance, enthusiasm, wisdom, knowledge, generosity and all forms of expansion in general. It rules actors, statesmen, clerics, professional people, religion, publishing and the distribution of many people over large areas.

Sometimes Jupiter makes you think you deserve everything, and you become sloppy, wasteful, careless and rude, prodigal and lawless, in the illusion that nothing can ever go wrong. Then there is the danger of over-confidence, exaggeration, undependability and over-indulgence.

Jupiter is the minimization of limitation and the emphasis on spirituality and potential. It is the thirst for knowledge and higher learning.

SATURN

Saturn circles our system in dark splendor with its mysterious rings, forcing us to be awakened to whatever we have neglected in the past. It will present real puzzles and problems to be solved, causing delays, obstacles and hindrances. By doing so, Saturn stirs our own sensitivity to those areas where we are laziest.

Here we must patiently develop *method,* and only through painstaking effort can our ends be achieved. It brings order to a horoscope and imposes reason just where we are feeling least reasonable. By creating limitations and boundary, Saturn shows the consequences of being human and demands that we accept the changing cycles inevitable in human life. Saturn rules time, old age and sobriety. It can bring depression, gloom, jealousy and greed, or serious acceptance of responsibilities out of which success will develop. With Saturn there is nothing to do but face facts. It rules laborers, stones, granite, rocks and crystals of all kinds.

The Outer Planets

The following three are the outer planets. They liberate human beings from cultural conditioning, and in that sense are the law breakers. In early times it was thought that Saturn was the last planet of the system—the outer limit beyond which we could never go. The discovery of the next three planets ushered in new phases of human history, revolution and technology.

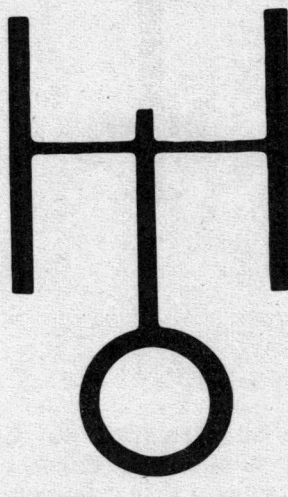

URANUS

Uranus rules unexpected change, upheaval, revolution. It is the symbol of total independence and asserts the freedom of an individual from all restriction and restraint. It is a breakthrough planet and indicates talent, originality and genius in a horoscope. It usually causes last-minute reversals and changes of plan, unwanted separations, accidents, catastrophes and eccentric behavior. It can add irrational rebelliousness and perverse bohemianism to a personality or a streak of unaffected brilliance in science and art. It rules technology, aviation and all forms of electrical and electronic advancement. It governs great leaps forward and topsy-turvy situations, and *always* turns things around at the last minute. Its effects are difficult to ever really predict, since it rules sudden last-minute decisions and events that come like lightning out of the blue.

NEPTUNE

Neptune dissolves existing reality the way the sea erodes the cliffs beside it. Its effects are subtle like the ringing of a buoy's bell in the fog. It suggests a reality higher than definition can usually describe. It awakens a sense of higher responsibility often causing guilt, worry, anxieties or delusions. Neptune is associated with all forms of escape and can make things seem a certain way so convincingly that you are absolutely sure of something that eventually turns out to be quite different.

It is the planet of illusion and therefore governs the invisible realms that lie beyond our ordinary minds, beyond our simple factual ability to prove what is "real." Treachery, deceit, disillusionment and disappointment are linked to Neptune. It describes a vague reality that promises eternity and the divine, yet in a manner so complex that we cannot really fathom it at all. At its worst Neptune is a cheap intoxicant; at its best it is the poetry, music and inspiration of the higher planes of spiritual love. It has dominion over movies, photographs and much of the arts.

PLUTO

Pluto lies at the outpost of our system and therefore rules finality in a horoscope—the final closing of chapters in your life, the passing of major milestones and points of development from which there is no return. It is a final wipeout, a closeout, an evacuation. It is a distant, subtle but powerful catalyst in all transformations that occur. It creates, destroys, then recreates. Sometimes Pluto starts its influence with a minor event or insignificant incident that might even go unnoticed. Slowly but surely, little by little, everything changes, until at last there has been a total transformation in the area of your life where Pluto has been operating. It rules mass thinking and the trends that society first rejects, then adopts and finally outgrows.

Pluto rules the dead and the underworld—all the powerful forces of creation and destruction that go on all the time beneath, around and above us. It can bring a lust for power with strong obsessions.

It is the planet that rules the metamorphoses of the caterpillar into a butterfly, for it symbolizes the capacity to change totally and forever a person's life style, way of thought and behavior.

FAMOUS PERSONALITIES

ARIES: Hans Christian Andersen, Pearl Bailey, Marlon Brando, Wernher Von Braun, Charlie Chaplin, Joan Crawford, Da Vinci, Bette Davis, Doris Day, W. C. Fields, Alec Guinness, Adolf Hitler, Billie Holiday, Thomas Jefferson, Nikita Khrushchev, Elton John, Arturo Toscanini, J. P. Morgan, Paul Robeson, Gloria Steinem, Lowell Thomas, Vincent van Gogh, Tennessee Williams

TAURUS: Fred Astaire, Charlote Brontë, Carol Burnett, Irving Berlin, Bing Crosby, Salvador Dali, Tchaikovsky, Queen Elizabeth II, Duke Ellington, Ella Fitzgerald, Henry Fonda, Sigmund Freud, Orson Welles, Joe Louis, Lenin, Karl Marx, Golda Meir, Eva Peron, Bertrand Russell, Shakespeare, Kate Smith, Benjamin Spock, Barbra Streisand, Shirley Temple, Harry Truman

GEMINI: Mikhail Baryshnikov, Boy George, Igor Stravinsky, Carlos Chavez, Walt Whitman, Bob Dylan, Ralph Waldo Emerson, Judy Garland, Paul Gauguin, Allen Ginsberg, Benny Goodman, Bob Hope, Burl Ives, John F. Kennedy, Peggy Lee, Marilyn Monroe, Joe Namath, Cole Porter, Laurence Olivier, Harriet Beecher Stowe, Queen Victoria, John Wayne, Frank Lloyd Wright

CANCER: "Dear Abby," David Brinkley, Yul Brynner, Pearl Buck, Marc Chagall, Jack Dempsey, Mildred (Babe) Zaharias, Mary Baker Eddy, Henry VIII, John Glenn, Ernest Hemingway, Lena Horne, Oscar Hammerstein, Helen Keller, Ann Landers, George Orwell, Nancy Reagan, Rembrandt, Richard Rodgers, Ginger Rogers, Rubens, Jean-Paul Sartre, O. J. Simpson

LEO: Neil Armstrong, Russell Baker, James Baldwin, Emily Brontë, Wilt Chamberlain, Julia Child, Cecil B. De Mille, Ogden Nash, Amelia Earhart, Edna Ferber, Arthur Goldberg, Dag Hammarskjöld, Alfred Hitchcock, Mick Jagger, George Meany, George Bernard Shaw, Napoleon, Jacqueline Onassis, Henry Ford, Francis Scott Key, Andy Warhol, Mae West, Orville Wright

VIRGO: Ingrid Bergman, Warren Burger, Maurice Chevalier, Agatha Christie, Sean Connery, Lafayette, Peter Falk, Greta Garbo, Althea Gibson, Arthur Godfrey, Goethe, Buddy Hackett, Michael Jackson, Lyndon Johnson, D. H. Lawrence, Sophia Loren, Grandma Moses, Arnold Palmer, Queen Elizabeth I, Walter Reuther, Peter Sellers, Lily Tomlin, George Wallace

LIBRA: Brigitte Bardot, Art Buchwald, Truman Capote, Dwight D. Eisenhower, William Faulkner, F. Scott Fitzgerald, Gandhi, George Gershwin, Micky Mantle, Helen Hayes, Vladimir Horowitz, Doris Lessing, Martina Navratalova, Eugene O'Neill, Luciano Pavarotti, Emily Post, Eleanor Roosevelt, Bruce Springsteen, Margaret Thatcher, Gore Vidal, Barbara Walters, Oscar Wilde

SCORPIO: Vivien Leigh, Richard Burton, Art Carney, Johnny Carson, Billy Graham, Grace Kelly, Walter Cronkite, Marie Curie, Charles de Gaulle, Linda Evans, Indira Gandhi, Theodore Roosevelt, Rock Hudson, Katherine Hepburn, Robert F. Kennedy, Billie Jean King, Martin Luther, Georgia O'Keeffe, Pablo Picasso, Jonas Salk, Alan Shepard, Robert Louis Stevenson

SAGITTARIUS: Jane Austen, Louisa May Alcott, Woody Allen, Beethoven, Willy Brandt, Mary Martin, William F. Buckley, Maria Callas, Winston Churchill, Noel Coward, Emily Dickinson, Walt Disney, Benjamin Disraeli, James Doolittle, Kirk Douglas, Chet Huntley, Jane Fonda, Chris Evert Lloyd, Margaret Mead, Charles Schulz, John Milton, Frank Sinatra, Steven Spielberg

CAPRICORN: Muhammad Ali, Isaac Asimov, Pablo Casals, Dizzy Dean, Marlene Dietrich, James Farmer, Ava Gardner, Barry Goldwater, Cary Grant, J. Edgar Hoover, Howard Hughes, Joan of Arc, Gypsy Rose Lee, Martin Luther King, Jr., Rudyard Kipling, Mao Tse-tung, Richard Nixon, Gamal Nasser, Louis Pasteur, Albert Schweitzer, Stalin, Benjamin Franklin, Elvis Presley

AQUARIUS: Marian Anderson, Susan B. Anthony, Jack Benny, Charles Darwin, Charles Dickens, Thomas Edison, John Barrymore, Clark Gable, Jascha Heifetz, Abraham Lincoln, John McEnroe, Yehudi Menuhin, Mozart, Jack Nicklaus, Ronald Reagan, Jackie Robinson, Norman Rockwell, Franklin D. Roosevelt, Gertrude Stein, Charles Lindbergh, Margaret Truman

PISCES: Edward Albee, Harry Belafonte, Alexander Graham Bell, Frank Borman, Chopin, Adelle Davis, Albert Einstein, Jackie Gleason, Winslow Homer, Edward M. Kennedy, Victor Hugo, Mike Mansfield, Michelangelo, Edna St. Vincent Millay, Liza Minelli, John Steinbeck, Linus Pauling, Ravel, Diana Ross, William Shirer, Elizabeth Taylor, George Washington

AQUARIUS

CHARACTER ANALYSIS

Of all the signs of the Zodiac, Aquarius is perhaps the most progressive. People born under this sign are usually quite tolerant and broadminded. There is a saying that most Aquarians are 50 years ahead of their time. As a rule they are unselfish and peace-loving. They are often more interested in helping others than they are in helping themselves. They think of mankind on a very broad scale and are interested in justice for all. All the wrongs that exist in the world appall them. They may spend a lifetime trying to set things right, in their own way.

The Aquarian does not believe in hanging onto old, useless values. He is for progress; for moving ahead and making a better world. It is important to him that peace and harmony exist in social situations; he'll accept nothing less than that.

Anything connected with the betterment of mankind interests him. He is also likely to have a useful hobby. In short, he is a person with a purpose in mind. General education methods and sociology are usually things that interest him greatly. He does not believe that mankind should be divided into rich and poor. He feels that everyone should be entitled to the same privileges no matter what his background. More often than not, people born under the sign of Aquarius have an intellectual nature. They usually know a lot about many things and they are sure of what they know. There is nothing superficial about them. They are eager to impart what they know to others. To them, it is more important to have a good mind than a full stomach. The Aquarian probably feels that man will eat out of necessity, but that his mind must be properly trained if he is to enjoy all that life has to offer. He holds that the world would be a better place if all men were intellectually responsible.

As has already been mentioned, the Aquarian is years ahead of time in his way of thinking. Others often find it hard to keep up with him. He is not afraid of change; on the contrary, he welcomes it. New ways of living are always of interest to him. The person born under this eleventh sign of the zodiac is eager to develop along creative lines—he is keen on new forms of organization or thought. Even in love matters, he tends to be creative. To some he may seem slightly mad, to others he is apt to seem a bit of a genius.

The Aquarian is interested in groups—how they are structured, their behavioral patterns and so on. He enjoys bringing people together. He wants to see everyone living in peace and harmony.

The individual holds little interest for him. He thinks in terms of masses of people. For him, this is life.

He surprises many people. The Aquarian always keeps others guessing. At times, he does not even know himself what his next step in life will be.

At times he may seem rather detached, disengaged. Others may feel he is sizing up everyone around him and making mental notes. The Aquarian believes in live and let live as an all-around way of getting on in the world. He would never try to dominate another; he respects the other man for his individuality. He believes in letting others express themselves as they want. He does not feel he has the right to direct another's life style. Others often find it difficult placing an Aquarian; he seems so full of contradictions at times—it's difficult to say he is one thing or the other.

The person born under this sign usually has his own set of laws to live by. Conventional rules and regulations, he feels, need not apply to him. He has his own rights and wrongs. To the average person he may seem downright unconventional. Others may think he is just trying to gain attention by shocking his neighbors, but this is far from the truth. The Aquarian does not believe in poses; he believes in what he does. The customs and dress of the average person say little to him. He may find it quite necessary to develop his own way of behaving and dressing in order to express the "real" him. He is an individualist. Original modes of behavior and thinking are something he cannot do without.

His head is generally full of plans and ideas. Because he is so often busy turning things over in his head, he is apt to seem a bit dreamy and "out of it" to others. At times, the Aquarian shoots his hopes too high and has to pay the consequences of being too unrealistic.

Health

On the whole, people born under the sign of Aquarius are good to look at. They may be slight of build, yet they are strong in a wiry sort of way. They have a strong resistance against illnesses, generally. They are healthy, for the most part, and know how to take care of themselves. They are usually interested in hygiene and take all sorts of precautions so that disease never has a chance to strike them. Physically they have little to worry about; their constitutions are strong and healthy.

Tensions and pressure, however, can cause them to become depressed, and this often has a bad effect on their overall health. But this is generally rare, for the Aquarian has the ability to remove himself from things that are disturbing. He can look at things in an objective way so that they do not really affect his spiritual balance.

It is important for the person born under this sign to oppose people who try to dominate him or drive him into a corner. He is not the kind of person who can allow someone to encroach upon his freedom. The strain of someone bearing down on him can have a bad influence on his well-being. At times, he may be downright nervous due to disturbing conditions. It is important that the Aquarian see to it that he has the proper amount of vitamins and minerals to help counteract his nervousness. He should try to see to it that his diet is well-balanced with plenty of fresh fruit and vegetables. He also needs peace and quiet and plenty of fresh air. A country place where he can retreat when the going gets rough would be ideal. Harmonious surroundings are important to him.

Still and all, he is not the kind of person who will hold his tongue if someone criticizes his ideals. He'll stand up for what he believes. His objective manner will protect him from injury to some extent.

The mind is important to the Aquarian. He can train himself to control it so that when he meets with minor setbacks or disturbances they do not really affect him.

The weak parts of his body are his ankles and calves. If he has an accident, quite often these areas are affected. Nervous and circulatory disorders sometimes bother him. The Aquarian who is not careful may become the victim of low blood pressure and anemia. By taking the proper vitamins and eating the proper food, he can prevent these ailments.

Occupation

The kind of occupation that generally interests someone born under the sign of Aquarius is work that has a bit of idealism to it—a job that has a philosophical outlook. It is important to someone born under this sign that he has a job suited to his particular talents and character. If it is not exactly his kind of work then it must be open-ended enough so that he can mold it to fit his particular need. He has to be creative in his work. Suggestions and new techniques are important to him. Quite often his place of business profits through his being allowed to approach the duties of his position in a creative manner.

He is a person who enjoys keeping busy. He believes in rolling up his sleeves and getting down to brass tacks immediately. He doesn't like to waste time when working. Quite often he is quicker than the people he works with and can finish his job in half the time it takes others to do it. He is energetic and enthusiastic about what he does. Many of the suggestions he has for improvements on the job are helpful. He is usually a great source of inspiration for his co-workers. Responsibility does not frighten him, but he would rather not take orders from someone else.

Quite often the mind of the Aquarian is turning over new plans and ideas, even while he is busy at work. His thoughts never rest. He is inventive in his way of thinking. Quite often the results of his mental endeavors benefit everyone. He is intrigued by things that are new and different. He is not afraid to try out a new work technique or method. He believes in modern ideas. Routine work is not apt to hold his interest for very long. He likes unusual chores; things that give him a chance to do something on his own. If he is tied down to a humdrum kind of job, he is not likely to be interested in doing his best. Employers may find him a bit trying and unreliable. Routine chores hold little interest for him; he is apt to work at them in spurts, but his attention will be easily distracted. If his work is dull, he is apt to begin with a bang (in an attempt to get it out of the way as soon as possible), but later his energy is likely to peter out and he may even allow himself to become careless.

If the people he works with are rather slow and unimaginative, the Aquarian is apt to become restless and impatient. If he feels that they do not make an effort to better themselves, he is likely to become a bit scornful.

Social work is an occupation well suited to someone born under this sign. He is more concerned for others than he is for himself. His self-sacrificing way is a feather in his cap, and the people he deals with are apt to put themselves in his hands completely, trusting him to do what is best for them. The Aquarian does well in rehabilitation work. He likes to help people help themselves. He is the kind of person who is cut out for service work.

Some Aquarians make good writers and journalists. They have sharp, acute minds and know how to translate their thoughts on paper so that others can benefit from them.

Art and all things related to culture attract the average Aquarian. Some of them make good painters and musicians. They know how to be critical in a constructive way. Often they make good art or music critics.

It is important that the Aquarian put his heart and soul into his creative work if he wants to attain the high goals he sets for himself. He can do well in any job where he is allowed to make use of his rich imagination. In strict business matters, he may not be able to function very well due to a tendency to dream. Some people born under this sign, in spite of their good intentions, only plan during their lives and never get around to putting their ideas into action. Then when things get to be too much for them, they allow their plans to slide.

Money to the average Aquarian is nice to have for what it can do. Money in itself has little interest for him. He is neither a splurger or a pennypincher. He generally makes use of his finances in what he feels is a practical way. He may use some of it to make progress for himself and others easier.

Some Aquarians come by money through their inventions or discoveries. They may work night and day for a long period of time before coming up with the answer or solution of a problem. However, this sort of research or investigatory work generally intrigues them.

The Aquarian is the kind of person who will work hard for success, but he is more pleased if it comes as a surprise.

Home and Family

The Aquarian is generally a very sociable person. He or she feels it is important to have a nice home—one where it is pleasant to entertain friends and associates. His taste is generally modern —although he may have a respect for old things. He is bound to have all the latest fixtures and appliances in his home. As soon as something becomes out-of-date or non-functional, he is likely to throw it out and get something that is in keeping with the times. Appliances that save on housework are a must for the Aquarian woman. She has more important things to do than attending to the drudgery of housekeeping.

Although the Aquarian is fond of having a lot of people about, he does have his moments when he has to be alone. He wants peace and quiet so he can think things out without being interrupted. Chances are he is a member of many kinds of clubs and organizations. He likes people of all kinds. But he also likes his privacy to be respected. When he feels that it is necessary to withdraw from the hubbub of the crowd, he does not appreciate others who try to prevent this.

Although he loves his home and family, he does not like them to play a dominating role in his life. He'll own up to his responsibilities but he does not want to have his duties shoved under his nose constantly. In short, he does not want to feel that he is tied down. He needs love and affection, as everyone does, but he needs to be independent too. At times, these may conflict with each other.

With children, the Aquarian is likely to get along very well. He does not treat them as his inferiors, but is apt to handle them as little people. He knows how to talk and reason with them just as he would someone his own age. Children, in turn, generally respect him for treating them as individuals. He does not oppress children but encourages them to develop their natural talents and to express their own personalities.

The Aquarian, at times, enjoys the direct and honest company of children to that of so-called adults. He knows how to keep children entertained with stories and games. In spite of his ability to be permissive, the average Aquarian makes it clear to the child that he will tolerate no nonsense from them. Children, understanding this, never misbehave while in the company of an Aquarian adult.

Social Relationships

The average Aquarian is cheerful and outgoing when around people. At home he may be rather quiet and pensive. Few people understand this sort of person very well, even though they may feel they do. Some Aquarians withdraw so often from social situations that it becomes a permanent habit. Some famous recluses were born under this eleventh sign of the zodiac.

Because he sometimes keeps himself apart, he seems rather standoffish and critical to those who do not understand him. The Aquarian is apt to make many friends in his life, but his quality for being unconsciously aloof may make it difficult for others to get to know him. His close friendships may be few.

He is optimistic by nature and always tends to look on the positive or bright side of social situations. This outlook makes it possible for him to get along well with all kinds of people—even if only for a limited amount of time. Some of his friends and acquaintances may seem rather strange and eccentric to others. His collection of friends is likely to encompass many extremes in personality types.

The Aquarian makes a good friend because of his many nice qualities and his tolerant disposition. He does well with business associates as a rule and with his loved ones.

The average Aquarian enjoys observing mankind in all its forms and variations. He is never quick to judge another. For him, no one is totally bad or good. He is willing to make excuses for others if he really feels that they mean well. At times, this works against him; people may take advantage of his tolerant ways and play him for the fool. He does not always learn from his mistakes. He is easily moved by hard-luck stories. He is always willing to give another the benefit of a doubt.

He is the kind of person who sticks by his friends and acquaintances. Many of the friends he makes he keeps for life. He is loyal and dependable. When friends are in trouble, they can always depend on him. He likes them to respect his individuality as much as he respects theirs. He is never apt to meddle in their private affairs but will lend a helping hand if asked.

LOVE AND MARRIAGE

The average Aquarian may not be as interested in love for himself, that is, on a person to person basis, as he is in love on a universal basis. When he or she does fall in love with someone it is usually because of some intellectual attraction he feels rather than for some physical or superficial quality the person of the opposite sex may have.

Love to the Aquarian is serious business. He is faithful. When looking for a mate or partner, he will be more interested in the person's intellectual capacities and emotional depths than in what his personality may seem to be like. If the person that interests him does not measure up to his standards, he ends the relationship then and there—often without an explanation.

Although the average Aquarian may be deeply interested in love and romance, he or she may occasionally seem rather cool. He is difficult to understand in the battlefield of love. As with other things, he has his particular rules which he feels he must follow. The Aquarian's lover may have a hard time trying to pin him down. He won't allow himself to be totally possessed. He believes in holding onto his sense of liberty and freedom. He would never make excessive demands of his loved one's freedom; he expects the same consideration. In spite of this attitude, he is generally quite affectionate and loving.

In love, Aquarians do not always know what they want. They may have a good many love affairs before they decide to settle down. The *idea* of love may mean more to an Aquarian than the *act* of loving.

When he or she does marry, the Aquarian is faithful and considerate, and enjoys family life, the peace and quiet of home. Aquarians' love may waver at times, but it will never stray.

Romance and the Aquarius Woman

Some Aquarian women may seem rather cool and aloof, on the one hand, while exuding a sort of sexual warmth and charm, on the other. They may not be particularly interested in sex. They are more often than not attracted to the mental capacities of a man. The purely physical attributes, no matter how attractive they may be, hold little interest for them. When she does fall in love, it is usually with a man who is her intellectual equal or superior. She makes a faithful wife or lover. The man to whom she gives her affection must live up to her expectations. If he does not, she is likely to drop him rather quickly.

Many men are apt to find this kind of woman both attractive and cold. She is not a very affectionate person as a rule. A possessive man is apt to be in for a lot of frustration while courting her. She has her own laws to live by. She will not submit to a man who wants to fashion her to fit his own needs. Freedom and privacy are important to her even after marriage. If the man she loves respects her for her individuality and allows her what she feels are her God-given rights, everything will run smoothly in their relationship. She is in need of warmth and affection. The right man can help her to develop her interest in these qualities. Although she is no flirt, she may have a good many romantic adventures behind her before she consents to marry and settle down.

She makes an excellent companion, spiritually and intellectually. She makes a faithful and devoted wife. It is important to her that she have all the latest household appliances—especially those that save time—for she is not very domestically inclined. Chances are that after marriage she will want to continue her career or interests outside the home.

She is loving when dealing with her family. She must have peace and harmony in her home. She will put her foot down if things upset her. Her husband or children must not make excessive demands of her. Home may tie her down more than she desires; at times she may feel the need to get out and do something for others. Her family may see this as a kind of neglectful behavior although it is not. She holds that her family is more than just a husband and children; she relates to the community in which she lives and feels that she has obligations to it. She is very conscientious in her relationships.

As a mother, she is ideal. She understands her children and treats them as equals. She is not a scold but her children would never step out of line, anyway. They respect her too much for that.

Romance and the Aquarius Man

The Aquarius man is generally quite broad-minded. His interests extend to the farthest horizons. Humanity means a lot to him. He is in love with people; this is more important to him, sometimes, than being in love with just one person.

He is the kind of a lover who can win a woman over by his intellectual charm. He is usually witty and a good conversationalist. His joy of life usually impresses members of the opposite sex. Liberty is important to him. He will take up with the woman he loves but never try to strap her down with dos and don'ts. He wants his loved one to respect his right to express himself as he desires. If she understands his deep interest in personal freedom, and accepts it, the relationship is bound to be an enjoyable one. If she becomes too possessive, he is apt to break the relationship without giving an explanation.

Chances are he will have quite a number of love affairs in his life before he thinks of marrying. Sometimes he is impulsive about love and falls for a woman rather quickly and without reason; later he may regret it. He is unpredictable in love. Some Aquarian men marry their loved ones after a relatively unhappy love affair and make good husbands. They may disappoint their loved ones while courting, but after they settle down they do their best to set matters right.

He is generally affectionate, although he may not be very demonstrative. He is kind and considerate; he would never take advantage of another's feelings. Every time he is in love he is serious—even if the affair is short-lived.

He is fair in all things. He is likely to treat strangers with the same courtesy and kindness as he treats his family. Everyone is equal to him. He won't act one way with one person, another way with another. He's honest and always the same as far as his personality is concerned.

He is a faithful husband and a responsible parent. His interests outside may take him away from home affairs quite often, however, he will never neglect his basic duties as a provider. He may have to be coaxed to stay home more often, from time to time.

Children love him. He is tolerant with them and enjoys seeing them developing their own personalities. He is not a disciplinarian; he does not have to be. He guides his offspring with ease.

Woman—Man

AQUARIUS WOMAN
ARIES MAN

In some ways, the Aries man resembles an intellectual mountain goat leaping from crag to crag. He has an insatiable thirst for knowledge. He's ambitious and is apt to have his finger in many pies. He can go far with a woman like you—someone attractive, quickwitted, and smart.

He is not interested in a clinging vine kind of wife, but someone who is there when he needs her, someone who listens and understands what he says, someone who can give advice if he should ever need it . . . which is not likely to be often. The Aries man wants a woman who will look good on his arm without hanging on it too heavily. He is looking for a woman who has both feet on the ground and yet is mysterious and enticing—a kind of domestic

Helen of Troy whose face or fine dinner can launch a thousand business deals if need be. That woman he's in search of sounds a little like you, doesn't she? If the shoe fits, put it on. You won't regret it.

The Aries man makes a good husband. He is faithful and attentive. He is an affectionate kind of man. He'll make you feel needed and loved. Love is a serious matter for the Aries man. He does not believe in flirting or playing the field, especially after he's found the woman of his dreams. He'll expect you to be as constant in your affection as he is in his. He'll expect you to be one hundred percent his; he won't put up with any nonsense while romancing you.

The Aries man may be pretty progressive and modern about many things; however, when it comes to pants wearing, he's downright conventional: it's strictly male attire. The best position you can take in the relationship is a supporting one. He's the boss and that's that. Once you have learned to accept that, you'll find the going easy.

The Aries man, with his endless energy and drive, likes to relax in the comfort of his home at the end of the day. The good homemaker can be sure of holding his love. He's keen on slippers and pipe and a comfortable armchair. If you see to it that everything in the house is where he expects to find it, you'll have no difficulty keeping the relationship on an even keel.

Life and love with an Aries man may be just the medicine you need. He'll be a good provider. He'll spoil you if he's financially able.

He's young at heart and can get along with children easily. He'll spoil them every chance he gets.

AQUARIUS WOMAN
TAURUS MAN

If you've got your heart set on a man born under the sign of Taurus, you'll have to learn the art of being patient. Taureans take their time about everything—even love.

The steady and deliberate Taurus man is a little slow on the draw; it may take him quite a while before he gets around to popping that question. For the woman who doesn't mind twiddling her thumbs, the waiting and anticipating almost always pays off in the end. Taurus men want to make sure that every step they take is a good one—particularly, if they feel that the path they're on is one that leads to the altar.

If you are in the mood for a whirlwind romance, you had better cast your net in shallower waters. Moreover, most Taureans prefer to do the angling themselves. They are not keen on women taking the lead; once she does, he's liable to drop her like a dead fish. If you let yourself get caught on his terms, you'll find that he's fallen for you—hook, line, and sinker.

The Taurus man is fond of a comfortable home life. It is very important to him. If you keep those home fires burning you will have no trouble keeping that flame in your Taurean's heart aglow. You have a talent for homemaking; use it. Your taste in furnishings is excellent. You know how to make a house come to life with colors and decorations.

Taurus, the strong, steady, and protective Bull may not be your idea of a man on the move; still, he's reliable. Perhaps he could be the anchor for your dreams and plans. He could help you to acquire a more balanced outlook and approach to your life. If you're given to impulsiveness, he could help you to curb it. He's the man who is always there when you need him.

When you tie the knot with a man born under Taurus, you can put away fears about creditors pounding on the front door. Taureans are practical about everything including bill-paying. When he carries you over that threshold, you can be certain that the entire house is paid for, not only the doorsill.

As a housewife, you won't have to worry about putting aside your many interests for the sake of back-breaking household chores. Your Taurus hubby will see to it that you have all the latest time-saving appliances and comforts.

Your children will be obedient and orderly. Your Taurus husband will see to that.

AQUARIUS WOMAN
GEMINI MAN

The Gemini man is quite a catch. Many a woman has set her cap for him and failed to bag him. Generally, Gemini men are intelligent, witty, and outgoing. Many of them tend to be rather versatile. The Gemini man could easily wind up being your better half.

One thing that causes a Twin's mind and affection to wander is a bore, and it is unlikely that an active woman like you would ever allow herself to be accused of being that. The Gemini man that has caught your heart will admire you for your ideas and intellect—perhaps even more than for your homemaking talents and good looks.

The woman who hitches up with a Twin needn't feel that once she's made her marriage vows that she'll have to store her interests and ambition in the attic somewhere. The Gemini man will admire you for your zeal and liveliness. He's the kind of guy who won't scowl if you let him shift for himself in the kitchen once in a while. In fact, he'll enjoy the challenge of wrestling with pots and pans himself for a change. Chances are, too, that he might turn out to be a better cook than you—that is, if he isn't already.

The man born under the sign of the Twins is a very active person. There aren't many women who have enough pep to keep up with him, but this should be no problem for a spry woman like you. The Gemini man is a dreamer, planner, and idealist. A woman with a strong personality could easily fill the role of rudder for her Gemini's ship-without-a-sail. If you are a cultivated, purposeful woman, he won't mind it too much. The intelligent Twin is often aware of his shortcomings and doesn't resent it if someone with better bearings than himself gives him a shove in the right direction—when it's needed. The average Gemini does not have serious ego-hangups and will even accept a well-deserved chewing out from his mate quite good-naturedly.

When you team up with a Gemini man, you'll probably always have a houseful of people to entertain—interesting people, too; Geminians find it hard to tolerate sluggish minds and dispositions.

People born under Gemini generally have two sides to their natures, as different as night and day. It's very easy for them to be happy-go-lucky one minute, then down in the dumps the next. They hate to be bored and will generally do anything to make their lives interesting, vivid, and action-packed.

Gemini men are always attractive to the opposite sex. He'll flirt occasionally, but it will never amount to anything serious.

As a father, he's a pushover; he loves children so much that he lets them do what they want.

AQUARIUS WOMAN
CANCER MAN

Chances are you won't hit it off too well with the man born under Cancer if your plans are love, but then, Cupid has been known to do some pretty unlikely things. The Cancerian is a very sensitive man—thin-skinned and occasionally moody. You've got to keep on your toes—and not step on his—if you're determined to make a go of the relationship.

The Cancer man may be lacking in some of the qualities you seek in a man, but when it comes to being faithful and being a good provider, he's hard to beat.

The perceptive woman will not mistake the Crab's quietness for sullenness or his thriftiness for pennypinching. In some respects, he is like that wise old owl out on a limb; he may look like he's dozing but actually he hasn't missed a thing. Cancerians often possess a well of knowledge about human behavior; they can come across with some pretty helpful advice to those in trouble or in need. He can certainly guide you in making investments both in time and money. He may not say much, but he's always got his wits about him.

The Crab may not be the match or catch for a woman like you; at times, you are likely to find him downright dull. True to his sign, he can be fairly cranky and crabby when handled the wrong way. He is perhaps more sensitive than he should be.

If you're smarter than your Cancer friend, be smart enough not to let him know. Never give him the idea that you think he's a little short on brain power. It would send him scurrying back into his shell—and all that ground lost in the relationship will perhaps never be recovered.

The Crab is happiest at home. Once settled down for the night or the weekend, wild horses couldn't drag him any farther than the gatepost—that is, unless those wild horses were dispatched by his mother. The Crab is sometimes a Momma's boy. If his mate does not put her foot down, he will see to it that his mother always comes first. No self-respecting wife would ever allow herself to play second fiddle—even if it's to her old gray-haired mother-in-law. With a little bit of tact, however, she'll find that slipping into that number-one position is as easy as pie (that legendary one his mother used to bake).

If you pamper your Cancer man, you'll find that "Mother" turns up increasingly less—at the front door as well as in conversations.

Cancerians make protective, proud, and patient fathers.

AQUARIUS WOMAN
LEO MAN

To know a man born under the sign of the Lion is not necessarily to love him—even though the temptation may be great. When he fixes most girls with his leonine double-whammy, it causes their hearts to pitter-pat and their minds to cloud over.

You are a little too sensible to allow yourself to be bowled over by a regal strut and a roar. Still, there's no denying that Leo has a way with women—even sensible women like yourself. Once he's swept a girl off her feet, it may be hard for her to scramble upright again. Still, you are no pushover for romantic charm, especially if you feel it's all show.

He'll wine you and dine you in the fanciest places. He'll croon to you under the moon and shower you with diamonds if he can get a hold of them . . . still, it would be wise to find out just how long that shower is going to last before consenting to be his wife.

Lions in love are hard to ignore, let alone brush off. Your no's will have a way of nudging him on until he feels he has you completely under his spell. Once mesmerized by this romantic powerhouse, you will most likely find yourself doing things you never dreamed of. Leos can be like vain pussycats when involved romantically. They like to be cuddled, curried, and tickled under the chin. This may not be your cup of tea exactly, still when you're romantically dealing with a man born under the sign of Leo, you'll find yourself doing all kinds of things to make him purr.

Although he may be big and magnanimous while trying to win you, he'll let out a blood-curdling roar if he thinks he's not getting the tender love and care he feels is his due. If you keep him well supplied with affection, you can be sure his eyes will never look for someone else and his heart will never wander.

Leo men often tend to be authoritarian—they are born to lord it over others in one way or another, it seems. If he is the top banana at his firm, he'll most likely do everything he can to stay on top. If he's not number one, he's most likely working on it and will be sitting on the throne before long.

You'll have more security than you can use if he is in a position to support you in the manner to which he feels you should be accustomed. He is apt to be too lavish, though—at least, by your standards.

You'll always have plenty of friends when you have a Leo for a mate. He's a natural-born friendmaker and entertainer. He loves to kick up his heels at a party.

As fathers, Leos tend to spoil their children no end.

AQUARIUS WOMAN
VIRGO MAN

The Virgo man is all business—at least he may seem so to you. He is usually very cool, calm, and collected. He's perhaps too much of a fuss-budget to wake up deep romantic interests in a woman like you. Torrid romancing to him is just so much sentimental mush. He can do without it and can make that quite evident in short order. He's keen on chastity and, if necessary, he can lead a sedentary, sexless life without caring too much about the fun others think he's missing. In short, you are liable to find him a first-class dud. He doesn't have much of an imagination; flights of fancy don't interest him. He is always correct and likes to be handled correctly. Almost everything about him is orderly. "There's a place for everything . . ." is likely to be an adage he'll fall upon quite regularly.

He does have an honest-to-goodness heart, believe it or not. The woman who finds herself strangely attracted to his cool, feet-flat-on-the-ground ways, will discover that his is a constant heart, not one that goes in for flings or sordid affairs. Virgos take an awfully long time to warm up to someone. A practical man, even in matters of the heart, he wants to know just what kind of person you are before he takes a chance on you.

The impulsive girl had better not make the mistake of kissing her Virgo friend on the street—even if it's only a peck on the cheek. He's not at all demonstrative and hates public displays of affection. Love, according to him, should be kept within the confines of one's home—with the curtains drawn. Once he believes that you are on the level with him as far as your love is concerned, you'll see how fast he can lose his cool. Virgos are considerate, gentle lovers. He'll spend a long time, though, getting to know you. He'll like you before he loves you.

A romance with a Virgo man can be a sometime—or, rather, a one-time—thing. If the bottom ever falls out, don't bother reaching for the adhesive tape. Nine times out of ten he won't care about patching up. He's a once-burnt twice-shy guy. When he crosses your telephone number out of his address book, he's crossing you out of his life for good.

Neat as a pin, he's thumbs-down on what he considers "sloppy" housekeeping. An ashtray with just one stubbed out cigarette in it can annoy him even if it's only two seconds old. Glassware should always sparkle and shine if you want to keep him happy.

If you marry him, keep your sunny-side up.

Your children should be kept as spotless as your house. Kids with dirty faces and hands displease him. Train them to be kind and courteous.

AQUARIUS WOMAN
LIBRA MAN

If there's a Libran in your life, you are most likely a very happy woman. Men born under this sign have a way with women. You'll always feel at ease in a Libran's company; you can be yourself when you're with him.

The Libra man can be moody at times. His moodiness is often puzzling. One moment he comes on hard and strong with declarations of his love, the next moment you find that he's left you like yesterday's mashed potatoes. He'll come back, though; don't worry. Librans are like that. Deep down inside he really knows what he wants, even though he may not appear to.

You'll appreciate his admiration of beauty and harmony. If

you're dressed to the teeth and never looked lovelier, you'll get a ready compliment—and one that's really meant. Librans don't indulge in idle flattery. If they don't like something, they are tactful enough to remain silent.

Librans will go to great lengths to preserve peace and harmony, even by telling a fat lie if necessary. They don't like showdowns or disagreeable confrontations. The frank woman is all for getting whatever is bothering her off her chest and out into the open, even if it comes out all wrong. To the Libran, making a clean breast of everything seems like sheer folly sometimes.

You may lose your patience while waiting for your Libra friend to make up his mind. It takes him ages sometimes to make a decision. He weighs both sides carefully before committing himself to anything. You seldom dillydally—at least about small things—and so it's likely that you will find it difficult to see eye to eye with a hesitating Libran when it comes to decision-making methods.

All in all, though, he is kind, considerate, and fair. He is interested in the "real" truth; he'll try to balance everything out until he has all the correct answers. It's not difficult for him to see both sides of a story.

He's a peace-loving man. The sight of blood is apt to turn his stomach.

Librans are not showoffs. Generally, they are well-balanced, modest people. Honest, wholesome, and affectionate, they are serious about every love encounter they have. If he should find that the girl he's dating is not really suited to him, he will end the relationship in such a tactful manner that no hard feelings will come about.

The Libra father is firm, gentle, and patient.

AQUARIUS WOMAN
SCORPIO MAN

Many find the Scorpio's sting a fate worse than death. When his anger breaks loose, you had better clear out of the vicinity.

The average Scorpio may strike you as a brute. He'll stick pins into the balloons of your plans and dreams if they don't line up with what he thinks is right. If you do anything to irritate him—just anything—you'll wish you hadn't. He'll give you a sounding out that would make you pack your bags and go back to Mother—if you were that kind of a girl.

The Scorpio man hates being tied down to home life—he would rather be out on the battlefield of life, belting away at whatever he feels is a just and worthy cause, instead of staying home nestled in a comfortable armchair with the evening paper. If you are a girl who has a homemaking streak, don't keep those home fires burning too brightly too long; you may just run out of firewood.

As passionate as he is in business affairs and politics, the Scorpio man still has plenty of pep and ginger stored away for lovemaking.

Most women are easily attracted to him—perhaps you are no exception. Those who allow a man born under this sign to sweep them off their feet, shortly find that they're dealing with a pepper pot of seething excitement. The Scorpio man is passionate with a capital P, you can be sure of that. But he's capable of dishing out as much pain as pleasure. Damsels with fluttering hearts who, when in the embrace of a Scorpio, think "This is it," had better be in a position moments later to realize that "Perhaps this isn't it."

Scorpios are blunt. An insult is likely to whiz out of his mouth quicker than a compliment.

If you're the kind of woman who can keep a stiff upper lip, take it on the chin, turn a deaf ear, and all of that, because you feel you are still under his love-spell in spite of everything: lots of luck.

If you have decided to take the bitter with the sweet, prepare yourself for a lot of ups and downs. Chances are you won't have as much time for your own affairs and interests as you'd like. The Scorpio's love of power may cause you to be at his constant beck and call.

Scorpios like fathering large families. They love children, but quite often they fail to live up to their responsibilities as a parent.

AQUARIUS WOMAN
SAGITTARIUS MAN

If you've set your cap for a man born under the sign of Sagittarius, you may have to apply an awful lot of strategy before you can persuade him to get down on bended knee. Although some Sagittarians may be marriage-shy, they're not ones to skitter away from romance. You'll find a love relationship with a Sagittarian—whether a fling or "the real thing"—a very enjoyable experience.

As a rule, Sagittarians are bright, happy, healthy people. They have a strong sense of fair play. Often they are a source of inspiration to others. They are full of drive and ideas.

You'll be taken by the Sagittarian's infectious grin and his light-hearted friendly nature. If you do wind up being the woman in his life, you'll find that he's apt to treat you more like a buddy than the love of his life. It's just his way. Sagittarians are often more chummy than romantic.

You'll admire his broadmindedness in most matters, including those of the heart. If, while dating you, he claims that he still wants to play the field, he'll expect you to enjoy the same liberty. Once he's promised to love, honor, and obey, however, he does just that. Marriage for him, once he's taken that big step, is very serious business.

The Sagittarius man is quick-witted. He has a genuine interest in equality. He hates prejudice and injustice. Generally, Sagittarians are good at sports. They love the great out-of-doors and respect wild life in all its forms.

He's not much of a homebody. Quite often he's occupied with far away places either in his daydreams or in reality. He enjoys being on the move. He's got ants in his pants and refuses to sit still for long stretches at a time. Humdrum routine—especially at home—bores him.

At the drop of a hat, he may ask you to whip off your apron and dine out for a change. He likes to surprise people.

He'll take great pride in showing you off to his friends. He'll always be considerate where your feelings are concerned; he will never embarrass or disappoint you intentionally.

His friendly, sun-shiny nature is capable of attracting many people. Like you, he's very tolerant when it comes to friends. You will most likely spend a great deal of time helping him entertain people.

Sagittarians are all thumbs when it comes to tiny tots. They develop an interest in children when they grow older and wiser.

AQUARIUS WOMAN
CAPRICORN MAN

A with-it girl like you is likely to find the average Capricorn man a bit of a drag. The man born under the sign of the Goat is often a closed person and difficult to get to know. Even if you do get to know him, you may not find him very interesting.

In romance, Capricorn men are a little on the rusty side. You'll probably have to make all the passes.

You may find his plodding manner irritating and his conservative, traditional ways downright maddening. He's not one to take chances on anything. "If it was good enough for my father, it's good enough for me" may be his motto. He follows a way that is tried and true.

Whenever adventure rears its tantalizing head, the Goat will turn the other way; he's just not interested.

He may be just as ambitious as you are—perhaps even more so—but his ways of accomplishing his aims are more subterranean or, at least, seem so. He operates from the background a good deal of the time. At a gathering you may never even notice him, but he's there, taking in everything, sizing everyone up, planning his next careful move.

Although Capricorns may be intellectual to a degree, it is not generally the kind of intelligence you appreciate. He may not be as quick or as bright as you; it may take him ages to understand a simple joke.

If you do decide to take up with a man born under this sign, you ought to be pretty good in the "cheering up" department. The Capricorn man often acts as though he's constantly being followed by a cloud of gloom.

The Capricorn man is happiest when in the comfort and privacy of his own home. The security possible within four walls can make him a happy man. He'll spend as much time as he can at home. If he is loaded down with extra work, he'll bring it home instead of working overtime at the office.

You'll most likely find yourself frequently confronted by his relatives. Family is very important to the Capricorn—*his* family that is. They had better take a pretty important place in your life, too, if you want to keep your home a happy one.

Although his caution in most matters may all but drive you up the wall, you'll find his concerned way with money is justified most of the time. He'll plan everything right down to the last penny.

He can be quite a scold with children. You'll have to step in and smooth things out.

AQUARIUS WOMAN
AQUARIUS MAN

Aquarians are extremely friendly and open, even with other Aquarians. Of all the signs, they are perhaps the most tolerant. In the thinking department they are often miles ahead of others, and with very little effort, it seems. As an Aquarian yourself, you will most likely find your Aquarian friend intriguing, and the relationship between two Aquarians is likely to be twice as challenging. Your own high respect for intelligence and fair play may be reason enough to settle your heart on another Water Bearer.

Aquarians love everybody, even their worst enemies—sometimes. Through your relationship with another Aquarian, you'll find yourself running into all sorts of people, ranging from near-genius to downright insane—and these are all friends that you'll share in common.

In the holding hands stage of your romance you may find that your Water Bearing friend has cold feet that may take quite a bit of warming up. More than likely, he'll just want to be your pal in the beginning. For him—as for you, that's an important step in any relationship—even love. The "poetry and flowers" stage will come later, perhaps some years later.

The Aquarian is all heart; still, when it comes to tying himself down to one person and for keeps, he is liable to hesitate. He may even try to get out of it if you give him half a chance—and as an Aquarian, you may be inclined to do just that. He's no Valentino and wouldn't want to be, but then, a Valentino isn't quite what you're looking for either. In fact, as an Aquarian yourself, you are bound to understand his hesitation—more or less. You are also likely to be more attracted by his broadmindedness and high moral standards than by his abilities to romance.

You won't find it difficult to look up to a man born under your sign, and the challenge is certain to be exciting. He can pierce through the most complicated problem as if it were a matter of two plus two. Others may find him too lofty or high-minded, but you're pretty much that way yourself.

In marriage you need never be afraid that his affection will wander. It stays put once he's hitched. He'll certainly admire you for your intelligence, and don't think that you have to stick close to the kitchen. Once you're married, he'll want you to pursue whatever you want in your quest for knowledge. You'll most likely have a minor squabble with him now and then, but never anything serious.

Still, even you may find his forgetfulness (added to your own) a little bothersome. His head is so full of ideas and plans that sometimes he seems like the absent-minded professor. Kids love him and vice versa. He's tolerant and open-minded with everybody, from the very young to the very old.

AQUARIUS WOMAN
PISCES MAN

The man born under Pisces is quite a dreamer. Sometime he's so wrapped up in his dreams that he's difficult to reach. To the average, ambitious woman, he may seem a little sluggish.

He's easy-going most of the time. He seems to take things in his stride. He'll entertain all kinds of views and opinions from just about anyone, nodding or smiling vaguely, giving the impression that he's with them one hundred percent while that may not be the case at all. His attitude may be "why bother" when he is confronted with someone wrong who thinks he's right. The Pisces man will seldom speak his mind if he thinks he'll be rigidly opposed.

The Pisces man is oversensitive at times—he's afraid of getting his feelings hurt. He'll sometimes imagine a personal affront when none's been made. Chances are you'll find this complex of his maddening; at times, you may feel like giving him a swift kick where it hurts the most. It won't do any good, though. It would just add fuel to the fire of his complex.

One thing you will admire about this man is his concern for people who are sickly or troubled. He'll make his shoulder available to anyone in the mood for a good cry. He can listen to one hard-luck story after another without seeming to tire. When his advice is asked, he is capable of coming across with some pretty important words of wisdom. He often knows what's bugging someone before that person is aware of it himself. It's almost intuitive with Pisceans, it seems. Still, at the end of the day, he looks forward to some peace and quiet. If you've got a problem on your mind, don't dump it into his lap at the end of the day. If you do, you're liable to find him short-tempered. He's a good listener but he can only take so much.

Pisces men are not aimless although they may seem so at times. The positive sort of Pisces man is quite often successful in his profession and is likely to wind up rich and influential. Material gain, however, is not a direct goal for a man born under this sign.

The weaker Piscean is usually content to stay put on the level where he happens to find himself. He won't complain too much if the roof leaks or the fence is in need of repair. He'll just shrug it off as a minor inconvenience. He's got more important things to think about, he'll say.

Because of their seemingly laissez-faire manner, people born under this sign are immensely popular with children. For tots they play the double role of confidant and playmate. It will never enter his mind to discipline a child, no matter how spoiled or incorrigible that child becomes.

Man—Woman

**AQUARIUS MAN
ARIES WOMAN**

The Aries woman is quite a charmer. When she tugs at the strings of your heart, you'll know it. She's a woman who's in search of a knight in shining armor. She is a very particular person with very high ideals. She won't accept anyone but the man of her dreams.

The Aries woman never plays around with passion; she means business when it comes to love.

Don't get the idea that she's a dewy-eyed miss. She isn't. In fact, she can be pretty practical and to-the-point when she wants. She's a girl with plenty of drive and ambition. With an Aries woman behind you, you are liable to go far in life. She knows how to help her man get ahead. She's full of wise advice; you only have to ask. In some cases, the Aries woman has a keen business sense; many of them become successful career women. There is nothing backward or retiring about her. She is equipped with a good brain and she knows how to use it.

Your union with her could be something strong, secure, and romantic. If both of you have your sights fixed in the same direction, there is almost nothing that you could not accomplish.

The Aries woman is proud and capable of being quite jealous. While you're with her, never cast your eye in another woman's direction. It could spell disaster for your relationship. The Aries woman won't put up with romantic nonsense when her heart is at stake.

If the Aries woman backs you up in your business affairs, you can be sure of succeeding. However, if she only is interested in advancing her own career and puts her interests before yours, she can be sure of rocking the boat. It will put a strain on the relationship. The over-ambitious Aries woman can be a pain in the neck and make you forget that you were once in love with her.

The cultivated Aries woman makes a wonderful wife and mother. She has a natural talent for homemaking. With a pot of paint and some wallpaper, she can transform the dreariest domicile into an abode of beauty and snug comfort. The perfect hostess—even when friends just happen by—she knows how to make guests feel at home.

You'll also admire your Arien because she knows how to stand on her own two feet. Hers is an independent nature. She won't break down and cry when things go wrong, but pick herself up and try to patch up matters.

The Aries woman makes a fine, affectionate mother.

AQUARIUS MAN
TAURUS WOMAN

The woman born under the sign of Taurus may lack a little of the sparkle and bubble you often like to find in a woman. The Taurus woman is generally down-to-earth and never flighty. It's important to her that she keep both feet flat on the ground. She is not fond of bounding all over the place, especially if she's under the impression that there's no profit in it.

On the other hand, if you hit if off with a Taurus woman, you won't be disappointed at all in the romance area. The Taurus woman is all woman and proud of it, too. She can be very devoted and loving once she decides that her relationship with you is no fly-by-night romance. Basically, she's a passionate person. In sex, she's direct and to-the-point. If she really loves you, she'll let you know she's yours—and without reservations. Better not flirt with other women once you've committed yourself to her. She is capable of being jealous and possessive.

She'll stick by you through thick and thin. It's almost certain that if the going ever gets rough, she'll not go running home to her mother. She can adjust to hard times just as graciously as she can to the good times.

Taureans are, on the whole, pretty even-tempered. They like to be treated with kindness. Pretty things and soft things make them purr like kittens.

You may find her a little slow and deliberate. She likes to be safe and sure about everything. Let her plod along if she likes; don't coax her but just let her take her own sweet time. Everything she does is done thoroughly and, generally, without mistakes. Don't deride her for being a kind of slow-poke. It could lead to flying pots and pans and a fireworks display that would put Bastille Day to shame. The Taurus woman doesn't anger readily but when prodded often enough, she's capable of letting loose with a cyclone of ill-will. If you treat her with kindness and consideration, you'll have no cause for complaint.

The Taurean loves doing things for her man. She's a whiz in the kitchen and can whip up feasts fit for a king if she thinks they'll be royally appreciated. She may not fully understand you, but she'll adore you and be faithful to you if she feels you're worthy of it.

The woman born under Taurus will make a wonderful mother. She knows how to keep her children well-loved, cuddled, and warm. She may find them difficult to manage, however, when they reach the teenage stage.

AQUARIUS MAN
GEMINI WOMAN

You may find a romance with a woman born under the sign of the Twins a many-splendored thing. In her you can find the intellectual companionship you often look for in a friend or mate. A

Gemini girl friend can appreciate your aims and desires because she travels pretty much the same road as you do intellectually—that is, at least part of the way. She may share your interest but she will lack your tenacity.

She suffers from itchy feet. She can be here, there all over the place and at the same time, or so it would seem. Her eagerness to move about may make you dizzy, still you'll enjoy and appreciate her liveliness and mental agility.

Geminians often have sparkling personalities; you'll be attracted by her warmth and grace. While she's on your arm you'll probably notice that many male eyes are drawn to her—she may even return a gaze or two, but don't let that worry you. All women born under this sign have nothing against a harmless flirt once in a while. They enjoy this sort of attention; if she feels she is already spoken for, however, she will never let it get out of hand.

Although she may not be as handy as you'd like in the kitchen, you'll never go hungry for a filling and tasty meal. She's as much in a hurry as you are, and won't feel like she's cheating by breaking out the instant mashed potatoes or the frozen peas. She may not be much of a good cook but she is clever; with a dash of this and a suggestion of that, she can make an uninteresting TV dinner taste like something out of a James Beard cookbook. Then, again, maybe you've struck it rich and have a Gemini girl friend who finds complicated recipes a challenge to her intellect. If so, you'll find every meal a tantalizing and mouth-watering surprise.

When you're beating your brains out over the Sunday crossword puzzle and find yourself stuck, just ask your Gemini girlie; she'll give you all the right answers without batting an eyelash.

Like you, she loves all kinds of people. You may even find that you're a bit more particular than she. Often all that a Geminian requires is that her friends be interesting—and stay interesting. One thing she's not able to abide is a dullard.

Leave the party-organizing to your Gemini sweetheart or mate, and you'll never have a chance to know what a dull moment is. She'll bring the swinger out in you if you give her half a chance.

A Gemini mother enjoys her children. Like them, she's often restless, adventurous, and easily bored.

AQUARIUS MAN
CANCER WOMAN

If you fall in love with a Cancer woman, be prepared for anything. Cancerians are sometimes difficult to understand when it comes to love. In one hour, she can unravel a whole gamut of emotions that will leave you in a tizzy. She'll keep you guessing, that's for sure.

You may find her a little too uncertain and sensitive for your liking. You'll most likely spend a good deal of time encouraging her—helping her to erase her foolish fears. Tell her she's a living doll a dozen times a day and you'll be well loved in return.

Be careful of the jokes you make when in her company. Don't let any of them revolve around her, her personal interests, or her family. If you do, you'll most likely reduce her to tears. She can't stand being made fun of. It will take bushels of roses and tons of chocolates—not to mention the apologies—to get her to come back out of her shell.

In matters of money-managing she may not easily come around to your way of thinking. Money will never burn a hole in her pocket. You may get the notion that your Cancerian sweetheart or mate is a direct descendent of Scrooge. If she has her way, she'll hang onto that first dollar you earned. She's not only that way with money, but with everything right on up from bakery string to jelly jars. She's a saver; she never throws anything away, no matter how trivial.

Once she returns your "I love you," you'll find you have an affectionate, self-scarificing, and devoted woman on your hands. Her love for you will never alter unless you want it to. She'll put you high upon a pedestal and will do everything—even if it's against your will—to keep you up there.

Cancer women love home life. For them, marriage is an easy step. They're domestic with a capital D. She'll do her best to make your home comfortable and cozy. She, herself, is more at ease at home then anywhere else. She makes an excellent hostess. The best in her comes out when she is in her own environment.

Cancer women make the best mothers of all the signs of the zodiac. She'll consider every complaint of her child a major catastrophe. With her, children always come first. If you're lucky, you'll run a close second. You'll perhaps see her as too devoted to the children. You may have a hard time convincing her that her apron strings are a little too long.

AQUARIUS MAN
LEO WOMAN

If you can manage a girl who likes to kick up her heels every now and again, then the Leo woman was made for you. You'll have to learn to put away jealous fears—or at least forget about them—when you take up with a woman born under this sign, because she's often the kind that makes heads turn and tongues wag. You don't necessarily have to believe any of what you hear—it's most likely just jealous gossip or wishful thinking. Take up with a

Leo woman and you'll be taking off on a romance full of fire and ice; be prepared to take the good things with the bad—the bitter with the sweet.

The Leo girl has more than a fair share of grace and glamour. She is aware of her charms and knows how to put them to good use. Needless to say, other women in her vicinity turn green with envy and will try anything short of shoving her into the nearest lake, in order to put her out of commission.

If she's captured your heart and fancy, woo her full-force if your intention is to eventually win her. Shower her with expensive gifts and promise her the moon—if you're in a position to go that far—then you'll find her resistance beginning to weaken. It's not that she's such a difficult cookie—she'll probably make a big fuss over you once she's decided you're the man for her—but she does enjoy a lot of attention. What's more, she feels she's entitled to it. Her mild arrogance, though, is becoming. The Leo woman knows how to transform the crime of excessive pride into a very charming misdemeanor. It sweeps most men right off their feet . . . rather, all men. Those who do not succumb to her leonine charm are few and far between.

If you've got an important business deal to clinch and you have doubts as to whether or not it will go over well, bring your Leo girl along to that business luncheon and it's a cinch that contract will be yours. She won't have to do or say anything—just be there, at your side. The grouchiest oil magnate can be transformed into a gushing, obedient schoolboy if there's a Leo woman in the room.

If you're rich and want to stay that way, don't give your Leo mate a free hand with the charge accounts and credit cards. If you're poor, the luxury-loving Leo will most likely never enter your life.

She makes a strict yet easy-going mother. She loves to pal around with her children.

AQUARIUS MAN
VIRGO WOMAN

The Virgo woman may be a little too difficult for you to understand at first. Her waters run deep. Even when you think you know her, don't take any bets on it. She's capable of keeping things hidden in the deep recesses of her womanly soul—things she'll only release when she's sure that you're the man she's been looking for. It may take her some time to come around to this decision. Virgo girls are finicky about almost everything; everything has to be letter-perfect before they're satisfied. Many of them have the idea that the only people who can do things correctly are Virgos.

Nothing offends a Virgo woman more than slovenly dress, sloppy character, or a careless display of affection. Make sure your tie is not crooked and your shoes sport a bright shine before you go calling on this lady. Keep your off-color jokes for the locker-room; she'll have none of that. Take her arm when crossing the street. Don't rush the romance. Trying to corner her in the back of a cab may be one way of striking out. Never criticize the way she looks—in fact, the best policy would be to agree with her as much as possible. Still, there's just so much a man can take; all those dos and don'ts you'll have to observe if you want to get to first base with a Virgo may be just a little too much to ask of you. After a few dates, you may come to the conclusion that she just isn't worth all that trouble. However, the Virgo woman is mysterious enough, generally speaking, to keep her men running back for more. Chances are you'll be intrigued by her airs and graces.

If love-making means a lot to you, you'll be disappointed at first in the cool ways of your Virgo girlie. However, under her glacial facade there lies a hot cauldron of seething excitement. If you're patient and artful in your romantic approach, you'll find that all that caution was well worth the trouble. When Virgos love, they don't stint. It's all or nothing as far as they're concerned. Once they're convinced that they love you, they go all the way right off the bat, tossing all cares to the wind.

One thing a Virgo woman can't stand in love is hypocrisy. They don't give a hoot about what the neighbors say, if their hearts tell them "Go ahead." They're very concerned with human truths—so much so that if their hearts stumble upon another fancy, they're liable to be true to that new heart-throb and leave you standing in the rain.

She's honest to her heart and will be as true to you as you are with her, generally. Do her wrong once, however, and it's farewell.

She's both strict and tender with children. As a mother she'll try to bring out the best in her children.

AQUARIUS MAN
LIBRA WOMAN

You'll probably find that the girl born under the sign of Libra is worth more than her weight in gold. She's a woman after your own heart.

With her, you'll always come first—make no mistake about that. She'll always be behind you 100 percent, no matter what you do. When you ask her advice about almost anything, you'll most likely get a very balanced and realistic opinion. She is good at thinking things out and never lets her emotions run away with her when clear logic is called for.

As a homemaker she is hard to beat. She is very concerned with harmony and balance. You can be sure she'll make your house a joy to live in; she'll see to it that the house is tastefully furnished and decorated. A Libran cannot stand filth or disarray—it gives her goose-bumps. Anything that does not radiate harmony, in fact, runs against her orderly grain.

She is chock-full of charm and womanly ways. She can sweep just about any man off his feet with one winning smile. When it comes to using her brains, she can out-think almost anyone and, sometimes, with half the effort. She is diplomatic enough, though, never to let this become glaringly apparent. She may even turn the conversation around so that you think you were the one who did all the brain-work. She couldn't care less, really, just as long as you wind up doing what is right.

The Libra woman will put you up on a pretty high pedestal. You are her man and her idol. She'll leave all the decision-making—large or small—up to you. She's not interested in running things and will only offer her assistance if she feels you really need it.

Some find her approach to reason masculine; however, in the areas of love and affection the Libra woman is *all* woman. She'll literally shower you with love and kisses during your romance with her. She doesn't believe in holding out. You shouldn't, either, if you want to hang onto her.

She is the kind of girl who likes to snuggle up to you in front of the fire on chilly autumn nights—the kind of girl who will bring you breakfast in bed on Sunday. She'll be very thoughtful about anything that concerns you. If anyone dares suggest you're not the grandest guy in the world, she'll give that person what-for. She'll defend you with her dying breath. The Libra woman will be everything you want her to be.

She'll be a sensitive and loving mother. Still, you'll always come before the children.

**AQUARIUS MAN
SCORPIO WOMAN**

The Scorpio woman can be a whirlwind of passion—perhaps too much passion to really suit you. When her temper flies, you'd better lock up the family heirlooms and take cover. When she chooses to be sweet, you're apt to think that butter wouldn't melt in her mouth . . . but, of course, it would.

The Scorpio woman can be as hot as a *tamale* or as cool as a cucumber, but whatever mood she's in, she's in it for real. She does not believe in poses or putting on airs.

The Scorpio woman is often sultry and seductive—her femme fatale charm can pierce through the hardest of hearts like a laser ray. She may not look like Mata Hari (quite often Scorpios resemble the tomboy next door) but once she's fixed you with her tantalizing eyes, you're a goner.

Life with the Scorpio woman will not be all smiles and smooth-sailing; when prompted she can unleash a gale of venom. Generally, she'll have the good grace to keep family battles within the walls of your home. When company visits, she's apt to give the impression that married life with you is one great big joy-ride. It's just one of her ways of expressing her loyalty to you, at least in front of others. She may fight you tooth and nail in the confines of your living room, but at a ball or during an evening out, she'll hang on your arm and have stars in her eyes.

Scorpio woman are good at keeping secrets. She may even keep a few buried from you if she feels like it.

Never cross her on even the smallest thing. When it comes to revenge, she's an eye-for-an-eye woman. She's not too keen on forgiveness, especially when she feels she's been wronged unjustly. You'd be well-advised not to give her any cause to be jealous, either. When the Scorpio woman sees green, your life will be made far from rosy. Once she's put you in the dog-house, you can be sure that you'll stay there a long time.

You may find life with the Scorpio woman too draining. Although she may be full of the old paprika, it's quite likely that she's not the kind of girl you'd like to spend the rest of your natural life with. You'd prefer someone gentler and not so hot-tempered, someone who can take the highs with the lows and not bellyache, someone who is flexible and understanding. If you've got your sights set on a shapely Socrpio, forget about that sweet girl of your dreams. A woman born under Scorpio can be heavenly, but she can also be the very devil when she chooses.

As a mother, a Scorpio woman is protective and encouraging.

AQUARIUS MAN
SAGITTARIUS WOMAN

You'll most likely never come across a more good-natured girl than the one born under the sign of Sagittarius. Generally, they're full of bounce and good cheer. Their sunny disposition seems almost permanent and can be relied upon even on the rainiest of days.

Women born under this sign are almost never malicious. If ever they seem to be, it is only seeming. Sagittarians are often a little short on tact and say literally anything that comes into their pretty little heads no matter what the occasion. Sometimes the words that tumble out of their mouths seem downright cutting and cruel. Still, no matter what she says, she means well. The Sagittarius woman is quite capable of losing some of her friends—and perhaps even some of yours—through a careless slip of the lip.

On the other hand, you are liable to appreciate her honesty and good intentions. To you, qualities of this sort play an important part in life. With a little patience and practice, you can probably help cure your Sagittarian of her loose tongue; in most cases, she'll give in to your better judgement and try to follow your advice to the letter.

Chances are she'll be the outdoors type of girl friend. Long hikes, fishing trips, and white-water canoeing will most likely appeal to her. She's a busy person; no one could ever call her a slouch. She sets great store in mobility. Her feet are itchy and she won't sit still for a minute if she doesn't have to.

She is great company most of the time and, generally, lots of fun. Even if your buddies drop by for poker and beer, she won't have any trouble fitting in.

On the whole, she is a very kind and sympathetic woman. If she feels she's made a mistake, she'll be the first to call your attention to it. She's not afraid to own up to her faults and shortcomings.

You might lose your patience with her once or twice. After she's seen how upset her shortsightedness or tendency to be a blabbermouth has made you, she'll do her best to straighten up.

The Sagittarian woman is not the kind who will pry into your business affairs. But she'll always be there, ready to offer advice if you need it. If you come home with red stains on your collar and you say it's paint and not lipstick, she'll believe you.

She'll seldom be suspicious; your word will almost always be good enough for her.

She is a wonderful and loving friend to her children.

AQUARIUS MAN
CAPRICORN WOMAN

If you are not a successful businessman or, at least, on your way to success, it's quite possible that a Capricorn woman will have no interest in entering your life. Generally speaking, she is a very security-minded female; she'll see to it that she invests her time only in sure things. Men who whittle away their time with one unsuccessful scheme or another, seldom attract a Capricorn. Men who are interested in getting somewhere in life and keep their noses close to the grindstone quite often have a Capricorn woman behind them, helping them to get ahead.

Although she is a kind of "climber," she is not what you could call cruel or hard-hearted. Beneath that cool, seemingly calculating, exterior, there's a warm and desirable woman. She just happens to think that it is as easy to fall in love with a rich or ambitious man as it is with a poor or lazy one. She's practical.

The Capricorn woman may be keenly interested in rising to the top, but she'll never be aggressive about it. She'll seldom step on someone's feet or nudge competitors away with her elbows. She's quiet about her desires. She sits, waits, and watches. When an opening or opportunity does appear, she'll latch onto it lickety-split. For an on-the-move man, an ambitious Capricorn wife or girl friend can be quite an asset. She can probably give you some very good advice about business matters. When you invite the boss and his wife for dinner, she'll charm them both right off the ground.

The Capricorn woman is thorough in whatever she does: cooking, cleaning, making a success out of life. Capricorns make excellent hostesses as well as guests. Generally, they are very well mannered and gracious, no matter what their backgrounds are. They seem to have a built-in sense of what is right. Crude behavior or a careless faux-pas can offend them no end.

If you should marry a woman born under Capricorn you need never worry about her going on a wild shopping spree. Capricorns are careful with every cent that comes into their hands. They understand the value of money better than most women and have no room in their lives for careless spending.

Capricorn girls are usually very fond of family—their own, that is. With them, family ties run very deep. Don't make jokes about her relatives; she won't stand for it. You'd better check her family out before you get down on bended knee; after your marriage you'll undoubtedly be seeing lots of them.

Capricorn mothers train their children to be polite and kind.

AQUARIUS MAN
AQUARIUS WOMAN

If you find that you've fallen head over heels for a woman born under the sign of the Water Bearer, you'd better fasten your safety belt. It may take you quite a while to actually discover what this girl is like—and even then, you may have nothing to go on but a string of vague hunches. The Aquarian is like a rainbow, full of bright and shining hues; she's like no other girl you've ever known. There is something elusive about her—something delightfully mysterious. You'll most likely never be able to put your finger on it. It's nothing calculated, either; Aquarians don't believe in phony charm.

There will never be a dull moment in your life with this Water Bearing woman; she seems to radiate adventure and magic. She'll most likely be the most open-minded and tolerant woman you've ever met. She has a strong dislike for injustice and prejudice. Narrow-mindedness runs against her grain.

She is very independent by nature and quite capable of shifting for herself if necessary. She may receive many proposals for marriage from all sorts of people without ever really taking them seriously. Marriage is a very big step for her; she wants to be sure she knows what she's getting into. If she thinks that it will seriously curb her independence and love of freedom, she's liable to shake her head and give the man his engagement ring back—if indeed she's let the romance get that far.

The line between friendship and romance is a pretty fuzzy one for an Aquarian. It's not difficult for her to remain buddy-buddy with an ex-lover. She's tolerant, remember? So, if you should see her on the arm of an old love, don't jump to any hasty conclusions.

She's not a jealous person herself and doesn't expect you to be either. You'll find her pretty much of a free spirit most of the time. Just when you think you know her inside-out, you'll discover that you don't really know her at all.

She's a very sympathetic and warm person; she can be helpful to people in need of assistance and advice.

She'll seldom be suspicious even if she has every right to be. If she loves a man, she'll forgive him just about anything. If he allows himself a little fling, chances are she'll just turn her head the other way. Her tolerance does have its limits, however, and her man should never press his luck at hanky-panky.

She makes a big-hearted mother; her good qualities rub off on her children.

AQUARIUS MAN
PISCES WOMAN

Many a man dreams of a Piscean kind of a girl. You're perhaps no exception. She's soft and cuddly—very domestic. She'll let you be the brains of the family; she's contented to just lean on your shoulder and let you be the master of the household.

She can be very ladylike and proper. Your business associates and friends will be dazzled by her warmth and femininity. Although she's a charmer, there is a lot more to her than just a pretty face. There is a brain ticking away behind that soft, womanly facade. You may never become aware of it—that is, until you're married to her. It's no cause for alarm, however; she'll most likely never use it against you.

If she feels you're botching up your married life through careless behavior or if she feels you could be earning more money than you do, she'll tell you about it. But any wife would, really. She will never try to usurp your position as head of the family.

No one had better dare say one uncomplimentary word about you in her presence. It's liable to cause her to break into tears. Pisces women are usually very sensitive beings. Their reaction to adversity, frustration, or anger is just a plain, good, old-fashioned cry. They can weep buckets when inclined.

She'll have an extra-special dinner waiting for you when you come home from an important business meeting. Don't bother to go into any of the details about the meeting, though, at the dinner table; she doesn't have much of a head for business matters usually, and is only too happy to leave that up to you.

She can do wonders with a house. She is very fond of soft and beautiful things. There will always be plenty of fresh-cut flowers around the house. She'll see that you always have plenty of socks and underwear in that top drawer of your dresser.

Treat her with tenderness and your relationship will be an enjoyable one. She's most likely fond of chocolates. A bunch of beautiful roses will never fail to make her eyes light up. See to it that you never forget her birthday or your anniversary. She won't. If you are patient and kind, you can keep a Pisces woman happy for a lifetime. She is, however, not without her faults. Her "sensitivity" may get on your nerves after a while. You may find her lacking in imagination and zest. You may even feel that she only uses her tears as a method of getting her own way.

She makes a strong, self-sacrificing mother. She'll find it difficult to refuse her children anything.

AQUARIUS

AQUARIUS
YEARLY FORECAST: 1987

*Forecast for 1987 Concerning Business and
Financial Matters, Job Prospects,
Travel, Health, Romance and Marriage
for Those Born with the Sun
in the Zodiacal Sign of Aquarius.
January 20–February 18*

The year 1987 has all the signs of being a rewarding and satisfying one for Aquarius. New friends can play an important part in your life. Both romantic and working relationships are favored. It is to your advantage to associate more with others. Although there may be recurring periods of minor upheaval in employment and commercial affairs, the greatest gains can be made through close cooperation and teamwork with others. Aquarius are not advised to follow the more independent streak in their natures this year. Efforts to bring your goods and services to the attention of a wider public through advertising can pay dividends. Money matters will run more smoothly. The financial judgments of Aquarius will be more reliable and effective. You are unlikely to have new serious health problems to contend with, but the condition of people you are fond of may not be as free of complications. While short trips and journeys can be productive, longer excursions will need meticulous planning. It is important not to remain aloof in any way from the people you work with. Combined efforts are the best policy this year. Marriages made in 1987 can develop into very happy partnerships. All marital affairs are likely to contain fewer problems. It will be easier to mantain domestic harmony. Single Aquarius can realize their heart's desire. There will be no shortage of opportunities for meeting prospective romantic partners. Sparetime activities are also likely to be most successful where they involve other people. Club and group membership can afford you great opportunity for personal satisfaction and enjoyment, especially if the aim of such organizations is to assist the suffering or underprivileged. Idealism can find outlets through teamwork. Aquarius will be presented with plenty of chances for putting their high standards and advanced ideas on life and mankind into operation. It is by following your ideals that you will attract people of principle, both as helpers and friends.

Throughout January and February, Aquarius should make extra efforts to render regular commercial activities more profitable. It is by continuing to pile on the pressure in business and career affairs that the greatest financial returns can be won. However, you are unlikely to have capital in hand where business finances are concerned, as any profits will probably have to be plowed back into new operations. Actual income can also be reduced by the need to repay borrowed money, especially if you have received loans from large commercial organizations. This need to struggle to maintain an acceptable momentum should lessen by the beginning of March. Conditions will then become more supportive for business enterprises. This is the time to capitalize on any upturn in business fortunes by launching publicity campaigns on both a major and minor scale. The excellent results of such campaigns will probably take you by surprise. Aquarius who have been forced by circumstances to work independently in business spheres can now meet compatible professional partners who help to lighten the load. Effective working relationships have a good chance of developing from March onward. A special characteristic of such partnerships will be that they allow you the maximum degree of freedom. There should be no need to compromise your standards or plans to meet the demands of people you have come to rely on. Land and property dealing can be favorably handled between April 20 and May 20. However, you are advised to avoid taking risks and gambles in the period from April 5 to May 20. While the whole year from March 2 onward favors joint efforts and teamwork, such cooperation can reach a peak of achievement and effectiveness between March 21 and April 19, and again between July 23 and August 22. Aquarius who have the greatest good for their fellow men and women in mind can meet with particular success in charitable works and in helping the needy in the period from November 22 to December 21.

There will be excellent chances in the period to March 1 for Aquarius to improve earnings and build up personal resources. You are likely to be offered better jobs during this time with accompanying wage increases. As with business finances, the advantages of extra income can be somewhat undermined by factors outside your control. Group and club activities can be more demanding financially. The idealistic impulses of Aquarius may lead them to finance humanitarian projects from personal resources. Extra expense can be incurred during this time by the health problems of friends or business colleagus. March 1 also sees the beginning of a period that is especially favorable for the self-employed and those who work on commission. It will be easier to expand markets and sell more goods. Acquaintances can help send more work your way. Employers will be in a receptive and sympathetic mood in the period from June 21 to July 22. This is a good time to approach them with requests for wage increases. Between August 23 and September 22 is the best time to seek refunds from overpaid taxes. This also marks the time when maintenance payments, insurance affairs and inheritances are best dealt with. Distant people and affairs can be helpful to finances between September 23 and October 22.

Aquarius should enter a more relaxed phase after the first two months of the year. Serious concern over money matters is likely to decrease, leaving you in a lighter frame of mind. When you put aside such worries, you may go to the other extreme, becoming too easygoing and frivolous. This in its own way can have a bad effect on your health. You can burn up mental and physical energy unnecessarily through overexcitableness. It is essential that you remain levelheaded and maintain your usual standard of achievement. Avoid aimless running around. This will only deplete your inner reserves and lead to nervous exhaustion. Any misuse of artificial stimulants will also have a deleterious effect on health. Keep strictly to prescribed doses if you have to take drugs or medication. There is also more need this year to keep alert and attentive when on the roads, either as a pedestrian or driver. Dreaminess and absentmindedness will invite accidents. Tools and machinery must be used with much greater attention to safety rules, especially between January 8 and February 19, and between May 21 and July 5. If you are traveling in distant places in the period from October 8 to November 23, special care must be taken with your health. You cannot afford to take risks. Aquarius may tend to run out of steam in the last ten days of the year. Efforts and exertions must be cut back accordingly.

A more active phase for travel should begin on March 2. You may have a desire to make many short trips, thinking that these will be productive. However, you should make only those journeys that are essential. It will be easier to burn up time and cash in unnecessary travel. While phone calls and letters will not give you the same exciting experiences and change afforded by trips, they can achieve the necessary results. It is important, however, that Aquarius do make changes. Get out of the rut, particularly at weekends. Travel to exotic or unfamiliar places will give your spirits a welcome lift, but such jouneys should not be started off the cuff. Careful planning is essential. All formalities, such as entry permits and visas, must be fully attended to. You cannot afford a casual approach to such matters.

Aquarius may prefer to take offers of more interesting work after March 2, even though this means a reduction in earnings. Work that suits you better can be provided by friends. It may be useful to arrange a number of job interviews on one trip. This period is also favorable for making trips in order to put in trial periods at prospective new jobs. Special interest should be given to jobs that entail working more closely with other people. You must resist any temptation to waste working time in idle chatter. Superiors will expect a good day's work for a good day's pay. May 21 to July 5 should be a heavy working period, with extra work loads and responsibilities to be shouldered. You are advised to do what you can toward gaining extra skills and qualifications that will make you more eligible for better jobs and positions. Between September 23 and October 22 is a good time for signing on for new training and other courses.

Aquarius are likely to have a strong urge to make new companions and acquaintances this year. Your efforts in relation to clubs and groups can be rewarded by meetings with new romantic partners. People you have known for long periods can suddenly become partners in a love affair. New romances may combine both physical attraction and a stimulating meeting of minds. The period from January 7 to February 4 may see terminations in existing relationships and the beginnings of new partnerships. Your need for a mate and urge for love will be especially strong between March 3 and 27, and between June 11 and July 4. Fortunately these are also times when it will be easier to meet romantic partners and fulfill your desires. It would be best to put off engagements until after March 1. July 30 to August 22 is the most favorable period for marriage ceremonies. Existing marriages will also blossom during this time. Aquarius must take care not to spoil things during this period by wild behavior or irresponsible actions. It will be easier to go overboard. Keep your expression of feelings to a level that spouses or sweethearts can tolerate. Don't suffocate others with too much affection. Altogether, 1987 should be a year that brings you together with people and one that also favors change in your financial affairs.

DAILY FORECAST
January–December 1987
JANUARY

1. THURSDAY. Quiet. The New Year starts off on a note that is very supportive of personal affairs. It would be advisable to go over plans made some time ago for the near future. There are likely to be changed circumstances, due perhaps to the Christmas break. Arrangements may have to be revised. Priorities may also have altered. Others will be ready to go along with any essential changes of plan. People will be more willing to fit in with your schedules and give what assistance they can to your affairs. It would be unwise to neglect business and other means of livelihood. Don't get so wrapped up in personal matters that you forget on which side your bread is buttered.

2. FRIDAY. Good. A short period of especially good fortune begins today for Aquarius. Wishes and desires that are close to your heart, and which nobody else knows about, can at last come to fruition. Even your wildest dreams may seem less farfetched. It is a good time for joining in organized recreational activities with others. Time spent with clubs and groups can give great satisfaction. It will also be good for introducing more efficient ways and means into business projects. Now is the time to cut out any dead wood in organizations and reduce overhead wherever possible. Visits to sick or lonely people will be greatly appreciated. Meetings behind closed doors will be most productive.

3. SATURDAY. Rewarding. Aquarius can give expression to their humanitarian impulses now. Conditions will help you to raise substantial sums if you are collecting money for charities and other worthy causes. As far as your own income is concerned, the use of a little imagination and hard thinking may give you the best chance of winning increases. You can swing things your way by manipulating events in the background. Evening hours are good for meeting with friends and associates with whom you have been out of touch. People from the past can supply contacts or suggestions that bring favorable financial results. Periods of solitude will allow you to find your feet and put your roots down deeper.

4. SUNDAY. Lucky. It seems that your finances are going to get a boost when you are least expecting it. Luck can come from surprising quarters. Current schemes that were designed to bring in extra cash can suddenly start to come up with the goods. Your spouse's relatives can be in a giving mood and may offer financial gifts or loans. It will be a good day for contacting business and employment associates out of office hours. A talk with a colleague or employer on the phone, or over a drink, can help to solve any problems. These probably cropped up at work or in commercial operations during the week. Try to tie up loose ends of projects nearing completion. You will have a freer hand for new ones.

5. MONDAY. Sensitive. This is no time to give into extravagant impulses. Spending must be restricted to essential purchases. If you splurge on unnecessary items, you will only take yourself to task later on. Rather, you should do what you can to build up your resources, especially by collecting any money you are owed. However, you are more likely to get what you are due by employing a diplomatic approach. Strong-arm tactics can backfire. Your love life will be most happy now. People with whom you have had only a nodding acquaintance can suddenly become romantic partners. It's a good time for planning marriages. Emotional problems must not be swept under the carpet for the sake of convenience.

6. TUESDAY. Variable. Aquarius who are hoping to have interviews today may be disappointed. They could be put off until another day, or canceled entirely. It can become impossible to contact important people, either by telephone or in person. Your need to inform others of a change of plan can be frustrated. Trips in your immediate vicinity should overcome problems connected with friendships, clubs or social affairs. Long-drawn-out discussions may come to nothing. Even when you seem to have negotiations in the bag, and have contracts to prove it, agreements may turn out to be not worth the paper they are printed on. Local people can introduce problems. These may relate to rights-of-way.

7. WEDNESDAY. Good. Today is very favorable for team efforts in business operations. It will also be good for pooling energy and resources with others to form business partnerships. It may be easier to see eye-to-eye with people working in close conjunction with you. Handle potential friction points in a rational way. Common agreements may be arrived at without much beating about the bush. Air travel should be pleasant and quick with no major holdups or delays. Friends can come forward with creative projects in mind, seeking your help to put them into practice. It may be to your advantage to help them get the show on the road. Surprise profits can come to sales representatives who are alert.

8. THURSDAY. Uncertain. Aquarius may not relish the idea of mixing with groups of people today, preferring, instead, to spend at least part of the day on their own. Your home can provide a safe and secure haven if you need to get away from the bustle and turmoil of the world. Old memories and thoughts about the past are likely to crowd in on you. In fact, if you are not careful, you will drown in nostalgia. If you are at home, and have energy to spare, you could constructively turn your attention to the household plumbing and drainage system. It would be a good opportunity for doing repairs or replacements. Employment and business problems will only get worse if you do not face them square on. Take the bull by the horns and save yourself some grief.

9. FRIDAY. Excellent. Important people will lean over backward to help the financial affairs of Aquarius. The day is good for approaching people in influential positions to ask for assistance in such matters. If legalities or rules and regulations stand in the way of your receiving such help, others may be prepared to disregard formalities. You are entirely likely to get the support you need against all the odds. It's a banner time for moving house and home. Real estate transactions are likely to work out in your favor. These should bring forth profitable results. Excellent results can also be achieved by wining and dining prominent people in the comfort of your home. Take advantage of these opportunities.

10. SATURDAY. Fair. Both creative energies and long attention spans will prevail for Aquarius today. It will be good, therefore, for following up on artistic and intellectual pursuits. All mental work will be easier to handle. While the early response to romantic advances can be extremely favorable, as Aquarius get better acquainted with new romantic partners, they are likely to find they have made a mistake. New love affairs can soon falter when you discover your partner is not really your type. Undercover operations and secret trips will work out favorably. Relatives can take you completely by surprise. They may even ask some impossible favor of you that could be difficult to grant.

11. SUNDAY. Disturbing. Unforeseen events can crop up and interfere with arrangements you have made with friends or loved ones. Pleasure may have to be sacrificed for the sake of needy elders or parents. Romance may play second fiddle to family emergencies. Those Aquarius who refuse to shoulder family duties, and follow their own inclinations, are likely to experience a lurking feeling of guilt. This will spoil their preferred activities if they attempt to undertake them. It would be wiser to tow the line. Rearrange your pleasure plans. Later on, you are advised to avoid risks and gambles like the plague. You can expect bad luck if you are putting money on horses or cards. When in doubt, play it safe.

12. MONDAY. Variable. Business finances can go through erratic ups and downs today. You are unlikely to receive the returns you had expected on investments. Conditions are not supportive for speculative commercial ventures. If you already have money tied up in such schemes, you may have a lot to worry about. Children may be in a mood where they will not want to be told or shown what to do. They may want to demonstrate their separateness from parents or elders. However, Aquarius are unlikely to sympathize with shows of defiance or independence. You should be able to keep the upper hand, even if such behavior takes you by surprise. The day is good for conducting important meetings.

13. TUESDAY. Deceptive. Aquarius will have to keep their wits about them to prevent this day from becoming a disaster. You are likely to be in a dreamy or muddleheaded state. Although it may be difficult to keep your mind on the task in hand, you must make every effort to counter tendencies to fall into reveries. Keep on the ball. Attention must not be allowed to wander. Accidents and mistakes can occur if your concentration lags. A practical approach is essential to employment activities. Aquarius employers must not treat employees like machines. While their whims and fancies should not be indulged, neither should their personal problems or working conditions be disregarded. Be open-minded.

14. WEDNESDAY. Mixed. Regular employment activities and means of livelihood can bring in extra cash now. Pay raises are in the cards. Overtime will pay well. Exceptional achievements will be well rewarded. However, it can be more difficult to make contact with employers or those in authority. They may seem rather distant and detached. This may lead Aquarius to think the worst. Don't read too much into the aloofness of superiors. You may not have all the energy you require available to you today. You are more likely to get run down from emotional rather than physical strain. Depression or worry will sap your vitality. This is nothing serious. Some extra rest will put you back in the game.

15. THURSDAY. Good. The day is favorable for all forms of teamwork and partnerships. Cooperative efforts can achieve much. Aquarius business people are advised to allow colleagues to handle publicity campaigns. They may have plenty of original ideas for attracting the attention of a wider public. Efforts to expand markets and win new customers through advertising can pay dividends. It's an excellent time for dealing with attorneys and law courts. If you are involved in legal proceedings, this is a good day for preparing a strong case with legal advisors. Marital tensions will be best resolved by straight talking. Problems will only worsen if they are kept bottled up. Get things out in the open.

16. FRIDAY. Rewarding. It's a good day for pooling efforts and resources with others to achieve your aims, especially if mature and experienced people are involved. Aquarius should seek to learn all they can from the knowledge of older people. Keep an open mind. Leave your prejudices and self-importance behind. Marriage breakups, and any associated maintenance payments, can be settled now with the minimum of bad feeling and complication. Activities shared with loved ones and mutual friends will help to cement friendships and bring couples closer together. Business finances should take an upward turn. Prospects for investment and other ventures are looking brighter again. Don't let opportunity slip away.

17. SATURDAY. Sensitive. Listen to what loved ones have to say today. They may have lively suggestions for outings and activities. Their exciting ideas will benefit you if you become involved. Projects or dreams that are dear to your heart can come to fruition now. They will do so through joint efforts of people with whom you work in close collaboration, or through the cooperation of emotional partners. Wishes can be fulfilled sooner than you ever expected. Be careful not to act or to judge people on faulty information. Check your facts before taking them as gospel. People will react strongly to wrongful accusations. Make sure you have full self-control if you are driving, even a short distance.

18. SUNDAY. Fair. This is a day when Aquarius can enjoy being more on their own. There will be no shortage of things to absorb your interest and attention if you spend part of the day alone. Conditions are favorable for digging and delving into books and collections. Solitude will allow you all the concentration you require to go deeply into subjects. It's a good day for allowing the imagination to take wing. You will again achieve the best results in artistic and inventive activities if you are in quiet surroundings. It's also a good time for checking through family and personal accounts, and for discussing the financial situation with spouses. Aquarius may not have cash to provide a romantic occasion.

19. MONDAY. Disturbing. Aquarius may abandon their excellent track record where honesty and integrity are concerned. Where joint finances are concerned, you may prefer to deal in double standards. Although you may not fully realize what you are doing, you may lay down conditions for others, and yet not abide by them yourself. Loved ones will not take kindly to seeing you spending freely when restrictions have been imposed on them. Harmony and cooperation can only be maintained if everyone is subject to the same standards. Friends might tempt you with wild and way-out money-making schemes. Aquarius would be foolish to get involved in such risky ventures.

20. TUESDAY. Deceptive. Aquarius should endeavor to take a broader view of things and widen their perspective. This is the time to abandon narrow views and prejudices. Look for new horizons. Embrace unfamiliar and untried ways. Adopt a more positive approach. It is by looking on the bright side that you will accomplish most. An optimistic attitude will summon up all the energy you need to reach the goals you set yourself. Don't take people and events in distant places at face value. There may be dishonesty and double-dealing going on behind the scenes. Even people you have formerly trusted can let you down badly. Be absolutely sure of your ground before making accusations.

21. WEDNESDAY. Good. This is another day when Aquarius should seek to explore new avenues and horizons. The day is good for all attempts to educate yourself further and broaden the mind. It's also favorable for starting retraining programs that will lead to improved job qualifications. It is likely that such activities will lead to meetings with people who become firm friends or romantic partners. You will probably be attracted to people who are on the same wave-length as you. Business finances can get a boost as a result of developments in distant places. Business contacts in other cities or areas will handle matters in a very satisfactory way. Your spouse's relatives will be in a more friendly mood.

22. THURSDAY. Demanding. Aquarius who are involved in overseas trading and travel may be in for a tricky day. You will have to stick absolutely to the letter of the law. Only then will you avoid trouble from officials. They are unlikely to turn a blind eye to even minor infringements of regulations, let alone larger ones.

It is not worth trying to pull the wool over the eyes of customs officials. Keep all your dealings open and aboveboard. If you have bright ideas and innovations to suggest at work, people in authority are unlikely to respond with much enthusiasm. Any hopes you have for stepping up the ladder of promotion can be disappointed. Likewise, applications for study grants may be turned down.

23. FRIDAY. Disquieting. Aquarius seem to be in a rather troubled mood at the moment. Conditions that affect work, business and external affairs will not be much to your liking. In fact, things can go very wrong for you. The circumstance you most want to avoid is likely to materialize. Such conditions will be a real test for the Aquarius strength of character and ability to persevere in the face of difficulty. You must rally your resources and take a positive stance. Don't allow negative feelings to paralyze you. You must remain positive if you are to steer events back on an optimistic course. Keep on the move. Look out for helpful contacts and useful information.

24. SATURDAY. Reflective. This will be a quieter and less pressured day, giving Aquarius the chance and the conditions for putting unsettled business and career affairs back on course. It should be possible to arrange sufficient time to yourself to do the necessary spadework. If you can give your full attention to the most pressing problems, much ground can be covered. While you can make good headway where means of livelihood are concerned, there may be a less favorable turn of events in your lovelife. It could be that you have asked or expected too much of loved ones recently. They now have a period of reaction. Close relationships can be in jeopardy. Don't neglect them.

25. SUNDAY. Mixed. Aquarius will enjoy the company of friends today. They will share activities with groups of people. It is not a day for solitariness. Let others know how you feel and what is on your mind. Associates will be in a receptive and sympathetic mood. They can take a keen interest in your ideas. Things you suggest are likely to be taken up. All forms of communication can be useful in furthering personal plans. Inquiries by phone can save time and trouble. Visits to museums and other places of interest will provide stimulation and pleasure. Things may not go according to plan later on. You may have to bide your time this evening. Patience is the watchword. Let others come to you.

26. MONDAY. Opportune. Aquarius will be able to take advantage of unsettled conditions or unexpected changes. Your ability to change direction suddenly, without losing your head, will stand you in good stead. Flexibility and a skill for taking opportunities as and when they come can bring great benefits. Public upheaval can provide circumstances that allow you to make a financial killing. Take full advantage of any freak or short-term demands for goods or services. Go into top gear to meet the needs of people in emergency situations. Friends can make lively and adventurous companions. There will be no need to fit in with the expectations of others.

27. TUESDAY. Fair. It's a good day for working more in the background, especially where professional and external affairs are concerned. This is a time when the humanitarian impulses of Aquarius can also do their personal reputations some good. Influential people can take favorable notice of your generosity and unselfishness. People will be more prepared to trust you on the basis of what you do for others. However, if you have any hopes of getting the upper hand by acquiring information before it becomes public knowledge, you are likely to be disappointed. Your attempts to get inside information will probably come to nothing. Take extra care on the roads. If you can, let someone else drive.

28. WEDNESDAY. Quiet. Aquarius can enjoy a more relaxed period now. There should be some release from the hustle and bustle of regular work and daily toil. This can leave you more time to yourself. Energy can be devoted to favorite pastimes and interests. You can catch up on personal activities like shopping. It's a good time also for cultivating contacts with people who work behind the scenes. It is people in hidden or unobtrusive positions who can bring opportunity your way. You can benefit from some direct self-questioning now. You cannot allow personal preferences to give you a distorted picture of people or events. An honest and unbiased appraisal will show you how the land really lies.

29. THURSDAY. Variable. This can be a lucky day for Aquarius. Events are likely to work out in your favor. People will be in a cooperative mood. Much can be accomplished by phone and letter. Communications you receive can bring good news or useful information. You can rely more on others, even on people whom you know only slightly. They will be prepared to go along with the course of action you suggest. Few obstacles will be placed in the way of Aquarius who go all out to achieve their goals. However, impulsive and hasty moves in employment and business affairs must be avoided. Decisions affecting work must be given careful and measured consideration.

30. FRIDAY. Buoyant. Aquarius can weave a special charm over others today. Your energy and appearance will seem especially attractive to people you meet. This will help you to drum up support and enthusiasm for pet projects and activities. Schemes designed to help others can get welcome and unexpected assistance. There should be no shortage of help and encouragement for putting idealistic ideas into practice. Your attractiveness can also have very favorable consequences in your lovelife. People you have known for some time can suddenly see you in a new and romantic light. Friends can put you in touch with people you take an immediate fancy to. Today, the world is your oyster. Enjoy it.

31. SATURDAY. Mixed. Conditions affecting business and professional matters will suit you very well. There will be opportunities on hand, and Aquarius will know just how to make the most of them. There should be room to expand regular commercial dealings. You will also feel quite confident to handle quantities of cash. The success you meet in dealing with money matters can win you the admiration and respect of others. People will be more ready to place their trust in you in the future on the basis of your achievements today. Although you are usually quick off-the-mark and swift in thought, developments in romance can leave even you disarmed. Keep your wits about you.

FEBRUARY

1. SUNDAY. Variable. Aquarius can get carried away on overgenerous impulses today. There is a chance that you will not know when to stop. There is no sense in giving to the point where your own finances are put in an embarrassing situation. It could also be that others are more than willing to take full advantage of your open genorosity. You must learn to discriminate between the justly deserving and those who are purely on the make. Keep your own economic limits in mind. People close to you may also try to take unfair advantage of you. It is essential that you let others know when you think they have pushed you too far. Set your limits and stick to them.

2. MONDAY. Deceptive. Check all facts you receive by letter or phone before you act on them. Information can be incorrectly relayed. Be extra careful when you are communicating news or instructions yourself. It will be easier to mislead associates or for them to misinterpret what you are saying. You may also get appointment times and phone numbers wrong. Meetings and contact points may not work out. People may react angrily if they are let down or left waiting. It will be up to you to let people in influential positions know what is on your mind. They could be more willing to supply help and support, but only when you include them in the picture. To do so will be to your advantage.

3. TUESDAY. Rewarding. Aquarius should keep on the move today. Make the rounds of contacts and associates. People you already know can, in turn, introduce you to others. These may prove to be most helpful in furthering your business or professional interests. You can miss valuable opportunities by staying in one spot. Let your imagination off the leash when dealing with artistic, inventive or mental activities. Don't limit your creative efforts by relying on traditional or familiar methods and styles. Break new ground wherever possible. Aquarius who deal in electrical goods and services are in for a bumper day. Don't shy away from making bold new decisions.

4. WEDNESDAY. Fair. This is another day when innovations and imaginative solutions should be sought. There will be plenty of room for making tasks easier and quicker by adopting a creative approach. Long drawn-out projects or overdue work can be brought to rapid conclusion by inventive means. Don't opt for the most obvious solutions. You will have the ability to think round corners now, so take advantage of it. Professional duties can force you to put in extra hours at work this evening. However, you won't be able to count on the understanding of family members. They are likely to feel neglected. It may be necessary to state your commitment to philanthropic endeavors in no uncertain terms.

5. THURSDAY. Difficult. Aquarius are likely to get the green light from important people to carry out their personal plans. Employers may be more conducive to giving you time off from regular employment activities. Just when you are set to put your plans into operation, duties and pressures associated with the home and family can cause you to abandon them. Conditions are unfavorable for property dealing. House buying should be put off until a more propitious day. Effort and expense given to home entertaining may prove unrewarding. Guests are unlikely to appreciate your hospitality. You may have to put your interests second to the needs of those around you.

6. FRIDAY. Disquieting. Youngsters can be a bit of a handful today. They are likely to be in a mischievous mood and require more supervision. They may also be irritable and need special attention. It may not be easy to see eye-to-eye with loved ones. If your point of view is not accepted, you must not take it as a personal insult. Disagreements can soon flare into fierce arguments, unless you maintain a rational and cool approach. Arrangements for outings or meetings with loved ones may not go according to plan. The course of romance may have to be replotted. This is not a good day for taking risks and gambles. Don't be tempted by tip-offs or attractive offers this evening.

7. SATURDAY. Quiet. Today will proceed at a slower and more relaxed pace. Aquarius will enjoy tranquil conditions. It's a good time for taking it easy and refueling your tanks. Engage in those activities which you find most restful or that take your mind off work and money problems. While leisure pursuits will be enjoyable, they should be kept within reason. Don't overstretch your capacities in the search for a good time. Candle-lit dinners and special entertainment shared with loved ones will give great pleasure. Visits to shows and night spots should prove enjoyable. The day is ideal for reading travel brochures and planning holidays.

8. SUNDAY. Creative. This can be a very productive day for artists and writers. All activities that require imaginative flair or mental concentration will yield good results. If you have recently struck a barren patch in creative endeavors, or are stuck on a particular problem, the way ahead should suddenly become clear. Aquarius will have a good grasp of expressive media. Ideas and feelings can be communicated with force and clarity. You should have success in raising money for humanitarian causes. People will find you very persuasive when it comes to standing up for the underprivileged and needy. Gambling should be avoided like the plague. It might even be illegal where you live.

9. MONDAY. Deceptive. Employment routines may be upset by unforeseen events. It may be necessary to stay at home to tend to loved ones who are sick. There will be a tendency for Aquarius to build castles in the sky. You will appear to be on another planet to the people around you. You will probably only be indulging thoughts and hopes of a romantic nature. Even this, though, will make for inefficiency. It will also make you more prone to accidents. You can miss valuable opportunities through daydreaming.

Unusual chances may come your way in regular employment activities, but you will need to be on-the-ball to take advantage of them. Sweethearts may be hiding something from you.

10. TUESDAY. Good. Aquarius will have better luck conducting transactions and negotiations today. It will be easier to reach favorable agreements with associates. It is a good time for finalizing long-term plans and putting your signature to contracts. There will be plenty of time to tie up the loose ends of overdue work and business. It is important that you clear the decks and keep your affairs running smoothly. You will have the concentration to attend to even the smallest details. Irritating minor jobs that you have put to one side are best completed now. Make sure you are eating well and keeping fit. Pay close attention to your health because it is of the utmost importance.

11. WEDNESDAY. Fair. Conditions will be much to your liking at work today, particularly during the morning. It could be that a lucky break comes your way early in the day. Hard work and diligence will not go unnoticed or unrewarded. Pay raises are in the cards for those who deserve them. It may be difficult to keep abreast of developments in your lovelife. Your own perceptions of romantic situations may not be entirely trustworthy. Aquarians will tend to project their own glamorized view of things onto others. Your appraisal of events is likely to be colored by the way you want things to go. You need to be more objective now, and to put your own needs second to those of loved ones.

12. THURSDAY. Confusing. Developments in professional and external affairs can follow a rather tangled course. It may be difficult to discern clear patterns for the time being. This is also a time when Aquarius are likely to feel the limitations imposed on their individuality. This may be the result of being one of a team or part of a business partnership. You would do better to look for the positive aspects of such cooperation. Avoid the temptation to rail against not having your own way entirely. Further obstacles may be thrown in your way. These may involve attention to rules, regulations and legal requirements. Regular trading activities may be slow as a result.

13. FRIDAY. Changeable. Aquarius are going to feel the pinch in partnerships of all kinds today. You just won't want to conform to the ideas, needs and plans of others. This applies to business, domestic or romantic relationships. You will want to do things your own way. The situation can be further aggravated by the need to give up exciting offers or preferred activities for the sake of loved ones or business colleagues. In spite of all this, it would be foolish to jeopardize any of the relationships you have carefully built. Cooperative efforts will still give the best results. The sooner you get over your reservations, the sooner you can make full and effective use of mutual alliances.

14. SATURDAY. Auspicious. Aquarius can uncover hidden knowledge by instigating their own research programs. Try digging to get to the bottom of things. Encyclopedias can be a mine of information. The day is good for abandoning the old and familiar and breaking new ground. Don't fall back on known and tried ways. Innovation and invention are possible. Look for the unconventional approach in all creative and mental activities. Give imagination a free hand. Originality can breed success now. Your humanitarian schemes are likely to get the backing and go-ahead from official sources. Influential people will be more sympathetic to your ideas for helping others.

15. SUNDAY. Variable. It may be necessary to discuss money matters with loved ones. It is unlikely that any constructive progress will be made. In fact, your points of view could be so opposed that sparks fly. It may be better to wait until both you and partners are in a more reasonable mood. Then thoroughly review family or joint finances. You would be ill-advised to use mutual funds to support the money-making projects of friends. Losses are more likely than gains. It can benefit Aquarius to get in touch with business colleagues, employers or other important people today. Do this in spite of it being a day off. It will be beneficial to air problems with such people.

16. MONDAY. Slow. Aquarius will be let off the hook so far as regular pressures and demands are concerned. This will allow you to draw back more into yourself and present a stronger face to the world. You should find the fortitude to be unaffected by little emotional and personal aggravations. You should also have more patience to deal with meticulous manual and practical tasks. While there is a short lull in the usual hustle and bustle, look ahead and lay plans for future activities. Now is the time for conferring with people who have in-depth knowledge of subjects or areas of interest to you. Fewer distractions make this an excellent day for reading and learning.

17. TUESDAY. Uncertain. Don't allow the pessimism of loved ones to interfere with your positive outlook. Spouses may attempt to pour cold water on your forward-looking plans. By all means, listen to what they have to say. They may have sound judgments to make. However, don't be dissuaded from positive action for the wrong reasons. External circumstances can force the ending of romantic attachments. Professional priorities, or family ties, may oblige you to move far away from loved ones. Don't be too forward in stating your plans and intentions to others. People may have shocked reactions if you confront them with too much at once. Subtlety is the order of the day.

18. WEDNESDAY. Mixed. You may hear from acquaintances in faraway places. It will give your spirits a lift. Distant affairs can take a turn for the better. Unexpected opportunities to travel may come your way. Aquarius can be selected by employers to undertake journeys connected with work. People in authority will be in a more sympathetic mood. They can be a source of good luck. Personal plans may win the approval of officials. You can make requests of people in high places with more confidence of success now. Aquarius connected with the production of newspapers, magazines and books, may be in for a difficult day. Your spouse's relatives may be unreceptive to your ideas or plans.

19. THURSDAY. Productive. You will have to keep your nose to the grindstone today. Avoid getting behind with schedules. Go into top gear now. Get as much done as possible. Keep in close touch with business contacts. Make sure any developments in the commercial world do not escape your notice. It is also advisable to pay extra attention to newspapers and news broadcasts. There may be political happenings that open up opportunities for you. Overseas developments may oblige you to make rapid decisions. Aquarius can have more success in contacting people who have proved elusive in the recent past. You may be in a position to drive a hard bargain if you are persistent. Hang in there.

20. FRIDAY. Good. There may be strong temptations for Aquarius to abandon their usual honesty and integrity. It may appear that personal advantage will come from going back on your word or playing the opportunist. All this is illusory. You will do yourself much more good in the long run by sticking to the course that you know to be best. It would be pointless to undermine the trust you have built up over long periods. Your reputation will increase ten-fold if you keep your side of the bargain. This may mean shouldering some hardship and inconvenience. You can inspire others with your energy and enthusiasm. Financiers will respond to your ideas and projects. Opportunity awaits.

FEBRUARY—AQUARIUS—1987 / **143**

21. SATURDAY. Disquieting. Aquarius are advised to keep matters relating to their financial situation to themselves. It may be better to keep people you would normally trust in the dark. Friends may inadvertently spill the beans in the wrong quarters. You may have to reach deeper into your pocket than you like in order to meet the costs associated with outings, entertainment and travel. This is not a good time for expounding your ideas and attitudes to groups of people. You are unlikely to meet a sympathetic ear. Deep antagonisms can be stirred up. Check all facts and figures before making irrevocable decisions. Mistakes are more likely to be made in haste.

22. SUNDAY. Worrisome. Aquarius may receive distress calls from close friends and acquaintances. You may have to ditch personal plans to help someone out of a tight corner. Loved ones may not be in the best of health. Their condition can cause anxiety and a change of plan. Specialist treatment may be required to get them back to fitness. You may have to respond to social invitations that you do not particularly relish. Although these will pull you away from favored pastimes and activities, you will probably be delighted that you went. Once again, people will not be too receptive to ideas that are far ahead of their time. Instead, listen to what others have to say.

23. MONDAY. Challenging. It is best to employ subtle and diplomatic means if you have to make requests for financial help from financiers or other important people. You are unlikely to succeed if you are too direct or overbearing. Enthusiasm or impatience must be contained if you are to reach your target. Don't let it all spill out prematurely. You can cover more ground in professional matters by working quietly and unobtrusively in the background. Without quite realizing it, Aquarius may be reluctant to face up to problems head on. You will be more prone to deluding yourself. You may prefer to sweep trouble under the carpet than to find solutions that could mean compromise.

24. TUESDAY. Important. You may have to try a number of different approaches before you win others over to your side. If you keep at it, you will succeed in gaining the cooperation and backing you require. Subtle and tactful means are again likely to be the most effective. Attempts to bludgeon others into towing the line will only fail. Do what you can to butter others up. You may even have to appeal to their vanity. Solo efforts are likely to fall short of the mark. Aquarius may have no choice but to muster support from others. If you have taken a fancy to someone, but are failing to get response, don't despair. It could be the other person is merely too shy to admit to feelings of a romantic nature.

25. WEDNESDAY. Disappointing. Aquarius can be bubbling over with original and inventive ideas. Family members, however, may try to dampen your enthusiasm to launch new ventures. In fact, you are likely to receive ultimatums if you insist on putting your plans into operation. Don't rush through work or opt for second-rate solutions. Shortcuts will be a case of haste makes waste. You may want to conclude long drawn-out affairs. You are advised to tie up loose ends carefully. The erratic and unconventional side of the Aquarius nature can come to the fore now. It may make people raise their eyebrows. Be careful not to put your reputation on the line.

26. THURSDAY. Good. You should have no problems drumming up assistance today. Friends and associates will be only too pleased to give what help they can. If you are planning humanitarian schemes that require official backing, you should gain a heartening response. It will also be easier to raise financial assistance for such enterprises. Organizations that are formed now to help the underprivileged and needy may soon be granted charitable status. Try seeking ways to economize the household budget. You may find it is cheaper in the long run to buy in bulk. Aquarius shoppers should have a particularly enjoyable and productive day in clothing stores and specialty shops.

27. FRIDAY. Encouraging. Conditions favor attempts to brighten up homes or build on extensions. These efforts will add to the comfort and efficiency of your surroundings. Home improvement schemes can prove to be good investments. Property values can increase. It will be easier to find the cash to fund such operations. Today is good for taking on overtime or extra duties at work. Aquarius should do all they can to boost incomes. You will need to keep on your toes to spot the chances for earning more money. If you feel that you are due for a pay raise, this is a good time to approach employers with such requests. They will be in a cheerful mood and are likely to give you a sympathetic hearing.

28. SATURDAY. Variable. This can be an unfavorable day for money matters. There may be trouble associated with club or group funds. Sums of money can go astray. Suspicion may fall on Aquarius. Personal or joint savings may be the source of disagreements. You may have to scrape the barrel of personal finances to help a friend in need. There may be brighter prospects in view where employment and professional interests are concerned. Influential people can be willing to put in a good word for you. They may arrange introductions or send opportunities your way. Later, the cloud hanging over financial affairs may disappear. It will become easier to raise money for charity.

MARCH

1. SUNDAY. Fair. Show the world a cheerful face today. Others will soon join in your positive mood. Look on the bright side, and see how much energy you generate. Aquarius must be more ready to forgive and forget. Don't judge others too harshly if they make a mess of things. Family members or people you work with can be clumsy and forgetful. Irritable reactions on your part won't improve the situation. Although you may run into difficulties where business activities are concerned, trouble will be minimized by the intervention of people in prominent positions. You may be a little too ready to take offence at others intervening. Best to keep a cool head.

2. MONDAY. Productive. Aquarius will meet people who put useful facts and inside information their way. If you are troubled with a legal problem, it can be worth your while to talk it over with friends. They may be more knowledgeable on legal matters than you realize. Don't give up too easily on talks designed to ease your business financial situation. If discussions have broken down, do your utmost to get them going again. Today is good for picking up the loose ends of abandoned business deals. Try to make a go of them again. Writers of historical, philosophical and other serious subjects should have a productive day. All academic and mental activities will benefit from continued efforts.

3. TUESDAY. Demanding. You may have to attend to family and household duties. These may interfere with your plans for outings with sweethearts. Married Aquarius may be obliged to reveal certain facts about past relationships that upset their spouse. Loved ones are likely to get even more incensed if you keep your past history to yourself. You should not be dishonest with them. However, a little censorship may be in order. Say only as much as is strictly necessary. Aquarius will have a very creative approach to work problems now. Quick and original thinking will show you shortcuts and new methods. Long-drawn-out financial transactions are best brought to a close as rapidly as possible.

4. WEDNESDAY. Sensitive. Interfering people or irritating circumstances can make for problems at home. Family members will be troubled by external affairs. Aquarius must try to see how important the career and employment aspirations of loved ones are to them. It would be unwise to dampen their enthusiasm or plans for a career in public or professional fields. Seek to give them all the all the encouragement and support you can. The buying and selling of property can have profitable results. It will be easier to get planning permission or official go-aheads for improvements to homes. Employers are likely to reward your efforts to get work finished ahead of schedule.

5. THURSDAY. Quiet. This can be a slow day at work. Aquarius may be given time off or allowed to bring work home. It would be best not to fritter away any time you have to yourself. This is the moment to catch up on any repair jobs that need attending to around the home. If you cannot manage maintenance and repair work yourself, arrange for professionals to come in. Do what you can by yourself. Today is good also for visiting parents and older relatives, especially if they are living alone and are rather lonely. You can gain much pleasure and enjoyment from entertaining and feeding friends and associates in your home environment. Your efforts will be thoroughly appreciated.

6. FRIDAY. Strenuous. All professional, employment and public affairs can go badly astray. They must be handled with extra skill. It will be easier for Aquarius to do and say things that cast a slur on their good names. Reputations must be protected. Tact and tolerance are essential now. Give all moves and decisions as much preconsideration as possible. Avoid hasty, impulsive actions. People who bear you a grudge in the business world may try to cast your commercial activities in a bad light. Unjust accusations may be made by people who are jealous of your successes. Find time to take it easy. Pursue the activities that you most enjoy. In the evening, pamper yourself.

7. SATURDAY. Disturbing. Youngsters will be in a mischievous mood. Parents may have to deal with delinquent or unruly behavior. Children may commit misdemeanors that bring them and parents into contact with the law. Financial compensations may be demanded of you. It would be wise to start the day with a stern warning. Your lovelife can be disrupted by requests from friends, club and group associates. Unavoidable social invitations may come your way. Aquarius who cannot resist taking a gamble today, could be in for very heavy losses. Conditions are extremely unfavorable for speculation. Leisure pursuits can be spoiled by health problems. Watch your diet carefully.

8. SUNDAY. Variable. Today can provide a happier contrast to recent troubles and turmoils. Get busy with jobs around the house and garden. Put financial and emotional problems on the back burner for the time being. Do what you can to take your mind off things that have been causing anxiety. Once you get started, you will soon get totally absorbed. Trips to beauty spots and places of interest will provide a welcome change. New experiences can help lift your spirits. Intellectual pursuits can be turned to profitable use. You must avoid depleting your energy by taking on too much. It's advisable not to make unnecessary journeys. You would probably find them a waste of time.

9. MONDAY. Good. Aquarius should strive to tie up all loose ends. Bring overdue business to a close. Clear the decks and get a fresh start on things. This is no time for half-hearted efforts at work. You have everything to gain by going into top gear. What you achieve now, over and above normal outputs, can both improve your standing and win excellent bonuses. Employers will be taking note of extra exertions. If you are bedevilled by feelings of drowsiness and fatigue it would be best to work against it. Don't go into a slump. A brisk walk or run can revitalize your system. On the other hand, don't overdo strenuous exercise.

10. TUESDAY. Easygoing. You cannot afford an over-casual approach to your health. You should be giving more rather than less attention to your physical condition. The importance of a balanced and nutritious diet cannot be underestimated. Any recent lack of energy or persistent physical symptoms may be the result of poor diet. Food should be taken at regular times and in relaxed conditions. Rushed meals will reduce their nutritious effects. Exercise too is essential to keep the body in a balanced and healthy state. Walks in the country are an excellent idea for Aquarius who live in towns and cities. Seek unpolluted air. Conditions at work will be easygoing and uneventful.

11. WEDNESDAY. Troubling. Aquarius may think that associates are not pulling their weight or are working below standard. It is unlikely that you will be seeing eye-to-eye with partners on matters of behavior. Loved ones' choice of color, design or clothes may leave you cold. Aquarius should hold their tendency to criticize in check. This is a side of your nature that can easily get out of hand with very destructive consequences. You won't get much satisfaction from bankers or financiers if you make approaches for loans or other financial requests. This is especially true where your business needs are involved. Arguments with loved ones are in the cards. Try to forestall them with tact and patience.

12. THURSDAY. Difficult. Unexpected bills and financial demands can come in now. Your economic resources will be put under strain. People to whom you owe money may be very insistent on repayment. It is likely that you will find it difficult to raise the cash in time. Avoid taking on any additional financial commitments until the situation settles down again. You may see the need to take out extra insurance on property and loved ones. However, the costs involved may be beyond your reach. Compromises will have to be made. You may not get the open channels you would like to important information and sources of knowledge. Officials can block your investigations. Take time to review future plans.

13. FRIDAY. Confusing. It may be better to avoid discussions of joint finances with partners for the time being. Nothing constructive is likely to come from such conferences. In fact, you may only stir up dissension and bad feeling. Loved ones can be uncooperative when it comes to putting economy measures into practice. Welcome financial boosts may come in the form of legacies. Confusion can also come in their wake. It may not be clear just who is the recipient or what amount has been left. Aquarius who handle money or real estate for others cannot afford to take any risks now. Don't be content with spoken agreements. The wishes of clients or associates must be recorded.

14. SATURDAY. Prosperous. Family members can make timely and generous gestures to Aquarius who are in trouble with partnership finances. Parents may see fit to give married children a financial boost. Tensions and disagreements within family groups can dissolve more easily than expected. Differences of opinion can be settled before they develop into ugly scenes. If you are trying to sell your house, don't take the first offer that comes. It seems you will have no trouble selling at a higher price. Be prepared to hang on for the top amount. A similar story applies to antiques and family heirlooms. Don't accept first quotes or reported prices. Get a second opinion. Wait for the best offers.

15. SUNDAY. Disturbing. You may see the right solution to put partnership finances back on course, but be unable to do much about it. Loved ones may not give much credence to your ideas. They will prefer to go their own way with spending. Aquarius can experience the frustration of being overruled or ignored. Friends can be an unsettling factor in money matters. Their ideas and outlook can change from moment to moment. It is best not to rely on them whatever. This can be a volatile day emotionally for Aquarius. Feelings may boil over without provocation. Keep a rein on your temper. The evening may bring an unexpected change.

16. MONDAY. Deceptive. It will be more difficult to obtain a true picture of people and events in distant places. First impressions can be misleading. People may give false reports in order to gain personal advantage. Aquarius can be attracted by exciting propositions and job descriptions. It is unlikely that such situations will live up to their claims. Be more skeptical and cautious. Look before you leap. Don't take things at face value. Beware of religious practitioners who spout high-sounding words. They may, in fact, have very dubious motives. It will be easier to spoil academic efforts by careless mistakes or by using wrong information. Check your sources thoroughly.

17. TUESDAY. Variable. It is a good day for conferring with tutors and academic people. If you are having trouble with your studies, teachers will soon get you back on the right track. Don't sweep problems under the carpet. Take every opportunity to seek advice. Aquarius can further their charitable and humanitarian projects by producing leaflets or information sheets. You may come across useful advertisements connected with such projects in publications. This is a good moment for Aquarius business people to consider retraining. Taking courses will increase your skills in management. You should not put too much trust in prominent people. They can let you down.

18. WEDNESDAY. Uncertain. Don't be heavy-handed when dealing with professional duties or employment affairs. It will be easier to tread on other peoples' toes. This can only make things more difficult for yourself in the future. Large measures of tact and diplomacy are called for. You would be ill-advised to go behind the backs of superiors or influential people. This is not the best moment to improvise new methods or to take shortcuts. This is not to say that you should follow the most obvious route or broadcast your intentions far and wide. In fact, the results of working in the background can do much to improve your reputation. You could come out on top in tricky situations.

19. THURSDAY. Sensitive. It would be unwise to neglect loved ones for the sake of professional and business activities. Try to arrive at a better balance between external affairs and home and family requirements. A tense atmosphere will soon build up at home if you do not pay attention. This can be a difficult day for handling the buying and selling of property. Such transactions need slow and measured consideration. Hasty moves can lead to blunders. Romance can also be badly affected by business pressures. Outings with sweethearts may have to be canceled. It is important that special efforts are made to compensate loved ones for your attentions spent elsewhere.

20. FRIDAY. Tricky. It won't be easy for Aquarius to steer financial transactions their way. In fact, negotiations can go up in smoke. It will be almost impossible to see eye-to-eye with business associates. Stark differences of opinion can lead to the breakdown of important discussions. You may have to reach deeper into your pocket than you would like to cover travel expenses. Friends and money will make a bad mix today. You may fall out with a pal and lose some cash in the bargain. Things will be looking up in club and group activities. Don't swerve from the path of truth and honesty. You can win friends for life by sticking to your guns.

21. SATURDAY. Special. The emphasis today is very much on affairs of the heart. Dreams and wishes you hold dear can at last come true. Unexpected developments can bring you close to people you are fond of. Someone you have taken a fancy to may return your affections. One way or another, romantic urges are likely to be fulfilled. People you have thought of only as friends can suddenly be seen in a romantic light. It may not be people of your own age who make the best romantic partners now. You could fall for someone much older or younger than yourself. Nothing is likely to interfere with your personal plans. In fact, people can be most obliging in this respect.

22. SUNDAY. Deceptive. You can have great trouble getting hold of people of prime importance. They are likely to be involved in family or recreational activities. This can be most irritating for Aquarius. There may be a crisis to deal with. The absence of influential associates can aggravate the situation. You may have to do much chasing around in an attempt to locate people. You may still not track them down. Talk over money matters with friends and acquaintances. Aquarius should avail themselves of the financial experience of others. It is essential for you to be very matter-of-fact. There is more chance of self-delusion. Proceed not only with caution but also with understanding.

23. MONDAY. Slow. The day is unlikely to build to the momentum that would help you put personal plans into operation. Although you may try to get things moving, they will probably grind to a halt again. Conditions will not be sufficiently supportive for you to push ahead in the way you had hoped. This is likely to be most irritating. Nothing will be gained from impatience or attempts to force the pace. It would be wiser to contain your energies for the time being. Events will heat up soon enough. Just be sure you are ready to act when the time comes. Nighttime driving can be especially hazardous. Lighting conditions and equipment may be at fault. Be sure your vehicle is safe.

24. TUESDAY. Good. In stark contrast to yesterday's frustrating conditions, everything should go Aquarius' way today. In fact, it could be that all your hopes and preparations in the last few weeks have been building up to this day. People who hold the power of decision and influence are likely to show whole-hearted support for your plans and projects. You should be able to swing into action now with official consent behind you. Great benefit can be derived from attempts to bring goods and services to the attention of a wider public. Publicity will prove a worthwhile investment. Your ability to embrace a wide spectrum of ideas will greatly appeal to others.

25. WEDNESDAY. Exciting. There may be a little self-doubt and lack of confidence to contend with. The support and encouragement you receive from those around you should carry you forward on a wave of enthusiasm. Don't hesitate to lean on friends and loved ones. They will be only too pleased to have an opportunity to demonstrate their affection for you. If personal plans seem doomed through lack of cash, it is likely that someone will come to the rescue with financial support. Your lovelife can suddenly go into a higher gear. A tiny flame of romance can build to a forest fire. Make sure you do not put the dampers on it.

26. THURSDAY. Happy. Exciting romantic developments can again provide the main focus of the day for those Aquarius who are in the running. In fact, marvellous and unusual experiences can come to those who are in a romantic mood. Aquarius should have no trouble in drawing romantic partners to themselves. Your charm and attractiveness will be at a peak. Others can fall for you in a big way. Your special charisma will also make any fundraising activities very successful. Large sums can be raised for charitable and humanitarian purposes. Aquarius will find it easier to forge good relations with people in authority. Influential people can decide to let bygones be bygones.

27. FRIDAY. Quiet. This will be a less eventful day. The absence of distractions will provide excellent conditions for mental concentration. Today is good for attending to expense sheets and accounts. Clear away any backlog of unanswered letters. It is a good time also to check income against expenses. Take steps to put any discrepancies right. Get a clear picture of your financial situation now. You will be able to plan with more certainty for the future. There will not be sufficient momentum to launch new money-making schemes with any chance of success. Be content with laying the foundations for future action. Advance planning will pay off later in the form of extra income.

28. SATURDAY. Variable. This is a good time for planning home improvements and making the necessary preparations. Make sure you are well equipped with paint, plaster, ladders, etc., if you are undertaking repairs or redecorations around the house. Now is also good for roof work and outside renovations. A surprise request for cash from a needy friend may put you in an awkward situation. In spite of pressing circumstances, it may be wiser if you decline such requests. People upon whom you rely can play hard to get. Important people will be disinclined to give a firm yes or no. When you press them for reasons, you are unlikely to obtain a satisfactory answer.

29. SUNDAY. Deceptive. Aquarius should employ some healthy skepticism today. People may try to purposely mislead you for their own benefit. Facts and information may be conveyed wrongly. Check thoroughly before you act or make decisions. Logical thought and a hard-headed approach are essential if you are to make a success of newly-launched projects. There is no point in going ahead with plans that simply won't stand up against the test of reason. Keep your feet on the ground. Avoid pie-in-the-sky thinking. People can misread your generous impulses and attempts to help others. Neighbors may be in a meddlesome mood. Find time to exercise.

30. MONDAY. Good. The mail may bring something that sets your heart thumping in happy anticipation. Aquarius may be presented with opportunities to put ideas that are way ahead of their time into operation. It is a good day for sticking your neck out. Conditions are encouraging for adventurous enterprises. Have the courage of your convictions. Air travel will be speedy and enjoyable. Conversations with unconventional people may give your approach and attitude to life a jog. You may see things in a new light as the result of such talks. Writers of adventure stories can have a field day. It is a good time for carrying out personal investigations and for delving into mysteries from the past.

31. TUESDAY. Changeable. In spite of appearances to the contrary, this is no time for complacency. You may feel you have done quite enough to win the respect of others. You may feel also that you have made sufficient headway with business and employment activities. Your inclination may be to put your feet up and let the world go by. If you do, events are likely to get ahead of you and force you to keep up the pace. Competitors are likely to move ahead of you if you let business operations slide. Past efforts can be wasted if you do not capitalize on them now. You can't afford to slack off in any of your regular business affairs. Keep on the ball and don't let anyone take advantage of you.

APRIL

1. WEDNESDAY. Routine. It is important that you do not neglect home and family affairs in favor of outside interests or responsibilities. Loved ones may need a little extra support and affection now. You may feel that a great stone has been taken from your back if you can bring overdue business to a speedy close. Try clearing the decks prior to making new starts. It is not a day for putting up with procrastination from others. Keep things on the move. If you are a collector of antiques, paintings or fine objects, your searches for such items will prove particularly successful today. The evening will be good for paying visits to, or communicating with, parents.

2. THURSDAY. Tricky. Your achievements in creative and intellectual fields today can win you respect and renown. Artists, writers and designers may be lauded by clients or the general public. All your past efforts and struggles will suddenly seem worthwhile. The tenderness and frankness you exhibit when dealing with children will make you a favorite with them. Youngsters will respond to directness. You will also know how to coax the best out of them. Aquarius may be put in a difficult position when confronted with the entertainment plans of loved ones. The costs involved are likely to be very steep. You won't want to disappoint anyone. Only you know how to escape from this dilemma.

3. FRIDAY. Mixed. You are likely to get just that degree of help and encouragement from influential people that turns a speculative venture into a success. People with money are more likely to chance it with risky schemes. If your vacation is coming up, but you find you are short of cash, it will be worth your while to request a holiday allowance from your employers. Although wining and dining business associates can bring benefits, it will probably set you back a pretty penny. The reactions of Aquarius may be a little rusty. You may not be as quick off the mark as you would like in sports and games activities. Unexpected defeats are likely. Try to take them in stride.

4. SATURDAY. Variable. There may be upheavals in your lovelife due to outside interferences. Plans could be disrupted by surprise events. Friends can be particularly heavy-handed now. Their bluntness of manner can make you see red. Their lack of delicacy may shock your own sense of propriety or upset your loved ones. Fine art objects and antiques make sensible investments now. You may be able to add a touch of class and beauty to home or working surroundings. You may acquire a valuable asset at the same time. An aggressive and direct approach may not win the best results in financial negotiations. Subtle means will be more effective and will go a long way to keeping good relationships.

5. SUNDAY. Slow. Aquarius may be feeling rather lazy today. It would be better to get yourself into action than waste the day lolling about. You won't feel pleased with yourself when you realize the time and opportunities you have wasted. Make good use of the day. Once you get started, you can cover much ground. You will be delighted with what you achieve. Beware of people who try to maneuver you into doing work that is rightly their responsibility. Efforts to bring in some extra cash can prove lucrative now. It may require a minimum of effort. Loved ones will respond to gestures of affection. Spend some time with them.

6. MONDAY. Challenging. Keep your wits about you at work today. Valuable opportunities for making extra cash will be lost if you daydream or get involved in chitchat. Books and information can come your way on diet and exercise. These are subjects that are well worth studying now. Your health is likely to benefit greatly. A visit to the doctor may be required if you have contracted flu or have more serious symptoms. It won't be easy to see eye-to-eye with other parties in financial transactions. In fact, negotiations can reach stalemate. They may have to be called off completely. Bankers could be insistent that loans are repaid immediately. Assure them you will meet regular payment schedules.

7. TUESDAY. Good. You will get better results today by working with others than by solo efforts. Loved ones will appreciate your help and will be ready to give assistance in return. Mutual cooperation and teamwork are the best policy today. You will be surprised at just how much you can achieve by pooling time and energy with sympathetic associates. Aquarius must take care not to overrule partners and dominate the scene. Teammates can have a tremendous contribution to make. If you curtail their freedom, you will only minimize their effectiveness. Your lovelife will contain some adventure. Let loved ones do the choosing now.

8. WEDNESDAY. Pleasant. Today is good for dealing with lawyers and law courts. Rules and regulations will provide fewer obstructions and hold-ups. Officials will tend to help things go more smoothly rather than slow them down. This is another day when cooperative efforts will be far more productive than individual action. Avail yourself of the support and assistance of others, wherever possible. Aquarius will be in a confident mood and will handle interviews and discussions with important people without trouble. This is not a day for digging in your heels or laying down the law yourself. You must be more prepared to be flexible and to meet others halfway. This will benefit you in the long run when you need full support and help.

9. THURSDAY. Changeable. This is a good day for popping the question or making plans for marriage ceremonies and honeymoons. Aquarius may have trouble finding associates who are as freethinking, not to say eccentric, as themselves. If you can find people whose unconventional approach appeals to you, they are likely to make excellent business partners or teammates. The emphasis is also on the less obvious and more original approach in legal affairs. Imaginative solutions can be found to legal problems.

Aquarius can break new ground in such matters. Later on, you are advised to avoid gambling and risk-taking like the plague. Play it safe. It will be far less painful than losing your shirt.

10. FRIDAY. Uncertain. Aquarius will make good investigators today. The results of your digging and delving can have valuable consequences for your professional affairs. An unusual fact that has attracted your attention may be just the tip of an iceberg. Make sure to follow up leads and intuitions. Don't be put off the scent by awkward people or situations. Your present grasp of financial matters can leave much to be desired. You won't find it easy to make the right decisions where money is concerned. Tricky financial conditions won't make your job any easier. It may be well to check with friends if you have made an appointment with them. They could be rather unreliable now.

11. SATURDAY. Disturbing. It won't be easy to keep mutual funds intact. Unexpected bills may come in which force you to draw on savings. Partners can have extravagant urges and dip into joint resources to finance shopping sprees. This can also be a good time to shift invested capital. It would be unwise to make any such moves without the advice of stockbrokers. You may be jumping out of the frying pan and into the fire if you attempt reinvestments on the basis of your own limited knowledge. Interest rates on borrowed cash can rise. Plans for old-age security, which you thought were watertight, can suddenly spring a few leaks. Pension plans may contain drawbacks. Review your retirement plans.

12. SUNDAY. Deceptive. This is a good day for beginning to draw up plans for holidays and travel. It could be unwise to assume there is any finality about such arrangements. It would well be that unscheduled events force you to change your ideas about exact locations and times chosen for vacations. Even though holidays may have to be put off, the homework you do now on resorts and travel arrangements will be most valuable in the future. Your open-minded attitude and tolerance can be seen by others as an indication of a weak will or lack of morals. It will be almost impossible to convince others of the validity of your point of view. It would be wisest to keep your ideas to yourself.

13. MONDAY. Variable. Aquarius will meet with success if they are setting up businesses or other operations in distant places that are likely to continue for an extended time. Overseas trading can be established on a firm basis. The time is good for importing and exporting ventures. It is favorable also for moving your home to foreign countries, providing you intend to make a long stay. You may see another side of your spouse's relatives which had up to now remained concealed. The help and encouragement they give you now can result in them becoming trusted friends. Your enthusiasm for future business plans may receive a cold reception from prominent people.

14. TUESDAY. Good. Now is the time make up your mind one way or the other over an issue that has kept you undecided for some time past. If you don't act now it may be too late. Don't wait for others to take the initiative. This is your chance to take action. You can play the game as well as anyone. It would be unwise to broadcast your business or professional plans and intentions too widely. Play your cards close to the chest. Competitors may jump on the bandwagon and reduce your chances of success if you let them in on the act. Cooperation should be sought from people who work in the background. Don't let opportunity slip from your fingers.

15. WEDNESDAY. Buoyant. This is no time to dig your heels in or to take an uncompromising stance in business or employment matters. You must be prepared to swim with the tide. Rigid expectations are likely to be disappointed. You may find yourself in a very fluid situation that requires a high degree of flexibility. Keep in step with the people and events around you. Good financial returns and rewards can be won. You may not have much luck trying to persuade people to your point of view through a logical approach. People will be more responsive if you appeal to their feelings. Professional duties may lead to romantic experiences. Don't hold back; enjoy yourself.

16. THURSDAY. Successful. Don't underestimate the influence of your friends. It may turn out that a pal has contacts in high places. These can be of great benefit to you. You may be given just the introduction you have been waiting for. Official permission can be obtained through the agency of friends. In club and group affairs, don't let others know what is on your mind for the time being. Shrewdness can pay dividends. If you are working in a group with humanitarian aims, you may even have to resort to a little cunning to make the best use of the resources available to you. A short journey can bring the realization of a heartfelt desire that much closer.

17. FRIDAY. Disquieting. It will be easier for Aquarius to misread people and situations. Your grasp of events may not be as accurate as you would like to think. Mistakes can be made with money. Family members can let you down. They may go back on their word or forget arrangements. You should be skeptical about what fellow workers tell you. They may be pulling your leg or purposely misleading you for their own ends. With creative and imaginative powers high, you should devote as much time as possible to artistic and inventive activities. Excellent results can be achieved. Your friends may weigh you down like a ton bricks. Break out on your own. Explore new horizons.

18. SATURDAY. Exciting. Friends will make lively and happy companions today. The day is good for group outings and for living it up at parties. Social gatherings will be fun. If you have nothing in particular planned for the day, your pals are likely to have some excellent suggestions. Although their ideas may not appeal to you at first, you will be delighted you shared their arrangements by the end of the day. It is a good time for involvement in new and unfamiliar activities or visits to strange places. You are more likely to receive the help and encouragement of influencial people, especially where organized group and recreational activities are concerned. These may involve club activities.

19. SUNDAY. Upsetting. You can meet people who provide valuable help and information. However, such contacts will prove less useful than expected due to hidden factors. Don't hold out too much hope for new associations even though they get off to a very promising start. While promises can be made with the best of intentions, it is very likely that they will be broken when it comes to the crunch. Loved ones can be a problem today. They may make unreasonable demands or make small problems into large ones. Spouses may use minor financial problems as a club with which to hit their Aquarius partners over the head. Try to avoid such confrontations. You will be in a sensitive mood.

20. MONDAY. Sensitive. Loved ones may still be in a rather agitated mood. If Aquarius treat them with a tender touch they will soon calm down and return to their more reasonable selves. Any irritable reactions, on the other hand, will be like throwing fuel on the fire. You are also advised to employ a diplomatic and subtle approach where money-making schemes are concerned. Don't hesitate to use your charm and to butter people up. However, you may talk till the cows come home in an attempt to persuade people of your point of view or integrity. On the other hand, a smile or gesture of reassurance at the right moment can move mountains, to say nothing of influencing people.

21. TUESDAY. Fair. This is no time to allow personal preferences to influence your choices in professional matters. Sentimentality must be left out of the reckoning. A hardheaded and factual approach is essential. If you judge a person's eligibility for a position by his or her personality rather than their efficiency and effectiveness, your own reputation may be called into question. Favorite hobbies and pastimes can develop into significant sources of income if they are given the right attention. Aquarius should spend some time enjoying themselves and having fun. Parents and guardians will have more success with children by adopting a firm approach. Let them know, once and for all, that you are the boss!

22. WEDNESDAY. Good. It can be important for you to put in a personal appearance where negotiations involving business finances are concerned. Don't delegate important matters. Your thinking can be particularly creative now. You will find original solutions to financial problems that would not occur to associates. Humdrum and well tried methods will not give the best results. Inspirational flair is required. Stick your neck out. Take the uncharted course. Money markets may be in a state of flux. It will be up to the astute Aquarius to take full advantage of unsettled conditions. There will be opportunities for increasing business profits if you act now.

23. THURSDAY. Variable. Unsuspected personal advantage can come from your generous impulses towards others, especially in financial ways. The philanthropic side of the Aquarius nature can find expression now in schemes designed to raise money for the needy and deserving. Conditions are very supportive for such enterprises. It is a good time for dealing with large commercial organizations. Such ventures may allow you to increase the scope and profitability of your business operations. You may have some adventurous urges where money is concerned. You are advised to steer well clear of gambling joints and race courses. Risk-taking can end in huge losses.

24. FRIDAY. Difficult. Heavy losses in business finances can force Aquarius to dig into personal resources to pay off debts or compensation to others. You cannot afford to get down in the mouth about such losses. You should keep on the ball. Take full advantage of the opportunities likely to come that will help you reverse these losses. You are more likely to miss your chances if you withdraw and feel sorry for yourself. Make sure you stay alert and clear-headed. If you keep your ear to the ground, you can pick up information that enables you to steer a successful course in speculative ventures. Friends can have valuable advice to give. You can gain much not only by listening but also by acting.

25. SATURDAY. Deceptive. Make your plans early and stick to them through thick and thin. If you just take the day as it comes, it will be easy to fritter your energy away without achieving much. People can be rather demanding. They may create obstacles to your reaching the goals you have set yourself. If you have a definite course of action, determination will win in the end. All facts and information relayed to you should be checked before you act upon it. Mistaken messages can lead Aquarius astray. Later on, social gatherings will provide opportunities for meeting new people who become firm friends. If you drink, don't drive. Ride home with a friend.

26. SUNDAY. Active. This is not a day for lazing about at home. Aquarius will enjoy being on the move today. Friends will make lively companions and may have some adventures planned. Arrange to join in the activities. New experiences can come your way if you follow the plans of close acquaintances. A tour of Sunday markets can be both enjoyable and productive. They will provide plenty of entertainment even if you decide to buy nothing. Later on, conditions will be excellent for organized sport and recreational activities. Make full use of any clubs or societies of which you are a member. Team efforts will be the most rewarding activities today. And you enjoy participation like that.

27. MONDAY. Fair. It would be best to keep new plans to yourself until they have gained a firmer footing. Don't draw unnecessary attention to ventures that are still in their early stages. Keep out of the limelight. Secrecy is of extra importance now. Today is good for working away from the public eye. Muse on the past and learn what lessons you can from previous experience. You will have only yourself to blame if you fall into the same traps again. Make sure you understand where you went wrong before. You may be drawn by circumstances or pushy people into abandoning your high standards and integrity. It is important that you stick to your guns whatever the pressures.

28. TUESDAY. Fortunate. There may not be much going on externally. However, this will be a very busy and important day for Aquarius in thought and feeling. The usefulness of self-reflection cannot be underestimated. Plans and new ideas may occur to you. New situations should be reviewed and pitfalls avoided. The preparations made now will stand you in good stead when the time for action comes. A psychic connection may seem to exist between you and influential people. They may have an intuition of your needs and ideas before you voice them. You are likely to receive sympathetic help from such quarters. Today is good for attempts to help the underprivileged.

29. WEDNESDAY. Quiet. There will be no dramatic developments or new problems to contend with today. Aquarius can put their energies into regular work activities and accomplish more than usual. Conditions will allow uninterrupted concentration. If you have fallen behind your schedule recently, this is the time to catch up. House buying or selling may not go as quickly as you would like. However, things are likely to go the way you want them to in time. Patience will be required. There is no point in trying to rush negotiations or push other parties along. Contemplations on the past can turn into suffocating nostalgia. Keep your thoughts on the present.

30. THURSDAY. Creative. You will have both the confidence and the creative inspiration to make an excellent job of any artistic or design work. You should also be able to give your undivided attention to intellectual pursuits and studies. Artists, writers and students will have a field day. What you achieve now will remove any doubts you have had about your competence and creative abilities. Your lovelife should take a decided turn for the better. New and exciting attachments can be formed. If you have taken a fancy to someone, you should ask the person to go out with you. How else do you expect to see if you get along? Engagements and marriages planned today can lead to happiness.

MAY

1. FRIDAY. Disturbing. Youngsters may be feeling under the weather. If Aquarius parents are worried about the condition of their children, medical advice should be sought. This is not the time to hope that symptoms will go away on their own. Your lovelife may be a bit thorny. Arguments can spoil time spent with loved ones. You will have to be very shrewd to avoid heavy losses in speculative enterprises. If you feel out of your depth in risky ventures, you had better leave them alone. Your creative and inventive outlets may be blocked today. You can have a hard time with artistic work or hobbies. It is a good time for relaxing exercise and meditation.

2. SATURDAY. Uncertain. If you have arranged to take extra work home to do over the weekend, you will get a lot done today. Those Aquarius who work from the home base will have a most productive day if they continue with regular routine. There may be room for change where household tasks and duties are concerned. It could be that certain family members are shouldering too much of the domestic burden. A redistribution of labor is called for. Aquarius must be careful not to be duped by appearances. Others may be keeping the whole truth from you. Concealed facts may need to be brought out into the light of day. Thinking over employment affairs would be wise later on in the day.

3. SUNDAY. Variable. Aquarius will be more vulnerable to infection and to getting run-down. It will be important to take extra care of your health. Don't take unnecessary risks. Relatives can be rather demanding. They may ask you to carry out chores for them. You may have to put off your plans in order to keep them company or give them assistance. They may be peeved by the actions of someone close to you and expect you to compensate in some way. Aquarius will appreciate some time spent in solitude. Quiet contemplation will help you get some order back into your thoughts. Reflect on recent events and bring situations into sharper focus.

4. MONDAY. Successful. You won't find it difficult to go into top gear at work today. You will finish work loads ahead of schedule. This will give you plenty of time to help others who may have gotten behind in their own jobs or who are laboring under increased work loads and difficult conditions. Lend a hand where you can. While such gestures of assistance are unlikely to involve you in too much effort, people can be eternally grateful for such help. Firm friendships can be cemented. Allow the considerate side of your nature to come to the forefront by giving service where it is needed. Today is good for visits to doctors and dentists and taking care of other health problems.

5. TUESDAY. Sensitive. Aquarius parents and guardians are advised to show a little leniency to children. This is not the best time to use strong disciplinary measures. They may be putting on a brave front while being upset or hurt inside. Gentle and understanding treatment can obtain the best results. It may be difficult to maintain harmony at home. Quarrels with loved ones are in the cards. In fact, there may be tensions with whomever you are in close contact today. Colleagues and associates in the business world are unlikely to come up to the high expectations you have of them. People who have a strong influence on your affairs may be in an unsympathetic mood today and of little help to you.

6. WEDNESDAY. Good. Members of business partnerships should be working together with more accord now. Returns on invested time, effort and cash should be increased as a result. You would do well to give needy friends whatever help they request of you. They will be only too pleased to pay back any good turns you do them. You may be in need of help yourself in the future. Children may attempt to exploit any differences of opinion between parents, especially if the issue at hand concerns them. Parents should endeavor to agree on the best course of action and then present a united front. Leisure pursuits and entertainment will bring satisfaction in the evening hours.

7. THURSDAY. Lucky. There should be opportunities to earn substantial extra amounts of cash. You may win an improved pay rate at work today. Future economic security should be looking much brighter. Any cash sums you receive are best deposited in safe accounts. Aquarius will meet with success if they have facts or information to track down. Today is good for background research and for digging beneath the surface of things. Financiers and bankers will be in a sympathetic mood. They may be prepared to stretch rules and regulations on your behalf. Loan periods can be extended. It is also a good time for settling controversies over inheritances out of court.

8. FRIDAY. Mixed. Today is good for making requests of people who have an important influence on your affairs. You are likely to get what you want. It may be necessary to seek the assistance of marriage or guidance counselors if marital or family problems have gotten out of hand. Beneficial help can come from official quarters. Money may become a bone of contention between financial partners or those who share the same account. Spending can get out of hand. Aquarius may have to control extravagant partners or spouses. Clear limits must be set on spending. Speculative ventures can prove disastrous. Don't invest in high-risk operations that promise the moon.

9. SATURDAY. Special. People you have known for a long time can become more than just friends now. Old acquaintances may be seen in a romantic light. Love affairs with such people can suddenly blossom. Aquarius may fall for people much older or younger than themselves. Romances on this basis can prove to be very happy. Single Aquarius looking for romantic involvement would do well to accept any invitations to social or group gatherings. It will be easier to meet prospective partners in such circumstances. This is not the time to hold back or play safe. Take the bull by the horns. Don't let minor problems prevent you from going after what you most want. Think positive.

10. SUNDAY. Disquieting. There may be an uncomfortable two-way pull between your own and your spouse's relatives. Arguments can develop between the two camps. Aquarius may be left in the middle not knowing who to side with. It may be better if you maintain a neutral position. Seek to act as peacemaker. Your own ability to embrace many points of view may be the very factor that can bring feuding family members together. You are well equipped to act as intermediary or referee. Your diplomatic skills can bring an end to family upheavals. People in distant places are more likely to act unjustly or be dishonest. They can behave in totally unreasonable ways. Be on guard.

11. MONDAY. Good. Aquarius will have more success with distant people and events now. You can probably get the better of awkward associates in other towns and cities. Any travel arrangements or ticket bookings you have to do are best attended to as early as possible. Places may not be available if you leave bookings until too late in the day. People you are intending to visit should also be contacted early in the morning. There is more chance of reaching them then to finalize plans. Personal plans may work out better than expected. They may contain unscheduled adventures. Future trends should be clearer now. There is much cause for optimism in financial affairs.

12. TUESDAY. Tricky. Secrecy can be vital to the success of new commercial operations. It would be suicidal to let competitors in on your plans and intentions. Wait till projects have gained a firm footing. Play your cards close to the chest. Carry out the ground work unobtrusively. You will have plenty to talk about after the successful launching of new enterprises. You may have extremely difficult conditions to contend with later on in the day. You may feel that it is not worth carrying on with your plans. The character of Aquarius people is likely to shine through and see them over the worst of problems. Don't give up too easily. If one method won't work, switch to another. If that's no good, try again.

13. WEDNESDAY. Disturbing. Professional and external affairs can run into opposition from official quarters. Permission and go-aheads may be denied you. This can lead to long delays or postponement for new enterprises. Aquarius enthusiasm and industry can be frustrated. Attempts to solve family discord through discussion are unlikely to meet with much success. In fact, airing problems may incense others still further. More upheavals could follow. This is not a good day for joint discussions in general. You are unlikely to make much headway with business negotiations. It is better to avoid committing yourself in writing or making final contractual agreements for the time being.

14. THURSDAY. Worrisome. The problems of children can be the cause for bitter disagreements between parents. Widely differing approaches may have to be thrashed out. Any business profits are best left in safe deposit accounts or put into rock-solid investment. Adventurous speculation with such monies can be ruinous. Risks are not worth the taking. You may have romantic feelings towards someone you have formerly thought of as just a friend. It may not be wise to make any advances to the person in question. They are unlikely to react favorably. It will be easy to overshoot the mark or attract opposition if you pursue heartfelt desires too assiduously.

15. FRIDAY. Variable. Both Aquarius and their associates may be rather keyed up today. People will tend to irritate you more than usual. You in turn will get on their nerves. While it won't be easy to get control of volatile emotions, make the attempt at least. If you let feelings of anger or frustration take over, the atmosphere will become very unpleasant. Friction can be minimized if Aquarius are prepared to be more flexible and fit in with the plans and ideas of others. If you try to have things all your own way, you will be inviting trouble. A love affair can spring up when you are least expecting it. You may be swept off your feet. This could be the most exciting event of the year, so far.

16. SATURDAY. Deceptive. Aquarius may be a little too naive and accepting today. You will let people get away with murder for the sake of keeping the peace. You must learn when to draw the line. People will take full advantage of you if you give them the chance. Don't take what others say as gospel. Some healthy skepticism may save you face as well as time and trouble. You can learn from the experience of older people who are no longer engaged in regular work. They will have useful suggestions that benefit your business or employment activities. Keep an open mind. Beware of being over optimistic. You may paint situations in brighter colors than they merit.

17. SUNDAY. Good. Discussions with influential people over a drink may prove rewarding. Business can be successfully conducted in informal surroundings. You may also meet important people unexpectedly with beneficial results. Entertaining superiors or business associates in the comfort of your own home will go smoothly. Such invitations can be both politic and enjoyable. Family members may have information or may send contacts your way that allow you to extend your business activities. This is no time to be brash or abrasive. The gentle approach will get the most favorable results. Confidentiality can play an important part in the success of your ventures.

18. MONDAY. Uncertain. You may have to sacrifice personal plans for the sake of business or career affairs. When checking your diary, you may notice that you have overlooked a prior engagement. You will have to replan the day accordingly. Aquarius may have to play down the more eccentric and unconventional side of their nature. It may be important not to draw unfavorable attention to yourself. Suppress any really wild urges. Don't underestimate the value of a good reputation. You cannot afford to lose your good name. Original ideas and inspiration can be channeled into creative and artistic work. Sporting activities will be most satisfactory and leave you exhilarated.

19. TUESDAY. Mixed. Friends are likely to get themselves into tight corners today. They will be very grateful for any help you give to extricate them. The personal presence of Aquarius will be very important to the successful outcome of business discussions. Your open and honest approach can help to win over opponents or fence-sitters. You may have better luck in winning financial backing for commercial operations than your colleagues. Avoid delegation where possible. It may be difficult to arrange time off work to attend to personal affairs. Ensure that you do a thorough job at work. Shoddy workmanship will get you into trouble and could posibly lead to your being let go.

20. WEDNESDAY. Enjoyable. Conditions are excellent for attempts to beautify the home. New curtains, a coat of paint or new furniture will all serve to brighten the place up. A change will be welcomed. A fresh look to your home will give a lift to the spirits of all who live there. Aquarius can raise substantial sums for charitable organizations or projects. The results of pushing ahead against difficult circumstances in business affairs can be most gratifying. By sticking to your guns in business transactions, you can win very favorable agreements. Farm and garden produce can be sold at a good profit. The day is also favorable for setting up secret sources of income against the possibility of hard times.

21. THURSDAY. Disconcerting. Your money difficulties you thought you had dealt with once and for all can crop up again. You must attempt to get to the very bottom of the matter now. Root out the problem. It is pointless to try to deal with old problems in the same old way. Take a fresh look. It appears that such difficulties are built into your way of life and habit patterns. They will require some thoroughgoing changes before you see the end of them. You must keep spending to a sensible level. Your financial situation is already under strain. You cannot afford to aggravate things. You may not get the support you would like in money matters from loved ones.

22. FRIDAY. Manageable. People in prominent positions may be in a sympathetic mood today. It will benefit Aquarius to contact them. Such contacts are just as well made by phone and letter as by personal calls. Keep trips and journeys to a minimum. You should take this opportunity to reach people in authority while conditions are so encouraging. Aquarius will have a good grasp of expressive media. Ideas and feelings are more easily communicated now. Inspiration can be channeled into practical work and activity. Later, relatives and neighbors may be in a touchy mood. Handle them with kid gloves if you want to avoid a showdown. Trivial matters can often be blown out of all proportion.

23. SATURDAY. Happy. You may receive something in the mail that puts a smile on your face. This can be a particularly successful day for writers. Scripts, articles and reports are more likely to receive a sympathetic reading from editors and other professional people. Your efforts and dedication can be rewarded with publication or extremely favorable responses. Close friends will make happy companions this weekend. You may feel like spending a lot of time with them. It is good to plan activities with them. Aquarius may have the urge to move into new homes with loved ones. Conditions are very favorable for such moves. Business finances can take a turn for the better.

24. SUNDAY. Good. Personal plans should work out just as you would hope. Today is good for excursions to the outdoors and places of interest. Short trips will give enjoyment and stimulation. You will enjoy an active day more than taking it easy at home. Aquarius may find the opportunity to act as peacemakers between feuding family factions. Help to disperse bad feelings and recrimination where you can. You may also have a role to play in neighborhood affairs. Local community workers may need all the help they can get. Aquarius may be able to launch their own community projects. Youngsters in particular may need guidance and encouragement in their leisure pursuits.

25. MONDAY. Rewarding. This will be an easygoing and pleasant kind of day. Everything will be as you would like it. There should be a total absence of irritations and problems. In fact, you may find that you have arrived at a plateau of happiness and satisfaction. The things you have been working for will fall into place now. There won't be much left to strive for, at least for the time being. Enjoy the lack of struggle while you can. Your lovelife will contain happy expriences. This can be the perfect day for introducing sweethearts to members of your family. You may have an urge to recall happy memories from the past. Go ahead and indulge yourself.

26. TUESDAY. Disquieting. Aquarius may not be too happy amid the hustle and bustle today. Home will seem a very safe and secure place to be. If you can arrange to work or stay at home, so much the better. It is probably the place where you will be most efficient and creative. Those who have to travel may be in for a most irritating time. It is unlikely that visits will be successful even if you reach your destination. Expect delays. Transport systems may be bedevilled by strikes and slowdowns. Traffic jams and diversions can make road travel a nightmare. Aquarius may meet with some success in productive shopping expeditions. But much will depend on what you are looking for.

27. WEDNESDAY. Successful. Today is good for launching operations that involve a high degree of risk. Aquarius will know just how to make the most of chancy situations. Try breaking new ground and taking up unfamiliar activities. Try your hand at a new sport. You can learn very quickly now. Look for ways of getting out of your rut and breaking old patterns that restrict your experience. Spare time activities can become additional sources of income. It may be good to take the products of a hobby to potential buyers or places of display. This is the time to make definite plans for your holiday. Pick up brochures from your local travel agent. It might be necessary to commit for hotel reservations very early.

28. THURSDAY. Mixed. Unexpected events can interfere with your personal plans. Activities may have to be rescheduled or canceled altogether. Be prepared for disappointments. Recently made plans for holidays can also run into trouble. This can be a blessing in disguise. You may be forced to make alternative arrangements that turn out far better than original plans. Get on the phone to check out second choices of places and times. Children may be in a particularly mischievous mood. Parents and guardians should let youngsters know their limits in no uncertain terms. It would be wise to appeal to the more responsible side of their natures. Give them the benefit of the doubt.

29. FRIDAY. Variable. During the morning, plan weekend activities with loved ones. Arrangements made now will allow you to make the most of your spare time. Aquarius will have to be on-the-ball if they are to make a success of speculative enterprises. Opportunities can come and go in a flash. Unless you are ready to seize your chances, little will be gained. Those who take advantage of such conditions can make a killing. Later on, your desire for enjoyment and gratification can get out of hand. Have your fun by all means, but don't overdo it. Your health and equilibrium will suffer if you overindulge yourself in pleasure-seeking. There is a limit on how much you can do if you don't get adequate rest.

30. SATURDAY. Good. This will be a satisfying and productive day for Aquarius. The kind of work or activity that you most enjoy will be the focus of your efforts today. There will be no shortage of opportunities to give others a helping hand. Assist the needy and underprivileged. Your humanitarian impulses will find deep fulfillment in service where it is most needed. Your own pleasure will come from seeing a smile on the face of another. A pleasant atmosphere should prevail at home. Any recent family tensions or arguments will have blown over by now. Heart-to-heart talks and gestures of affection should bring sweethearts closer together, but if that turns out not to be the case, there will be trouble.

31. SUNDAY. Quiet. The month ends on an easygoing note. There will be no new problems to contend with today. The day can be productively spent working on jobs around the home and garden. It is a good time also for mechanical tasks such as working on your car. Make sure you give some attention to physical fitness. Go jogging or visit the local swimming pool. Take a walk in the park or woods and fill your lungs with fresh air. If you keep your body in trim, you will appear most attractive to others. You will also do a lot for your self-confidence. Your health can also benfit from a change of diet. You might try vegetarian food for a while.

JUNE

1. MONDAY. Changeable. Aquarius can get tangled in legal complications today. It is unlikely that you will have to deal with them alone. Influential people will come to your aid and help extricate you. Don't take unnecessary risks where your health is concerned. Any illnesses, however slight, are best treated by a doctor. They could be more serious than you imagine. It is advisable to play it safe even though the diagnosis reveals nothing of importance. Your fears at least will be put to rest. You must not level accusations at others on the basis of shaky or incomplete information. The trickery of others may test your patience to the limit.

2. TUESDAY. Sensitive. Valuable cooperation can come from people much older or younger than yourself. There may be opportunities for teaming up with such people on a more permanent basis. Love affairs can begin with people who are not of your age bracket. Keep an open mind today. You can learn much from the experience of others. People you live or work with, in particular, will have important advice or suggestions to make. Loved ones may have a tendency to be underhanded or calculating. They may try to draw you into arguments to work off some irritability of their own. This can lead to confrontations at home. Try to defuse the situation. This day is also good for dealing with lawyers.

3. WEDNESDAY. Important. If you have need of a loan or have other financial problems today, it will be worth your while talking to a bank manager. You are likely to find him in a sympathetic mood. Favorable arrangements will be easier to reach. Aquarius will need to be on their toes to make the most of any investigations they undertake today. Valuable information will be missed if you are half-asleep while engaging in research work. You will need to be clear-headed in order to follow up promising leads. Letters will be an efficient way of sorting out taxation and insurance problems. Other financial matters, as well, can benefit from a timely letter, provided it is to the point and accurate.

4. THURSDAY. Disturbing. If you have inherited money or have alimony payments to settle in court, the chances are the rulings will not go in your favor. Legacies may be awarded to other parties. Payments of alimony will be heavier than expected. Aquarius will not fare well with employers if they make requests for higher pensions. You may just have to accept the existing arrangement as far as old-age security goes. Aquarius who deal with the financial accounts of others may run into trouble with tax officials. There may also be problems if you look after other people's belongings. It will be easier for Aquarius to jump to conclusions over the remarks of others. Look closely before you leap.

5. FRIDAY. Variable. This is a good day for doing some direct talking with loved ones concerning mutual resources. Together you should find ways of reducing household expenditures and perhaps ways of increasing income. Money spent on home improvement can prove a worthwhile investment. The gain in terms of potential selling price can be substantial. Love affairs can be guided toward deeper levels of feeling and understanding. While family finances are in a rather shaky state, it would be foolish to take on new financial risks. The speculative schemes of friends are best avoided. Aquarius may be rather shocked to find out certain things about people they know.

6. SATURDAY. Deceptive. Aquarius will have to keep their wits about them to avoid having the wool pulled over their eyes. Distant people or those from foreign lands may purposely try to mislead you. They may simply withhold the whole truth. You should take what they have to say with a grain of salt. You may find it difficult to focus your mind on studies or intellectual pursuits. The mind will wander off onto other things. Dwelling on the past can also interfere with the planning you should be doing for the future. You must knuckle under if a large part of the day is not to be wasted. There may be friction with fellow workers. Find time to exercise, even if you just go for a long walk.

7. SUNDAY. Uncertain. You may spend a lot of time and money on travel to no avail. You will end up wishing you had stayed at home. Avoid travel wherever possible. Put off essential journeys until conditions are more conducive. Your spouse's relatives may prove unreliable. It would be best not to trust any promises they make. Breaking unfamiliar ground in academic training or self-study activities will be rewarding. Aquarius will respond favorably to new teaching methods and soon adjust to new subjects. Your understanding of life can be deepened by books you find on a friend's bookshelf. This is a day for putting an end to indecision and taking the plunge. Win or lose, you are committed.

8. MONDAY. Fair. You may run into complications in your professional life. Your own anxieties about your career can introduce even worse problems. You must keep things in perspective. There may be circumstances that threaten your reputation. You must be careful to avoid situations that could cast you in a bad light. Valuable help can be given to your business operations by people who work behind the scenes. Make full use of any contacts you have inside relevant organizations. Avail yourself of any overtime opportunities later on. Aquarius will have a knack for finding shortcuts or answers to tricky problems today. So put this talent to good use while it is evident.

9. TUESDAY. Strenuous. Aquarius can have a productive day in business and public affairs. It will be easier to find a way around difficult people and situations. The wheels can be made to start turning again after long delays. Conditions are not sufficiently supportive for attempts to launch new ventures. Efforts given in this direction will simply peter out before achieving a firm footing. People who have some say over your activities may curtail your freedom by favors or insisting that certain work or activities are carried out. This can interfere with your spare-time plans. It seems you will have no choice but to do as you are asked for now. Things will improve. You must be patient.

10. WEDNESDAY. Disquieting. Business activities can suffer a setback today. Your business reputation may take a plunge. Associates will lose faith in your judgment for the time being. Business may fall off. Don't be surprised if profits don't come up to expectations. Your desire for love and affection may be stronger than ever. It may not be so easy to find a suitable partner if you don't already have one. Parties and social gatherings may be completely devoid of people you fancy. Friends are likely to be in a grumpy and demanding mood. Aquarius may do better to avoid their company. You may even decide to cancel plans for a get-together if they have already been made.

11. THURSDAY. Mixed. Loved ones may be under the weather. In fact, they may be suffering from serious health problems. If there are worrying symptoms, you must call in the doctor. This is not the time to hope that illness will go away of its own accord. Aquarius may suffer disappointment where their holiday plans are concerned. Unforeseeable circumstances at work can force employers to insist on a change of holiday dates. It will be easier to meet interesting new people who become firm friends. Aquarians should also take this opportunity to look up old friends. Broken relationships can be mended. Parties and being with groups of people will give you great pleasure.

12. FRIDAY. Difficult. Others are more likely to stay sitting on the fence or hidden in their shell than to enter the fray. Don't expect them to echo your ability to make clear decisions at the moment. They may remain noncommittal for some time. Don't be taken in by the superficial aspect of things. People and situations can appear in a false light on first acquaintance. Commitment should be withheld until you are more familiar with the situation. People who work in unobtrusive ways and places may be able to give you just the help you need in professional and commercial affairs. Take advantage of this while you can, because it is sometimes difficult to find such assistance. Real know-how is a rare commodity.

13. SATURDAY. Disturbing. Allowing yourself to get run down and continuing to work hard can have an adverse affect on your health. You may push yourself to your physical and emotional limits without quite realizing it. It is essential that Aquarius take their activities at a steady pace. Set yourself reasonable goals to achieve. Pool your resources. Tools and machinery may be dangerous to operate today. Watch out for objects left by others in your path. Make sure the car's emergency brake is on when you park it. Follow all safety rules to the letter. It will be difficult to track down people you urgently want to see. Don't neglect your family and loved ones.

14. SUNDAY. Harmonious. This can be a marvelous day for affairs of the heart. Aquarius will appear in a most desirable light to others. It will be easier to attract compatible partners. Romantic urges are more likely to be fulfilled. Your achievements in artistic fields and intellectual pursuits will not go unnoticed by people who matter. Commendations are likely. Honors can be won in further education courses. The more eccentric side of Aquarius' nature may need to be held in check. You cannot afford to upset the applecart now. Give your impulses for self-expression in creative work full scope. Your facility in handling expressive media will yield rewarding results.

15. MONDAY. Lucky. Grit and determination are the key words for today. Aquarius can benefit from pushing ahead against all the odds. Don't be put off by difficulties. Don't accept defeat where you feel there is still a chance of success. While one or two lucky breaks can come your way, it is important that you do not get carried away by a little success. You will be inviting trouble if you do not keep your feet firmly on the ground. Keep on your guard. Problems can descend when you least expect them. Your abilities can come to the attention of people in prominent positions. They may be prepared to take a financial risk with your projects, an indication that they have faith in you.

16. TUESDAY. Uncertain. You have already worked hard to lay the foundations for new money-making schemes. You cannot afford now to sit back and wait for the cash to roll in. You must be attentive to ways of ensuring profitability. Creative marketing can pay dividends. Commercial enterprises will benefit enormously from an innovative approach. It won't be the organizations or companies that are in the forefront that make the best investments for your capital. Those less known may prove a better bet. While regular commercial operations are likely to earn more, don't throw away profit by sticking your neck out too far. You could bite off more than you can chew.

17. WEDNESDAY. Variable. Aquarius should not be content with half-hearted efforts at work. It will be to your own advantage to put a little more effort into routine employment activities. Achievements over and above what is normally expected of you may be rewarded with a pay raise. By astute thinking you may find unlikely ways of introducing economy measures. There may also be opportunities to bring in extra cash providing you keep on the ball. Don't respond positively to any requests for financial loans that you receive from friends. Complications can arise in such circumstances. They may result in broken friendships or never seeing your money again. Play it safe today.

18. THURSDAY. Quiet. With less pressure on you at work, there should be time to catch up on overdue paperwork or letter writing. Take advantage of the lull in regular employment activities to get your affairs in order. Clear the decks and get ready for more active times ahead. Conversations with people living in your vicinity will fill you in on the latest neighborhood developments. If you have articles to sell or are looking for a new position, placing an advertisement in the local paper can help your endeavors. You can save yourself the time and money spent on travel by using the phone or a letter to make contacts, often with no loss of effectiveness. But if you must travel, avoid air travel.

19. FRIDAY. Changeable. Aquarius may be in a rather dreamy state. It is essential that you abandon your wandering thoughts and focus your mind on the job in hand. Problems will arise if you are only half awake. Employers will not be too pleased with slackers. It will be easier to make mistakes today if you are totaling up figures or making difficult calculations. It would be advisable to check over such work especially if large sums of money are involved. Aquarius will be happy in the company of friends and acquaintances. Parties and social gatherings will be fun. Car driving requires extra care. Don't mix drinking and driving no matter how capable you feel. And don't let anyone else try either.

20. SATURDAY. Good. People living close by may do you a good turn. You may have to call on a neighbor for help. You won't have much trouble handling writing activities today in spite of your own reluctance to begin. In fact, what you achieve in mental and academic matters now will restore your confidence in your own abilities in these fields. You can get welcome assistance with favorite pastimes and subjects of interest from people who are engaged in similar activities. Aquarius parents may have occasion to feel proud of their offspring. Their achievements or behavior under difficult conditions will be most gratifying. Your lovelife should be happy and you can look forward to a happy, relaxing weekend.

21. SUNDAY. Fair. You may not be in the mood to mix with crowds or groups today. At least for part of the time, you will be happier spending time on your own in quiet contemplation. Aquarius may be feeling a little vulnerable and sensitive. They may require the protection of the home environment as a consequence. Don't worry about family members getting funny ideas about you. They can be most sympathetic to behavioral quirks or antisocial impulses. Go into your shell if that is what you want to do. You will come out feeling much the stronger. For Aquarius who fancy a more active day, the activities of friends can provide you with stimulation and interest.

22. MONDAY. Encouraging. You are likely to get offers of help from family members who want to make life a little easier for you. You may be relieved of household chores or given assistance with extra work you bring home. Such cooperation can be a real boon. Your energy reserves may be at a rather low ebb. You will soon restore your vigor if you can just take things easy. Do less rather than more. At work you may have to fight for your rights. Others may try to take advantage of you or push you into untenable positions. Be prepared to stand your ground. You may have to demonstrate very clearly that you are not easily manipulated or intimidated by others.

23. TUESDAY. Easygoing. There won't be much to bother you today. You should be able to take things at a very easy pace. Demands at work will slacken for the time being. You may be able to arrange time off in which to enjoy yourself. Outlets for artistic endeavors are likely to attract you. Allow your creative imagination to take wing. It could be that you are not using your talents to the fullest. Get them out of mothballs. You will not have much energy for active sports. Quieter games and recreational activities will be most refreshing. You will enjoy being in the company of children. Now is a good time for a visit to a travel agent to make holiday plans if you want to be assured of good accommodations.

24. WEDNESDAY. Disquieting. While a new love affair may get off to a good start today, it is unlikely to continue happily for long. Romance can end in disappointment. Aquarius may allow their generosity to get the better of down-to-earth common sense. You cannot afford to be openhanded to the point of jeopardizing your own financial position. Give to needy friends and loved ones by all means, but don't forget that you also have to eat and pay the bills. People are unlikely to return your feelings of warmth and affection. In fact, expressions of love can be thrown back in your face. Older people may try to dissuade you from taking financial risks. They may be right.

25. THURSDAY. Routine. You will be able to make good progress with regular work activities. An absence of other pressures and distractions will enable you to focus your mind and energies on work in hand. Take advantage of the encouraging conditions to cover as much ground as possible. Your health will be more vulnerable than usual to infection or strain. Don't push yourself to the limits. Make sure you eat well. Try to get to bed early tonight. Today is good for a tour of shops and stores. Try to be economy-minded. Savings can be made if you decide to buy in quantity. A new domestic pet will give children special pleasure. Find opportunity for exercise.

26. FRIDAY. Successful. Try to get a good start as early as possible. You can make productive headway if you get to work much earlier than usual. What you achieve as a result in professional and business affairs will reap increased financial rewards. Aquarius are likely to be in a sharp and efficient mood. This will allow you to do a thorough job of all that you undertake. The quality of your work may win favorable notice from employers and colleagues. It is a good day for taking pride in your work. During the afternoon, you should think ahead to future business engagements and plan accordingly. Good jobs can be found in the evening newspapers if you are in the market for one.

27. SATURDAY. Troubling. Aquarius are again likely to be rather sensitive in health and body. Muscle strain is in the cards. Get help if there are heavy weights to be lifted. If you are in the same room as someone with the flu or a cold, you are almost certain to catch it. Those who work in close proximity to people with more serious infections, must take rigorous precautions to avoid becoming ill. If possible, you should stay out of these areas altogether. Your own body defenses may not provide the usual natural protection. Unless you have made definite social plans this evening, you are likely to get bored and restless. Get out of the house. Take in a movie perhaps.

28. SUNDAY. Deceptive. There is not much point in trying to discuss matters with colleagues or employers outside of the office. Informal arrangements are unlikely to be successful today. Influential people will probably be tied up with their own affairs. They may be impossible to contact. Your enthusiasm for helping the needy and underprivileged can be dampened by the opposition of officials. People who make the rules can make it difficult for you to go ahead with projects for charity. Marital and partnership problems that have been lurking beneath the surface for some time may finally come out into the open. They will have to be dealt with effectively. Try discussing them with your partner.

29. MONDAY. Variable. Aquarius can cover more ground by teaming up with older and and more experienced people than they can through solo efforts. Seek cooperation with those who have a wise and measured outlook. It would also be sensible to share financial problems with business associates. They are likely to come forward with funds and advice that go a long way to solving your difficulties. You will not have much energy available today. You should make the best possible use of the little you do have. Restrict your activities and undertakings to those that are most essential. Aquarius can be very persuasive convincing people in authority of their point of view.

30. TUESDAY: Mixed. Sweethearts and spouses should be in a loving and happy mood. Activities shared with them will run very smoothly. It is a good time for sorting out difficult domestic problems. Loved ones will be more ready to go along with your recommendations. They may have very sensible suggestions of their own to make. Aquarius may be given an extra measure of freedom by their spouses now. Those who have just become involved in new romantic relationships may have a difficult time that could lead to a disappointing end. Partners in these situations may tend to change to the point of exasperation on your part. It is doubtful you will stay for the final act.

JULY

1. WEDNESDAY. Good. This is not a day for dealing with small fry. Your best bet in commercial terms is with the bigger business organizations. Conditions in regular employment activities will be much to your liking. In fact, the future will begin to look distinctly rosy as a result of developments today. Long-term financial security will become more assured. Unexpected funds could come to you in the form of tax rebates. Because of special circumstances, you may find you have more take-home pay. Employers may find a way to reduce the amount of tax Aquarius workers have to pay. Do all you can to boost joint resources with loved ones and business partners.

2. THURSDAY. Demanding. If Aquarius have something to investigate today, it will be easier for them to go barking up the wrong tree. Your enthusiasm may blind you to the futility of your quest. Stand back to get a more objective view of what you are doing. Keep a broad overview. While Aquarius are noted for being leaders in the field, whatever the activity, they must be careful that inventiveness and originality does not get out of hand today. You can get too far ahead and miss the point altogether. Keep a firm rein on the urge to spend extravagantly. Rulings on the amount of alimony to be paid to ex-spouses may not go in favor of Aquarius. The evening is best left for relaxation.

3. FRIDAY. Tricky. Aquarius cannot count on their thinking being sharp and clear today. A sense of confusion is likely to spoil studies or intellectual work. It would be unwise to trust distant people at the moment. They are likely to take unfair advantage of the distance that separates you. They may pass incorrect information to you in the knowledge that it will be difficult for you to check the facts. Don't act on the information contained in long-distance communications. First make sure of your ground. Aquarius who have interviews with possible employers will tend to make a good impression. Be more prepared to bend to circumstances at work. Stay flexible and be willing to make changes.

4. SATURDAY. Productive. Events that concern you in distant places should take a turn for the better now. It will be easier to get things straight and to find ways around obstructions. You may run into difficulty in study and learning activities. You have everything to gain by sticking to your guns. Don't throw away all the hard work you have done because the going gets a little heavy for the time being. There may be bitter disagreements with friends. Bad feelings will soon blow over. It would be better to seek the advice and experience of people who are experts in their field than to rely on your own limited knowledge. Pay special attention to a loved one.

5. SUNDAY. Variable. You should do all you can to avoid head-on confrontations with your spouse's relatives. Events at work may not run smoothly. Aquarius may be obliged to take on more than their fair share of the work. This is likely to produce angry reactions in you. Tools and machinery carry a higher potential for danger and accidents today. Safety rules must be strictly adhered to. Don't rush any manual work you have to do. Car driving and maintenance can be particularly hazardous unless you take extra care. It will be easier for single Aquarius to link up with new romantic partners. You will be placed in a situation where meetings occur naturally.

6. MONDAY. Pleasant. You can gain advantages in regular employment affairs by getting in gear as early as possible this morning. It will be easier to get some time alone with superiors to discuss important matters in privacy. Employers are likely to be in a sympathetic mood. Take this opportunity to air any grievances or make special requests. It could be that you are in line for a promotional step or raise in pay. Your past achievements and record will stand you in good stead. What you achieve today can win the favorable notice of those in authority. If you have to undergo a medical checkup today, there is every likelihood that the report should be encouraging.

7. TUESDAY. Opportune. Luck is with you. You can afford to stick your neck out. It can be particularly worthwhile to take a gamble in professional or business affairs. You may miss valuable opportunities if you stick to known and tried ways. When acting in the public arena, Aquarius will have to let others know exactly where they stand and what their course of action is likely to be. This is the time to follow your aspirations right through. Once you have established your targets, you should go all-out to achieve them. There won't be much that can stand in your way or prevent you from making significant advances in your particular field. Take the bull by the horns and act with decisiveness.

8. WEDNESDAY. Strenuous. Conditions affecting business finances can be rather unpredictable. Aquarius should soon gain control with beneficial results. It will be easier to raise funds for commercial enterprises once you have understood the fluctuating nature of the situation. You may have need to call on friends and acquaintances for a helping hand. They are unlikely to be found wanting. You should gain the cooperation you need in both public and private affairs. Later on, people may ask favors of you in return for help previously given. With your generous streak, this should not be any hardship for you. But be on guard against being used by someone who is not altogether trustworthy.

9. THURSDAY. Fair. Things are unlikely to go the way you would like in club or group activities that involve you. No matter how hard you try to maintain the present status quo, the winds of change are blowing. You can't fight the inevitable. In other areas of your life, heartfelt hopes and desires can suddenly come to fruition. A goal you have kept secretly in mind for some time can unexpectedly come within easy reach. Friends will make good teammates or business partners now. Their contribution to getting a new joint venture under way can make success that much more likely. Profits should be very encouraging from such partnerships. Short journeys can be productive.

10. FRIDAY. Disturbing. It would be better not to draw unnecessary attention to yourself at work today. Proceed with your activities as unobtrusively as possible. This is not the time to raise any grievances or ask for favors. Employers will want to avoid complications. They are unlikely to give definite answers even if you can get through to them. They will only have their minds on efficiency and profit. Your health is likely to be a little run down. You may not want to put in an appearance at work at all. It may be difficult to gauge where you stand in a love affair. Loved ones may be very reluctant to show their feelings. It would be in your best interests to take a stand and clarify your position.

11. SATURDAY. Worrisome. Journeys are not recommended. People involved in your travel plans are likely to be unreliable. They may forget arrangements or go back on their word. Much time and money may be spent to no avail. If you must travel, it would be best to cover yourself by making phone calls where possible to check arrangements. Try not to get too angry over disappointments. If you allow your nerves to get on edge, your physical health is likely to suffer. Frustrating situations should be forgotten as quickly as possible. Don't dwell on your misfortunes or bad luck. At least you can count on the support and help of loved ones. Work will be more satisfying.

12. SUNDAY. Good. Don't try to hurry newly launched ventures. Let them establish themselves in their own good time. You will only spoil chances of success later if you try to force the pace at the beginning. Don't look for immediate changes. Introduce new arrangements or methods gradually, especially in the personal sphere of your life. You cannot afford to be involved in undercover operations now. Keep your activities well out in the open. Keep records of transactions and other activities. You may be called upon to produce proof at a later time. Associates will value your honesty and high standards. Spend time with your family or loved ones, especially if you have been away a great deal.

13. MONDAY. Encouraging. People you know only slightly can give welcome assistance. Your personal plans are likely to run more smoothly as a result. You will achieve more by teaming up with others than you will through individual efforts. The talents and abilities of associates can complement your own strengths and weaknesses perfectly. Efficient partnerships will be easier to form. Aquarius will be happy sharing their recreational activities with groups of people. You may also have a special role to play in neighborhood affairs. Aquarius can initiate new ideas or plans for putting community projects forward. You may make new friends in the bargain. Enjoy yourself.

14. TUESDAY. Challenging. This is not the time to take a rigid stance, especially where money-making is involved. Aquarius must be prepared to swim with the tide if they are hoping for financial successes. For once, your high ideals are likely to be a drawback. You will have to accept the world as a place of compromises. You cannot afford to turn your back on people because they have a markedly different outlook than you. Let the more generous side of your nature that respects differences of opinion come to the fore. Pay raises are on the cards for family members. Joint resources may get a boost. However, there may be some repayment demands to face up to.

15. WEDNESDAY. Manageable. This is a good time to suggest to your boss that you are due for a pay raise. Employers should be in a generous mood. Officials and others in authority are more likely to take a personal interest in your money problems. They may go out of their way to make things easier for you by providing loans or introductions. Aquarius must be careful that the more unconventional side of their nature does not take people by surprise or give them a nasty shock. Be as steady and cool-headed as you can. This is not the right time to dig your heels in and take a stand on issues. Friendships can be a little sensitive now and more vulnerable to breakups.

16. THURSDAY. Difficult. Today will be easy to whittle away in endless chitchat. You must knuckle under in employment activities. You may have to be quite firm with fellow workers if you are to focus your attention on the work at hand. They will be only too ready to load their problems on you or grab your attention in other ways. There may be a disappointment in romance. Sweethearts may stand you up or fail to make a call you are expecting. It may be necessary to let others know exactly what your limits are. People will take you for granted unless you speak your mind. Lay it on the line in no uncertain terms. Stick to your guns and don't waver. Others will respect you for it.

17. FRIDAY. Variable. This is the time to open up and let in new and exciting ideas. Give the inventive streak in you free rein. You may be rather uptight at the moment and inhibiting your creative flow. All written and academic work, in particular, will be much more enjoyable if you can tap an original vein. Don't be content with working to formula when you could be breaking new and interesting ground. People in authority can be sticklers for detail and discipline. Don't try to pull any punches with them. You will be judged by the company you and your associates keep now. Avoid people who may cast a shadow on your reputation. Why risk doing yourself an injustice if you don't have to?

18. SATURDAY. Tricky. Aquarius can take confident control in organizing humanitarian projects. You will know how to get the best out of people and what task they can perform within a team. Substantial sums can be raised for charity and great help given to the needy and underprivileged. Today is good for attending to small-scale maintenance jobs around the home. It may be difficult to avoid domestic tensions building up. A battlefield can develop where you and your partner have to cross paths. It will be largely up to you to preserve the peace. It would be inviting trouble to patronize loved ones or make them feel left out in the cold. It would be wise to do something special with them.

19. SUNDAY. Good. Aquarius can bring a light touch to efforts given to brightening up the home. You will have a good eye for color and pattern if you are choosing paints or wallpaper. Today is also good for buying new furniture and other household goods at Sunday bargain stores. If your family has not yet met your sweetheart, this is an excellent day to break the ice. You may be having trouble winding up a situation that has been dragging on too long. It could be because you are taking too narrow a view. You may discover a way out by stepping back and taking a more detached view because you can't see the woods for the trees.

20. MONDAY. Fortunate. Aquarius may receive help from someone influential with the buying or selling of homes or land. You may need professional guidance to ensure you obtain the best deal possible. Both private and professional dealers in antiques should have a lucky day. Old and rare articles can fetch extremely good prices. Big profits can be made. Troubles at home may be playing on your mind or interfering with your performance at work. It would be best to let your boss know of the problem. Superiors can take a very sympathetic view of personal problems. They will probably suggest you go home to sort things out. The evening should be better for harmony at home.

21. TUESDAY. Uncertain. It may be necessary to take legal action if large organizations or powerful individuals try to push you around. You must make it clear that you are not going to stand for any nonsense. People will more readily take advantage of you on other occasions unless you stop them now. Seek legal advice if there has been a flagrant transgression of your rights. Unforeseen circumstances can force you to give up plans for outings and entertainment. You may have to promise some kind of compensation to loved ones who will be very disappointed by such changes. It would be unwise to put too much faith in the words of your boss. It is best to be cautious.

22. WEDNESDAY. Sensitive. Children are more likely to run into trouble or become confused unless they are given more guidance and reassurance. It will not be necessary to limit their freedom. However, they should not be expected to cope with situations with which they have little experience. You are likely to feel the squeeze in financial matters today. A cluster of bills may put pressure on your resources. Whatever the external factors are, it is unlikely that you will have any spare cash for speculative ventures. The lovelife of single Aquarius will enter a more hopeful phase now. You can meet new partners, especially while traveling by air or sea. The most likely opportunity would occur on a ship.

23. THURSDAY. Deceptive. You cannot afford to have a casual attitude to your health now. It would be wise to get medical advice if you feel ill, especially if symptoms have been around for a few days. You may be risking a more serious condition if minor ailments are not nipped in the bud. There may be tricky conditions to contend with at work. Bosses or co-workers may try to load you with chores or duties that are not your responsibility. You must again make it clear that you are not going to be pushed around or exploited. You will only win respect by standing up for your rights. Applications for new jobs can meet with success. A change might improve your outlook.

24. FRIDAY. Enjoyable. Conditions at work will be more to your liking. Working procedures will be running so smoothly that even dull jobs will contain a measure of satisfaction. Personal fulfilment will come from work well done. The quality of the work you do and the efficiency with which you do it may attract the favorable notice of employers. It is a good day for ensuring that offices, factories and workshops are well-equipped. It is important to fill any gaps with new machinery or tools. If you have been thinking about getting a domestic pet, this is a good day for doing so. Later on, a love affair can blossom from rather unpromising beginnings. This could be what you have been hoping for.

25. SATURDAY. Mixed. This is another day when you need to take extra care of your health and physical well-being. It will be easier to catch infections and chills or to over-strain your system. You also can't afford to be hasty or slipshod in your undertakings. Accidents can happen to those who are in a rush. Approach all tasks in a steady and calm way. This can be an arduous day for those who have to put in an appearance at work. Absent colleagues can mean that extra responsibilities fall to you. Employers may have set quota targets very high. It will be possible to show more care and consideration in relationships with loved ones and spouses from now on and it would make sense.

26. SUNDAY. Fair. Problems that have been rumbling beneath the surface of close relationships may finally burst out into the open. Once they are out, you must deal with the issues to ensure that the same problems do not recur. Partners should be encouraged to get worries off their chests. Happiness will not be possible while there is still unresolved tension. Once you have reached a better understanding, it will also be easier to deal with minor irritations and difficulties. Aquarius must beware of the critical side of their nature becoming too destructive. You may just have to learn to live with the shortcomings of others. You can't change people to suit your expectations.

27. MONDAY. Good. It is through cooperative efforts that you can find outlets for your creative impulses and ideas. Individual action may not provide sufficient scope to really put innovations to the test. Join company with others where possible. Seek out people who complement your own abilities and qualities. There can be unexpected developments in a friendship. Someone you have known for a long time purely as a friend will suddenly appear in a romantic light. A happy love affair can result. Today is favorable for putting your signature to new contracts and partnership agreements. It is wise to confer with legal advisers on out-of-court settlements or the signing of important documents.

28. TUESDAY. Rewarding. Devoting time to esoteric and spiritual studies will be satisfying. Aquarius can also gain much from practicing yoga and meditational disciplines. Digging into subjects of interest can be most fruitful. Secret investigations can reveal hidden facts and information. Today is favorable for visits to museums and libraries. Advantages can be gained through background maneuvers. This is the time to pull strings where you can. Make full use of inside contacts. Large-scale business operations will fare well. Dealings with large commercial organizations can bring excellent results. Profitable new investments can be made if you strike while the iron is hot.

29. WEDNESDAY. Variable. Settlements of alimony payments to or from ex-spouses may run into difficulties. If you are expecting to receive money, property or assets left to you in wills, there may also be problems that prevent you realizing your hopes. Other relatives may dispute legacies. Stock markets are likely to be in a state of flux and unpredictable. Aquarius will have to stay on their toes if they are to keep abreast of changing fortunes. Quick thinking will allow you to take full advantage of unsettled conditions with lucrative results. People dear to you may be rather unreliable at the moment. Arrangements may fall through leaving you stranded for lack of alternate plans.

30. THURSDAY. Sensitive. Legal affairs should not be treated lightly. Seek professional advice if you have a court hearing to attend. Make sure you have adequate representation. Loved ones should be in an optimistic mood and will have a very positive influence on Aquarius. They may lift you out of a gloomy state and show you that every cloud has a silver lining. You must not allow prominent people to dampen your energy and enthusiasm for reaching the goals you have set yourself. Provided you can employ patience and perseverance, you can overcome whatever obstacles are placed in your path. A down-to-earth attitude is essential to all future planning. This is not a time to daydream.

31. FRIDAY. Pleasant. Long journeys for professional purposes can be especially productive. Acquaintances who live in distant places or who have traveled far to see you can provide welcome help and encouragement. A friend will probably be happy to put you up if you have to stay in a distant place overnight. Today is good for conferences with teachers and other professional educators. They will help you make decisions or solve problems regarding studies and academic work. The advice of experienced tutors will show you the way forward. Disputes between family factions are more easily settled now. If your spouse and your parents are the main protagonists, you may need to be the mediator.

AUGUST

1. SATURDAY. Changeable. This is a good moment to break with the past and seek new directions. It could be the time to take up new courses of study or learning activities. It is also favorable for becoming involved in new subjects of interest, spiritual teachings and movements. Aquarius may need new fuel to fire their imagination and fresh experience to reinvigorate their thinking. Books can provide a mine of information and inspiration. Visits to museums can be most stimulating. Family members may be a drag on your time and energy. Journeys can take longer than the time you have allocated them. Don't be too ready to take others at their word. Be skeptical, but also ready to admit you're wrong.

2. SUNDAY. Uncertain. It will be easy today to adopt an unnecessarily gloomy outlook in business and professional matters. If you go purely by the facts, you will see that there is no cause for alarm or despondency. If you let your imagination run away with you, the end of the world may seem to be upon you. Don't make molehills into mountains. Keep things in perspective. It is a good moment for inviting associates out for a meal or a drink. Such informal contact can stand you in good stead in the future. Try to cultivate bonds of trust and goodwill. Obstacles can get in the way of putting personal plans into operation.

3. MONDAY. Harmonious. Personal visits to business associates nearby can be very helpful in clinching business deals. Letters mailed or received now can bring benefits to your professional or public work. Ideas and plans are more easily expressed in written form. Information put down in writing can also give the people you send it to more time for contemplation. Background research into matters that could have an important bearing on future business plans will go well. Aquarius will make good judges and referees now. Your ability to hold a neutral position can be important to solving disputes and disagreements. Pay special attention to loved ones today. Their morale may need a boost.

4. TUESDAY. Good. It will appear to people in authority that cooperative efforts give the best results. You may have to follow your boss's instructions to work in teams. You may have to abandon individual plans and schedules as a result. It is a good day for proposing marriage or accepting such offers. A deep romantic desire can come true. Plans you have hoped and worked for over a long period of time may come to fruition. Dreams of setting up a home with loved ones can come closer to realization. Officials are more likely to give permission for the establishment of new organizations, especially if these have humanitarian aims. But beware of any haphazard undertakings.

5. WEDNESDAY. Fair. Aquarius will have to be quick from the start to keep up with changing conditions affecting business finances. It will be very difficult to predict just which way the wind will blow in commercial activities. You must be ready to make snap decisions when the time comes. If you feel a little slow-witted and dreamy today, it would be better to get business colleagues to monitor fluid situations. They are more likely to be on the ball. They will also be better at keeping cool under stress. Friends can make reliable partners if you are launching new and unusual projects. Conditions make Aquarius rather edgy. Try to keep a cool head in all your affairs.

6. THURSDAY. Deceptive. You may experience strong religious feelings today. They may be coupled with a deep desire to give service to your fellow man. You will find it most satisfying to put these feelings into action rather than preserving them as ideas. It will be easier for Aquarius to delude themselves or allow others to pull the wool over their eyes. Choices and decisions need extra care and consideration. Extraneous factors can cloud your judgment. You may need to use more impartiality. Advertisements can paint more attractive descriptions of jobs than they truly merit. Learning the full facts can be a disappointing experience. Be wary of excessive claims.

7. FRIDAY. Pleasant. You are unlikely to get support or funding for short-term and risky ventures. Bankers, financiers and other influential people will be more interested in safe enterprises that yield predictable returns on capital. If you have anxieties about your future job security or likelihood of promotion, it would be advisable to take up such issues with employers. They will be in an understanding mood and are likely to give you positive reassurance. It is a good time for pooling business resources with other commercial operators even if it means going through legal procedures. Tie up loose ends of existing affairs and prepare for more active times ahead.

8. SATURDAY. Disquieting. Teamwork and partnerships can contain difficulties. It won't be easy to see eye-to-eye with spouses or people who work closely with you. Your differing ideas on how best to proceed can result in a stalemate. It is important to keep your reputation in mind today. Be discriminating when it comes to joining forces with movements or concerns. Avoid contact with dubious organizations or people. It is not advisable to give second place to loved ones in favor of personal plans and aspirations. They may react sharply to being left out in the cold. Be careful not to ride roughshod over the feelings of others in romantic affairs. You may have had occasion to do so in the past, with bad results.

9. SUNDAY. Demanding. It is still important to give more consideration to the needs of others than to your own personal interests. Even when loved ones are not needful of your attention, it is probably best that you not ignore them to follow your own devices. It would be foolish to take unnecessary risks now by overriding rules and regulations. Play by the book. People in authority can come down on you like a ton of bricks. Don't step too far out of line. Use more of the diplomatic approach. Loved ones can be in a sensitive mood. They are likely to over-react if you say things about them to others. Don't be inconsiderate to those closest to you. How would you like it?

10. MONDAY. Variable. Beware of your prejudices today. Take things as they come without judging them by expectations. You may get invitations and propositions from unusual or strange quarters. You may miss valuable opportunities if you pass them by without due consideration. Your intuitions regarding money matters are likely to be right. It would be unwise to go rushing into risky financial ventures on the basis of a hunch. You must ensure that you are treading on firm ground before committing large sums of cash. Caution should also govern your mental endeavors. It is not advisable to get too enthusiastic about your ideas until they have been tried and tested.

11. TUESDAY. Mixed. Conditions affecting financial matters can be rather unsettled. It would be foolish for Aquarius to change their plans. Once you have decided on a sensible course of action you should stick to it. Money can be lost through indecision. Friends will come up with original and forward-looking projects. They may attempt to involve you in them. Stay clear. It will be money down the drain if you take the bait. Business colleagues, on the other hand, will have a much sounder grasp of commercial affairs. You may be doing yourself a favor by leaving matters in their hands for the time being. This is a time for sensible down-to-earth thinking. You should have no trouble doing so.

12. WEDNESDAY. Misleading. Don't jump to conclusions about things you heard said. It will be easier to misinterpret information received today. It is all the more important to make your own attempts at communication clear and concise. Others are more prone to misinterpreting your words. Aquarius should check the facts before acting on doubtful information. People can mistrust the motives for your generosity. Even though you go out of your way to help someone, suspicion can fall on you. Others will find it hard to believe that you are not in it for yourself. It would be best not to buy goods from door-to-door salespeople. You are likely to regret your purchases later.

13. THURSDAY. Good. Any expectations of bad luck on the 13th will almost certainly be denied. In fact, things should go very much your way. Aquarius will be the focus of sweethearts' or spouses' affections. Engagements made today can develop into happy marriages. Existing marriages should reach new heights of affection and understanding. Harmony should rule supreme in domestic affairs. Loved ones can go out of their way to ensure that you are happy and comfortable. Even your shortcomings are likely to be overlooked by the people who love you. Aquarius can put their signatures to official documents and agreements without qualms. Legal matters should go your way today.

14. FRIDAY. Manageable. If you are launching new business ventures, it would be wise to accompany the send-off with a lively publicity campaign. Advertising can attract wide and favorable attention. This is a day when it may be more sensible to keep your altruistic urges under cover. Others will not understand your desire to help needy and underprivileged people. Your generosity and desire to help those less fortunate can make people feel guilty and small. They are more likely to judge you as a crank than appreciate your efforts. Their reactions will arouse hostile feelings toward you. A visit to your parents will give them pleasure and will allow you to shake off recent unpleasant encounters.

15. SATURDAY. Troubling. Domestic tensions are likely. However, it won't be too difficult to mend the fences. It will be tricky but more beneficial to root out the underlying causes of conflict. Solutions are there to be found if both parties are prepared to work hard at it. Do some straight talking. This is not a good day for finalizing property deals. It would be better to wait for more favorable conditions before reaching the final terms of agreement on real estate transactions. Loved ones can be demanding and uneasy. Their Aquarius mates can help to ease them out of discontentment by entertaining them with a special treat. Allow them to decide just what that should be.

16. SUNDAY. Variable. Trouble may be brewing at home. Members of the family may want things all their own way. They will be prepared to trample on others to get it. This is bound to cause resentment and quarrels. You may find yourself powerless to affect such situations positively. If you try to calm troubled waters, you may simply aggravate the situation further. Aquarius won't be able to be sufficiently neutral to act as peacemakers. You would do better to leave well alone. If you are engaged in work with government departments on official projects, there may be some exciting developments today. New ground will be broken and new discoveries made.

17. MONDAY. Uncertain. You may have to go through some major changes and upheavals in your lovelife. Such changes will be for the best in the long run. New patterns will take some getting used to. They can give a relationship a new lease on life once you are acclimated. It could be that you have been employing double standards. You may take freedoms for yourself that you deny to loved ones. Such imbalances must be set straight. Resentments will build to the breaking point if things are allowed to continue in this way. A rather gloomy evening may be in store for you. Pleasure pursuits are unlikely to give the happiness you are seeking. It will be up to you to decide how to end this cycle.

18. TUESDAY. Sensitive. Children can take advantage of you today. They may get out of hand unless limits are clearly defined for them. They are likely to need more reassurance and guidance now. Your high hopes of success in commercial operations may be dashed. The foundations you have laid for business activities could be less sound than you imagined. Unexpected developments could have been avoided had you made more careful plans. They could mean a reduction in profits. Your professional worries are likely to get swept away this evening. Romance will be in the air. It is a good day for spending time with loved ones or making contact by phone or letter, depending on the circumstances.

19. WEDNESDAY. Deceptive. This is not the time to take things for granted in employment affairs. Even though you have been through the same working routines a thousand times before, you must stay on your toes. If you don't attend to work at hand, things can go wrong. Mistakes or accidents are likely. Stay alert. Others will appear to be hale and hearty one minute, then taken seriously ill the next. You cannot rely on the health of co-workers. The absence of fellow workers will give you the opportunity to put in some overtime. Later on, this may draw the favorable notice of employers. A surprising reward may be in the offing. This could be in the form of an important promotion or a large raise.

20. THURSDAY. Quiet. Business can slow to a snail's pace today. Sales and customers can hit a low. People won't have the money or the inclination to make purchases. Such quiet conditions will give you a chance to catch up on jobs you have been putting off for some time. Irritating paperwork and unanswered letters can be gotten out of the say now. Bring some order into your affairs. Give some attention to making things neat and tidy. You would do better to keep active today rather than ponder the future or dwell on the past. Your health can benefit from trying new diets and getting plenty of exercise. Get outdoors for a hike or jog. It is far better to stay healthy than collect medical benefits.

21. FRIDAY. Changeable. You may not have as much support as you have come to expect at work. The work force may be reduced through illness and resignations. This can mean that Aquarius have to shoulder more work and responsibility. It is important that you take extra care of your health if you have more work to deal with. You could suffer a setback if you push yourself to the limit now. It will be easier to reach favorable agreements in transactions and negotiations. It is best to put new partnership arrangements in writing. Great benefit can come from pooling your energies and resources with others in business ventures. Avoid high-risk entanglements.

22. SATURDAY. Fair. Legal matters you thought were finished once and for all can return to plague you. A close acquaintance may be on hand to show you a more thorough solution to such difficulties. Marital problems may also rise to the surface again. Aquarius will begin to lose patience with repetitive emotional conflicts. These must be taken in stride. There will be no progress if you attempt to sweep difficulties under the carpet. They will simply fester out of sight and create an uneasy atmosphere. The air should clear toward the end of the day. Aquarius can then begin to enjoy themselves. Spending the evening with friends will be fun. There could be a special reason for a party.

23. SUNDAY. Good. Aquarius are by nature both tolerant and understanding. You should do even more now to see the world from other people's points of view. This will only help to increase your understanding. Do all you can to embrace the outlook of others. The deeper your understanding of human nature grows, the greater the service you can render to others. Cooperative efforts will achieve more than individual action. Partnerships will run smoothly and without friction. Harmony should also reign in emotional relationships. Bonds of affection between marriage partners can be strengthened. Look for a present for a loved one while shopping in Sunday markets.

24. MONDAY. Slow. Aquarius who handle money or possessions for others need to take extra precautions to avoid loss or theft. There is no room for overconfidence where other people's assets are concerned. You cannot allow sentiment to overrule your business sense. If friends are in some way connected to your activities in commerce, they may ask for special favors or lure you off the straight and narrow path in other ways. It is essential that you stick to what you know is right even at the expense of a pal's feelings. Try to arrange to be alone for at least part of the day. You can accomplish much if you carve out a block of time for yourself. And you will not resent demands on your time by others as much.

25. TUESDAY. Mixed. It will be difficult to get to the bottom of things. People will tend to see research and investigations as snooping and spying. You will have to be most diplomatic if you have questions to ask. Even then, you are likely to be turned down. People will be interested in keeping secrets hidden and their privacy intact. Patience and perseverance will get you round such obstacles. You may pick up valuable information with regard to professional and business affairs. Financiers and bankers will lend a sympathetic ear to business problems. You are unlikely to get much satisfaction out of employers and bosses. Find time to exercise. You will feel better and may even be less tired.

26. WEDNESDAY. Routine. The pace will be slow today. In the absence of new pressures and problems you can give some constructive attention to smaller scale money matters. Make sure that insurance policies are fully paid up and still cover your needs. Today is also good for getting accounts in order so there is less work to do when the tax man calls. A visit or call to your accountant will tell how much you might end up owing the government. Find time to give some attention to old-age security. It would be advisable to make a comparative study of the various pension and retirement plans available. Extravagant spending must be avoided if you expect to live within your budget. Debts can mount up fast.

27. THURSDAY. Important. It will be hard to predict just which way romance is going to develop. All the indications can point in one direction, then suddenly change. Affairs that seem to be getting off to a good start may soon end in disappointment. It may be necessary to face up to the fact that a dull and habitual relationship has had its day. With diplomatic handling, it should be possible to terminate love affairs without rancor. Ex-lovers can remain friends. In matters relating to business finances, there may be a need to seek the advice of more experienced people. Your spouse's parents will enjoy a visit this evening and may offer a solution to problems.

28. FRIDAY. Variable. You may be provoked by rude and overbearing superiors. It would be better to keep quiet than express your indignation. You will probably be taking on stronger forces than you realize if you speak your mind. Bosses are likely to retain the upper hand. You will need the support of fellow workers if you are going to bring any effective pressure to bear on unreasonable employers. Solo battles are doomed to failure. Back off for now and prepare your case unobtrusively if you intend to take the matter further. If you are suddenly faced with a financial crisis, bankers may be willing to act as arbitrators. Find time to relax this evening. That shouldn't be difficult during the summer.

29. SATURDAY. Fair. Your success in commercial ventures may mean demand for your goods or services will grow quicker than you can keep up with. Business may have to farmed out to other concerns. Aquarius may not enjoy being too much in the public eye just now. You will probably be happier in a less visible position. You can certainly get more done by working in seclusion. Projects in the making should be treated confidentially until they are ready to be put into action. Today is good for all forms of investigative work. It will be easier to find sponsorship for research projects, especially from official sources. In love affairs the bonds of affection can be strengthened.

30. SUNDAY. Productive. You may not feel much like joining in activities with family or friends. All you enthusiasm will be for private interests and projects you are nurturing. Those people who might otherwise make demands on your time and attention will be engaged elsewhere. You will be left to your own devices. Aquarius can blossom once they are in secluded surroundings. You will certainly be able to attend to those activities that most absorb you. Creative ideas you come up with now can be turned into moneymakers. Such additional earnings can give family resources a boost. Be prepared to follow your hunches. Look at projects from a new perspective.

31. MONDAY. Sensitive. Developments in club and group affairs may not be at all to your liking. Your first impulse will be to do everything in your power to reverse decisions. You may want to run organizations according to your own principles. It would be unwise to throw your weight around or lay down the law as you see it. You are more likely to achieve your ends by subtle means. If you try to forcefully muscle in on the act, you will only antagonize the people in charge. Aquarius will have luck in direct contact with the officers of large business organizations. Lucrative deals can be forged. Negotiations are likely to go your way provided you have laid your plans well. It won't happen automatically.

SEPTEMBER

1. TUESDAY. Disturbing. Mistakes can be made that adversely affect business finances. Whether you are responsible or not, you may have to foot the bill. Aquarius may have to carry the burden for others. Friends will not make cheerful companions today. They may be rather distant and tight-lipped, making conversation very laborious. In other spheres, this will be an unfavorable day for communication. It would be unwise to discuss your ideas and opinions with others during club or group activities. Others won't be in a receptive mood. The Aquarius outlook will be a little too far over the heads of others for them to take any real interest.

2. WEDNESDAY. Variable. Things will be looking up today. Developments will be much to your liking. This will put you in a happier frame of mind. The more light-hearted and open side of your nature will be encouraged to come forward. Journeys can be productive and will expose you to interesting experiences. Your thinking will be sharp and creative. Academic and intellectual activities will run like clockwork. Aquarius writers should have a lively and stimulating day where their work is concerned. General conditions may close in on you later on. You may feel the need to pull in your horns. It may be necessary to conceal certain things from other people. Keep a low profile.

3. THURSDAY. Enjoyable. This is a good day for keeping the future economic security of yourself and your dependents firmly in mind. Seize any opportunity that may improve future income or help boost your savings. Consider new insurance or pension plans. More active methods are likely to hold the best financial prospects. Financial partners are unlikely to raise any objection for using mutual funds to back new commercial operations. There should be plenty of cash in the kitty for such enterprises. Today is good for meetings behind closed doors. Secret love affairs will bring pleasure. However, romantic partners can lead you on with promises they can't keep.

4. FRIDAY. Tricky. You should think twice before becoming involved in undercover operations. Concealed activities will have a tendency to foul up. Others involved in confidential activities may take advantage of the cloak-and-dagger conditions. Aquarius may be put in a tight corner. Your hopes of making advances through secrecy are unlikely to be realized. You may instead have more problems than you bargained for. Loved ones can be difficult. There may be hard choices to make concerning your allegiance to new romantic partners or acquaintances of long standing. The returns on recent investments are likely to be disappointing.

5. SATURDAY. Good. You can be very persuasive convincing others to fall in with your plans. People may at first show reluctance and doubt the viability of your schemes. However, you will soon put their minds at rest. You should get all the cooperation you need in personal arrangements. Aquarius may not be fully using talents and manual skills that could provide an additional source of income. You are advised to examine what there is in your repertoire that could bring in some extra cash. This is a good chance to make steady progress with projects that will take some time to realize their full potential. Such work will be rewarding from both a monetary and a personal viewpoint.

6. SUNDAY. Successful. The self-confidence of Aquarius will get a boost from developments today. People will be ready to take a lively interest in your ideas and outlook. Stimulating dialogues should ensue. There may also be a more practical outcome. People are more likely to be impressed with your business or public projects. They can offer encouragement and energetic assistance. Later on, your efforts on behalf of charitable organizations can raise substantial sums for the needy and underprivileged. This is also the time to put original ideas into practice. They may meet with considerable financial success as well as with praise from those in high places.

7. MONDAY. Upsetting. There is not much point in making requests today for favors from people in prominent positions. They will almost certainly turn you down. Your financial situation may feel a squeeze today. Taxation on personal earnings may be increased. If you are involved in legal proceedings, you are unlikely to come out on top. Your case may be overturned by unforeseen evidence or your opponent bending the law. Heavy financial demands may have to be met out of savings funds. Existing avenues of income may be threatened. You may not be able to rely on the backup earnings of loved ones. There is a chance they will also face a financial crisis.

8. TUESDAY. Disquieting. Hopes of raising loans through your bank or arranging more time to pay off existing loans are likely to be disappointed. You may run into obstacles if you are digging around for facts and information beneath the surface of things. People will be very reluctant to let you in on their secrets.

Access to books and records will not come easily. Only very persistent searches are likely to meet with any measure of success. From lunchtime onward, Aquarius will need to be extra cautious if they are driving vehicles. If you allow your mind to wander, you will be inviting trouble. Don't put your trust in people only recently met. Wait till you know them better.

9. WEDNESDAY. Rewarding. Give what help you can to those around you, especially to people who live in your vicinity. A good turn done now will stand you in good stead in times to come. Acquaintances made today can develop into firm friendships or happy romantic relationships. Long-term partnerships can result. If you have been trying to collect money you are owned for some time, a visit to the person or people concerned may meet with success today. There will be very little to distract you from activities requiring unbroken mental concentration. You can cover much ground in academic or intellectual pursuits. Detailed and intricate manual work will also be rewarding.

10. THURSDAY. Sensitive. This is the time to let your true feelings come out. You will probably be bubbling over with enthusiasm and excitement. This can have a very positive effect on others. There should be no need to put on a false front in an attempt to impress others. Your inner optimism will do a far better job in winning people over or getting the best out of them. Your optimistic outlook must be balanced with a practical and down-to-earth attitude. It will be easy to build castles in the air that come tumbling down at the first test. Groups that contain both sweethearts and friends may be tense and uneasy. Your positive attitude might smooth troubled waters.

11. FRIDAY. Variable. You could be giving too much time and attention to outside interests at the expense of home and family responsibilities. If so, this is the time to redress the balance. If you continue to neglect loved ones for the sake of ambitious urges and external affairs, you may have trouble on your hands. Homelife may become extremely uncomfortable. Loved ones will not be prepared to play second fiddle indefinitely. Split your time more evenly between professional and domestic affairs. Conditions are very favorable for moving your home and for the buying or selling of property. It is a good time also for acquiring land as an investment or for use as a vacation spot.

12. SATURDAY. Useful. Today is good for getting your home into better shape. A fresh coat of paint and perhaps some new furniture will brighten the place up. Family resources are likely to be in a healthy enough state to finance a few household cosmetics. The spirits of everyone involved will benefit from a change in the surroundings. This is no time for Aquarius to draw fixed and rigid lines in domestic affairs. Give others a chance to put forward their points of view. If you try to dominate the scene, others will feel resentful. Be more elastic in your approach. Demonstrating your affection for sweethearts in a more tangible way can go a long way toward deepening romantic relationships.

13. SUNDAY. Pleasant. It won't be difficult to find more time to give to favorite pastimes and hobbies. You will have an inventive streak now that can be constructively channeled into such activities. The company of children will give you pleasure. They will also appreciate your help and guidance. You spouse's relatives could make an unplanned visit or make contact by phone. Although Aquarius may not have a superabundance of physical energy, sporting activities can be great fun. You may be quite content to sit on the sidelines and watch others put in the hard work. The evening will be good for going over travel brochures and making holiday plans for the whole family.

14. MONDAY. Disturbing. Commercial enterprises that carry a high risk factor can run into trouble. The money you have already invested may prove insufficient to carry you over this rough time. If a new injection of cash is demanded, it would be unwise to borrow for that purpose. Even if you approach bankers and financiers for loans or special requests, you are unlikely to get what you want. Business finances will go through a very unpredictable phase. It will be necessary to keep a close watch on the rise and fall of economic conditions so that essential adjustments can be made as soon as possible. The needs of youngsters can prove costly. However, you should not neglect them.

15. TUESDAY. Mixed. Loved ones can get carried away on extravagant impulses. It will be up to Aquarius to rein in their free-spending partners. You cannot afford the risk of joint accounts running into the red. Timely action will avoid this. This is no time to be heavy-handed in financial transactions. You may be rather overbearing and blunt without quite realizing it. Employ a more tactful approach. People will respond more favorably to a lighter touch. Both creative inspiration and mental concentration will be at your disposal today. Artistic and intellectual pursuits will be easier and more enjoyable. You are likely to be in a state of elation by bedtime.

16. WEDNESDAY. Changeable. Your thoughts are likely to run wild today. It will be more difficult to focus your attention on work at hand. Unless you keep on the ball, mistakes you will probably make will necessitate starting all over again. Make a decision to dismiss daydreams the moment they come into your mind. You can get the better of wayward thoughts if you really try. Although you may have exciting and original business plans to present to prospective backers, they are unlikely to see your ideas in a favorable light. Going over accounts and taxation matters with accountants and attending to insurance affairs will prove beneficial later on. They will also be helpful to you at tax time.

17. THURSDAY. Fair. Aquarius workers will make a very favorable impression on employers today. Your achievements can win you special notice. It may be made apparent that your employment position is rock solid. You are likely to be much more confident about future job security. However, any special treatment you receive could be resented by your co-workers. You may have to make it clear that you are only receiving just rewards. This is a good time to stand back and make an objective assessment of your true capacities and shortcomings. You may want to decide what you should aim for in the future and what is beyond your reach. Take stock of your achievements.

18. FRIDAY. Disquieting. On this day in particular, you cannot afford to go back on your word or let others down. It would be better to go through with arrangements even at the cost of personal inconvenience. You may feel that you can travel lighter without the encumbering presence of others. However, people will be very upset if you leave them behind or decide on solo action. If others have reasonable expectations of involvement in your affairs, these must be honored. You will be asking for trouble if you put your desire to get ahead before your regard and responsibilities to loved ones. Try to put yourself in the place of those who are close to you. Don't neglect their needs.

19. SATURDAY. Good. Do not try to force the pace in activities that require cooperative efforts. Don't expect immediate results. Adopt a more restrained and measured approach to all teamwork. Pooling energies and resources with others will reap great benefits. However, Aquarius may have to give up some of their much loved freedom. This will be a relatively minor factor compared with the advantages gained through other people's support. Letters sent to people who are experts in their field can elicit valuable information and advice. Travel can be both productive and enjoyable, providing you do not move too far from base. Short trips are best today unless you are going on vacation.

20. SUNDAY. Harmonious. Aquarius who are getting married today can look forward to a happy occasion and a successful partnerhip. The wedding of a frriend may afford much pleasure to all concerned. It may be up to Aquarius to keep loved ones anchored in practical reality. They may have a tendency to dream too optimistically about the future. It is essential that they keep their feet on the ground and take life one step at a time. Keep your guard up when dealing with people who reside in or have traveled from distant places. They may have a nasty surprise in store for you. Later, you should follow any impulses to be alone. A little seclusion will help you to order your thoughts.

21. MONDAY. Strenuous. Your energy and enthusiasm is likely to be in the right place today. However, essential funds may be missing that would enable you to push through your ideas and aspirations. It is advisable to play things strictly by the book in all matters relating to taxes. Mistakes should be scrupulously avoided. Any deliberate attempts to avoid payment of taxes will land you in all sorts of trouble. Keep fully up to date on all financial commitments. It is unlikely that you will be granted leniency where alimony payments to ex-spouses are concerned. Bargain buys may be offered in the shops you frequently visit. But beware of shoddy merchandise that may be offered.

22. TUESDAY. Variable. It would be best to avoid the purchase of electrical goods and equipment. Such items may be found in poor working order when you get them home. It can be very difficult to exchange them or to get refunds. A friend in need may make a surprising request for a loan. You should think twice before acquiescing. You may be saving both yourself and your friend a lot of trouble by refusing his petitions. Aquarius will find opportunities for stimulating discussions on more serious topics with friends and close acquaintances. Horizons can be broadened through such interchanges. Creative ideas will abound. It will be up to you to capitalize on them.

23. WEDNESDAY. Deceptive. Aquarius may lose their usually calm and cool demeanor today and become prey to volatile emotions. It won't be so easy to stay detached and on top of things. Your ability to make rational choices will be impaired by sentimental or emotional considerations. The citadel of the intellect may be taken by storm. Passionate feelings can surface for someone with whom you have had a purely intellectual relationship. Love affairs can develop with academic or professional associates. You can do worse than to follow the dictates of your heart. Cold reason can be an insufficient guide. Follow your intuition today and try to use good judgment.

24. THURSDAY. Encouraging. Don't be content with a humdrum or predictable approach today. There is room for invention and creativity. Academic and intellectual pursuits, in particular, will benefit from more original thinking. Aquarius will respond well to the challenge of new educational and training endeavors. These can provide the stimulation and mind-stretching you are seeking. You will not be happy if you get stuck in a rut. Business interests in distant places will receive a boost. Overseas developments can have profitable consequences for commercial enterprises closer to home. Injecting some creative thinking into club and group affairs will prove very beneficial.

25. FRIDAY. Fair. This is not a good moment to draw unnecessary attention to your business activities. New projects especially should be nurtured away from the glare of publicity or public scrutiny. Avoid following the most obvious course. Use more subtle approaches. Wait until foundations are well laid before letting your plans be known. Although your motives for involvement in humanitarian projects will probably be purely unselfish, there may also be some welcome rewards in terms of personal reputation. Commercial and professional affairs are likely to pick up momentum later in the day. Forward planning and preparation can stand you in good stead for future growth of your business.

26. SATURDAY. Disquieting. Before attempts are made to launch new projects, it would be better to wait until conditions pick up again. They will not be sufficiently supportive to make fresh moves profitable, especially in commerce. Business contacts will probably be involved in family and personal activities. This forces a standstill on ambitious Aquarius. For the time being, it would be unwise to retrace your steps or alter details in an attempt to be constructively active. More harm than good can come from this. Long-distance communications may fail to make contact. You must be patient if your are to succeed. The time for action will come, but may take some patient waiting.

27. SUNDAY. Confusing. Friends can exhibit strange and uncharacteristic behavior. It may be motivated by hidden resentment. Bad feeling is likely to poison the air for some time. Acquaintances will find it hard to make a clean breast of it. In fact, things can come to such a pass that relationships will be endangered. Aquarius should do all they can to draw tense and moody asssociates out of themselves. Some straight talking can save the day and a friendship. Accepting invitations to parties and social gatherings will be rewarding. Mixing with groups of people can lead to meetings with valuable contacts. Aims and aspirations can come closer to realization as a result.

28. MONDAY. Uncertain. Aquarius cannot afford to stick to rigid lines of action now. You may find yourself in a tight corner where business finances are concerned. A way out of difficulties can be found, providing you adopt a more elastic approach. Flexibility can work wonders. Narrow thinking may have landed you in trouble in the first place. Be prepared to swim with the tide. It is advisable to take what superiors or other prominent people have to say to you with a grain of salt. Promises can be broken when it comes to the test. You should be well pleased with your lovelife. Some areas of tension, however, remain to be sorted out. This is understandable, but there will be solutions if you work at it.

29. TUESDAY. Variable. It won't be easy to see eye-to-eye with business associates today. Discussions on how best to spend or invest capital can lead to strong disagreements. Knocking your heads together is unlikely to produce a working solution. The trouble could lie in the fact that neither party is well enough informed. The way to agreement may lie in attempts to gain clearer insight into economic conditions and in getting hold of the latest information on subjects in question. Once you understand all the options, answers may be self-evident. Happy love affairs can be shared with people much older or younger than yourself.

30. WEDNESDAY. Good. The morning is favorable for undercover activities. It is good for meetings behind closed doors and for making confidential agreements. It would be wise to ensure that foundations are firmly laid before embarking on the more active phases of enterprises. Keep plans and arrangements in the dark until they can be put into operation. Secrecy can bring advantages now. Don't be too ready to show your hand ahead of time. It is a good day for turning over a new leaf and adopting new approaches. Cut out the dead wood where possible. Outdated techniques and ideas will only hamper your progress. Make constructive efforts on behalf of the needy and underprivileged. Each person can make a difference in the life of somebody less fortunate than themselves.

OCTOBER

1. THURSDAY. Mixed. Don't take your worries too seriously at the moment. Anxieties can prove groundless. Much time and energy can be consumed in pointless speculation. Look on the bright side. Optimism will be rewarded. It would be unwise to entrust neighbors with important tasks. They may be extremely absentminded. They can also be rather uncommunicative and withdrawn for reasons of their own. Try handling legal disputes through unofficial channels. Agreements are more speedily arrived at out of court. It will be easier for Aquarius to jump to conclusions about others on the basis of their behavior. Judgment should be reserved until you are better acquainted with all the facts. There are always two sides to disagreements.

2. FRIDAY. Fair. This is a day for playing it safe. The more eccentric and unconventional side of the Aquarius nature may have to be held in check. You will not achieve desired results if you go all out to add kudos to your name. In fact, your reputation is more likely to suffer from such attempts. Let success and recognition come in its own good time. The motives of teachers and other important people who give you a hand up the ladder of success may not be entirely unselfish. They could stand to benefit from any advantage that comes to you. Keep this in mind to avoid complications later. Friends can help you through a crisis of confidence. They can give you good advice and lend a sympathetic ear.

3. SATURDAY. Rewarding. Do not divulge the contents of private conversations to other parties. You will be inviting the wrath of associates if you spill the beans. More favorable results can come from discussing business transactions over a drink than through official meetings. It is a good day for making special arrangements with sweethearts during the morning. Plans made early can result in a very pleasant evening. Aquarius will enjoy being on the move today. By being more active you can meet new people who develop into firm friends. Old friends and acquaintances can put you in touch with new ones. Others will enjoy being in the company of Aquarius today.

4. SUNDAY. Successful. Even though this is a rest day, Aquarius should keep on the alert for the opportunity to earn extra money. Shopkeepers and traders will have a field day if they open up. There will be no shortage of Sunday shoppers. It is a good time for buying in quantity. Money can be saved on purchases made today. Restaurant owners can also do a very good business. There will be no need for Aquarius to be reserved about their views and ideas now. In fact, it is through straight talking that you will most impress others with your honesty and integrity. The confidence people place in you can have lucrative results. Today is also good for visiting parks and places of interest.

5. MONDAY. Changeable. Someone you had previously thought of as a good friend can suddenly appear in a romantic light. You may have a very fulfilling love affair on your hands. Old friends can make very compatible romantic partners. Personal resources should be conserved rather than thrown around with abandon. Keep future bills and financial commitments in mind if you feel an extravagant urge. Avoid unnecessary purchases made on the spur of the moment. Disagreements are likely with people who share funds and finances with you. It is probable that both parties have been rather short-sighted about joint resources. Accusation will not solve the problems. Stay calm and talk things over.

6. TUESDAY. Deceptive. This is a day when precision and clarity of expression are essential in all attempts at communication. Statements that convey their meaning clearly as far as you are concerned may appear totally ambiguous to others. Use plain words. If you have vital information or messages to pass on, it is advisable to check that they have been received in straightforward form. Mistakes and misunderstandings can haunt today like a wandering ghost. It may take some wily questioning to get the whole truth out of relatives. They may be sitting on important facts or deliberately misleading you for their own ends. It is not the time for making special requests of people in authority.

7. WEDNESDAY. Productive. Today is favorable for intellectual and academic pursuits that require creative flair and original thinking. Writers of fiction should have a field day. Inventive ideas will abound. People you work with or someone you recently met can put valuable opportunities your way. Their intervention can mean the successful outcome of personal plans. They may be very ready to make a personal sacrifice for your sake. Loved ones can fail to see the serious side of Aquarius idealism and futuristic thinking. They may look upon such activities as game playing. Even though you try to convince them of your earnest intentions, they are unlikely to be impressed.

8. THURSDAY. Sensitive. Creative activities and projects can be brought to conclusion on a high note now. Aquarius will know just how to round off artistic activities to greatest effect. It may be better to avoid mention of business and professional interests at home. Loved ones can be extremely unreceptive to such news. They may have their mind on matters closer to home. Family members may be in a rather sensitive mood and may require gentle handling. They will be more inclined to come out of their shells if they see signs of consideration and kindness. Gestures of affection will carry more weight than words. An evening at home will be enjoyable and worthwhile.

9. FRIDAY. Disquieting. Problems can arise over work and projects done in the past. Aquarius may be obliged to correct unsatisfactory work. There is also the chance that current projects nearing completion will have to be restarted from scratch due to mistakes made early on. Neighbors may interfere with family and domestic affairs, stirring up trouble and causing arguments. Short trips are unlikely to be particularly productive. It would be well to avoid them if possible. This is not the best day for putting your signature to final agreement on property or employment matters. Promising leads may be hard to follow up. You will have to be persistent in order to succeed.

10. SATURDAY. Good. Aquarius are probably crying out for a change of scene. This can be an excellent weekend for a visit to the country or seaside. New places and faces will give your spirits a lift. If you cannot travel far, visit places of interest and beauty in your local vicinity. Museums and art galleries may provide a stimulating change. Time spent with children can be both fun and constructive. Parties given for youngsters should be a great success. They will appreciate any encouragement and guidance you can give them with special interests and activities. Aquarius may get the green light from influential people on a project you have long dreamed of and yearned to complete.

11. SUNDAY. Uncertain. Aquarius may have time on their hands today. You may be at your wit's end to find some diversion or entertainment. Pleasure and enjoyment will not be easily found. Loved ones may not be in the mood to help relieve the boredom. Their health could be a little shaky and may even give you cause for concern. The day is good for communicating with people in distant places who have an important say in your affairs. Unexpected difficulties can be encountered in study and academic pursuits. It would be better to seek the help of tutors or other professional help. Don't try to muddle through on your own. The results will only lead to frustration.

12. MONDAY. Variable. Friends may be in a contrary mood and may make last minute changes to joint arrangements. Your hopes of enjoying outings or entertainment with your pals can be dashed. Commercial operations that carry a high risk factor are more likely to flounder through mismanagement. You may not have been giving business ventures the guidance they need. It is important to monitor such affairs very closely now. Make the necessary adjustments as soon as possible. Later in the day, devote some time to favorite pastimes and hobbies. The satisfaction derived from the activities you most enjoy can make your day. Find time to exercise daily, if possible, and keep fit.

13. TUESDAY. Fair. You may wake up feeling anxious and unrested from a night of worrying dreams. These can put you off your stride for the first part of the day. Your self-confidence may be shaken for the moment, but you will soon snap out of such moods when you see what the day has to offer. There will be challenges and valuable opportunities where professional and employment prospects are concerned. You will have to be on the ball to make the best use of them. Conditions favor the finalizing of contractual agreements. Today will be good also for setting up advertising campaigns with a strong theatrical touch. Give your creative powers full rein.

14. WEDNESDAY. Disturbing. This is a day when flexibility can save you a lot of trouble. There may be developments at work which throw you off rhythm. Employees may reorganize work patterns or procedures. The quicker you can adapt, the quicker you will settle down again. Your mind may also be caught up in anxieties about the future. Your thoughts may wander, imagining various possibilities. It will be difficult to focus your mind on immediate tasks. It is important that you snap out of such reveries. Accidents can happen if you are only half concentrating. It may prove impossible to get a sympathetic hearing from people in official positions. This is not the time to ask for a raise.

15. THURSDAY. Harmonious. You can cover ground at a surprisingly quick pace by joining forces with others. Cooperative efforts will be more effective than individual action. Projects that rely on joint resources will also make rapid headway. The day is good for tackling new activities and for breaking new ground. It will be easier to break with old ways and habits. Problems relating to the law will soon be cleared up by an attorney. Seek professional advice where there are legal difficulties. The threads of a broken relationship can be picked up now. Friendships can be reforged. Loved ones may not take kindly to such news. Jealousy may be the real motive for their mistrust of another.

16. FRIDAY. Mixed. It is important for Aquarius business people not to get out on a limb. Stay in close contact with commerical developments and with those people who are important to your operations. It will be easier to get out of step with associates and partners and to work counter productively to their efforts. There is also the danger that information will be wrongly conveyed. Unnecessary confusion may result. Check to see that the correct message has gotten through. It will be difficult to drum up support from business people through discussion of issues. Friends can help you out of a tight spot with sensible suggestions. You were probably too upset to work out a solution.

17. SATURDAY. Useful. Aquarius may have more luck winning influential people over to their side. Permission for development or funding for projects can be secured. In fact, your confidence will be boosted by the enthusiastic response of prominent people. Officials may be lenient in their interpretation of rules and regulations governing importing and exporting activities. As a result, trading can be more profitable. It would be better to bide your time when it comes to finalizing plans and arrangements for the future. Unexpected factors can emerge to upset your designs. Keep an open mind and a flexible approach until you are closer to the time for action. Do not try to rush things.

18. SUNDAY. Worrisome. Tensions and difficulties that have been beneath the surface in a love affair can suddenly erupt. Close relationships will benefit by giving problems an airing. However, Aquarius may find themselves with difficult decisions to make. Loved ones may want to cement partnerships more permanently. You may well find such demands too restrictive. Faced with an ultimatum, you will have to come down off the fence unless you can convince your sweetheart that things are best kept as they are. You may discover ways today for giving personal funds a boost. Background research into business affairs will stand you in good stead when the time for action arrives.

19. MONDAY. Upsetting. News of the death or serious illness of close friends or relatives may arrive. The physical condition of loved ones or spouses may necessitate a period of convalescence in special surroundings or under specialist treatment. This can set joint resources back a bit. Faced with the health needs of loved ones, you will have to draw on hard-earned funds. It won't be easy to get to the heart of the matter with friends. They could be intent on concealing facts and information. Sums of money that were not previously paid in taxes may have to be paid now. Avoid eccentric behavior. You need to remain rational and cool-headed now.

20. TUESDAY. Tricky. It may be more difficult than expected to sever connections with associates and set out on a new path. This may not be the most sensible course for you to follow anyway. Half-finished business will only return to haunt you in the future. It is best to turn and face the problem head-on. Obligations must be honored. There can be no positive outcome from shirking responsibilities. It is important not to credit yourself with more knowledge and skill than you actually possess. It will be easier to get carried away by the praise others lavish on you. You may become swell-headed. Take things at a steady pace. Find ways to make your diet healthier.

21. WEDNESDAY. Good. Providing you keep a practical and down-to-earth outlook, plans made for the future should prove very successful. As soon as you allow an over-optimistic view to color your aims, you will be courting disaster. Don't confuse fact and fantasy. Attempts to improve your skills, knowledge and understanding may meet with some setbacks. They should not be easily given up. You have much to gain by pushing ahead with self-improvement projects. Seek the counsel of wiser and more experienced people if you cannot surmount problems alone. Now is the time for adding books to your library. Items made in foreign countries can prove to be worthwhile purchases.

22. THURSDAY. Pleasant. Don't rely on your own limited knowledge when expert advice and insights can be sought. Professional people will be more willing to offer the fruits of their experience. This can be a day of success for writers and publishers. Manuscripts that have been submitted for reading are likely to be accepted for publication. Magazines can provide useful information and contain subjects of great interest. Contact with people in distant places will fill gaps in your knowledge regarding distant events. There won't be much to distract you from activities requiring unbroken mental concentration. You can make good progress with academic and self-improvement studies.

23. FRIDAY. Disquieting. Caution is advisable in employment and professional affairs in spite of indications to the contrary. Just when you start to take things for granted, they can begin to go very wrong. If you stay on the alert, danger can be averted. Announcements made public should be worded with great diplomacy. It will be easier to stir up adverse reactions. They could rebound on you with unfortunate consequences. You may need a lawyer to check business agreements you are required to sign. Documents may contain pitfalls. The warmth of the Aquarius personality can win over even the most difficult people now. Your charm may even spark a new romance which could become a flame.

24. SATURDAY. Enjoyable. This may be the end of the working week for you, but you may still see fit to devote part of the day to business and employment affairs. Problems may arise that need immediate attention. In general it would be better to deal with details and minor matters. Tie up the loose ends of small jobs and undertakings. You are unlikely to meet much success if you try to get larger scale activities under way. Conditions are not sufficiently supportive for attempts to launch major new projects. Friends will make lively and cheerful companions today. They may have some adventurous plans up their sleeves. They will want you to join in the fun. Enjoy yourself.

25. SUNDAY. Exciting. Today is favorable for plotting the course of future club and group activities. Arrangements for outings and other events should prove very successful. Excellent progress can be made in attempts to broaden the horizons of your own knowledge and to gain greater understanding of yourself. Strongly held desires and aspirations can come closer to realization as a result of the work you do on yourself now. Conditions are good for going all out to attain new qualifications and skills. Friends may interest you in subjects and pursuits of a more serious or mystical bent. You may become fascinated in spiritual or occult affairs. A visit to the library will spark your interest.

26. MONDAY. Fair. This is a day for throwing away crutches and reaching for the independence Aquarius so much desire. The time has come to test your own strengths and weaknesses. If you become too reliant on the support and encouragement of others, you may miss out on exciting new opportunities. Be prepared to strike out into uncharted territory. Let go and take the plunge. Firm friendships can develop with people met purely by chance. Push ahead with academic and intellectual pursuits. Aquarius thinking will be alert and to the point. A letter may bring heartening news that puts a smile on your face for the rest of the day. Time spent with family will be rewarding.

27. TUESDAY. Deceptive. Today facts and figures you may receive will be in a jumbled form. Even information released by official sources can be faulty or misleading. Aquarius are advised to cover themselves by checking on the accuracy of all information. It would be unwise to act on received knowledge if there is a glimmer of doubt as to its reliability. People should not be taken at face value. They may turn out to be wolves in sheep's clothing. People who harbor ill feelings toward you can appear all charm and smiles, even while they plot your downfall. Aquarius should make full use of contacts or informants who are well-placed. They will keep you informed of developments on business affairs.

28. WEDNESDAY. Variable. You may feel a little coldness on the part of sweethearts. It will probably indicate that their feelings for you are stronger than they would like to admit. Aquarius should reassure loved ones as to their own feelings. Romantic partners may need to be drawn out. Favorable agreements can be made with people who carry a lot of influence in business circles. Contracts can be signed with confidence. Business conducted at this level may require extra effort and diligence from Aquarius. It will be easy to endanger your position by an off-hand manner. You must convince associates of your serious intentions. Keep your options open and be ready to act at a momen't notice.

29. THURSDAY. Changeable. Aquarius are more likely to express things in ambiguous ways that leave others wondering just what you mean. It would be better to use straightforward language if you want to avoid misunderstanding. What you see as poetry, others may see as misleading. People will not be receptive to overly futuristic ideas. Today is good for channeling energies into charity schemes. Official approval may be obtained for projects designed to help the needy and underprivileged. Useful advice and insight can come from people you meet again after a long period of separation. Don't give away more than is necessary. It is time to be a little cagey. People are sometimes not what they seem.

30. FRIDAY. Productive. Aquarius probably have the experience necessary to make a success of current affairs in the personal sphere of their lives. It is just a question of drawing on lessons from the past and capitalizing on them. Don't make the same mistakes again. With the wisdom of the past added to your innate abilities, there is no reason why your aspirations should not be reached. Publicity campaigns must be handled with tact and subtlety. It will be easy to project the opposite impression of the one intended. Aquarius generosity and love of mankind can come to the fore now and will be gratefully received. Strange as it may seem, those who give benefit as much as those who receive.

31. SATURDAY. Fortunate. Your finances may receive a surprise boost. Prizes or inheritances may come out of the blue. Artists, designers and architects should find themselves in the money today. All work that requires creative flair is likely to pull in the cash. Works of art will fetch high prices. Today is good for attempts to raise money for charity or other causes. People who carry a lot of sway in public affairs are likely to do all in their power to lend support to your interests. This assistance can come from the purest of motives. They will simply be intent on making the way as smooth as possible for you. Quiet conditions will suit Aquarius who have work to do at home.

NOVEMBER

1. SUNDAY. Disturbing. Your freedom of choice or movement may be restricted by older people, particularly parents. They may use emotional or financial levers to hem you in. Aquarius may have to contend with emotional blackmail. People will try to make you feel guilty if you fail to do their bidding. Others may try to curtail your independent ways. You will become despondent if they succeed. Do all you can to hold your own. Investigations into financial dealings can reveal wrongdoings. Money markets are likely to be in an unsettled state. You cannot afford to hold tight if you want to keep abreast of fluid conditions. Use caution and keep your options open. You must be ready to act fast.

2. MONDAY. Misleading. It would be unwise to take job descriptions or advertisements at face value. Situations can be made to sound more attractive than they are in fact. It would be sensible to make a thorough check before making a commitment. Contracts and other important documents can contain loopholes or escape clauses. Seek professional advice before you put your signature to important agreements. The motives of people in prominent positions can be rather suspect now. They will pull strings and manipulate situations merely to make their own positions stronger. Aquarius should maintain their honesty and integrity even in the face of corruption, despite pressure to overlook it.

3. TUESDAY. Uncertain. Journeys made on the spur of the moment are unlikely to be either enjoyable or productive. In fact, they may waste time and cash and leave you in a bad mood. People will not be in a receptive state of mind. It will be difficult to get your point of view across. Attempts to contact people by phone or letter can fail. It is a frustrating day for conveying messages or gaining information. Involvement in neighborhood projects will run smoothly. Favorable progress can be made in club and group affairs, particularly where laying foundations for the future are concerned. Later on, you will enjoy a chat with neighbors or family members. They will have important news.

4. WEDNESDAY. Variable. Today, make sure that any confidential papers, letters or other important documents are kept under lock and key. Prying eyes and light fingers may be abroad. It will be easier today to lose passports, driving licenses and bank cards. Make sure they are secure if you are going out. Wallets should be carried in a front pocket and shopping bags kept tightly closed as protection against thieves and pickpockets. Later on, the home will be a haven of peace and tranquillity. Spend the evening in cozy domestic surroundings with loved ones. Your mind is likely to wander over old times. Affectionate memories will come to mind, and be enjoyed with others.

5. THURSDAY. Troubling. Aquarius probably won't be in the best of moods upon waking this morning. Feeling of irritability are likely to prevail. It is important that loved ones are not made to bear the brunt of your moodiness and frustration. It would be better to get on the move earlier than usual. You may have to work off the grumpiness in household chores or employment activities. Help can be difficult to obtain from superiors or people in authority. Their own self-interest is likely to be put before the needs of others. Special requests may be turned down. Officials can raise objections to property deals or plans for building home extensions. These will be legitimate and you may not overturn them.

6. FRIDAY. Quiet. A slight lull in the usual hustle and bustle will enable Aquarius to tie up the loose ends of outstanding affairs. Every effort should be made to conclude business that has overrun the time allocated for it. You should be able to devote your full attention to closing out such tasks. Parents will appreciate a visit, letter or phone call from you. Keep them informed of events in your life. Aquarius who collect antiques, stamps or works of art should have a productive day. Excellent items can be had at reasonable prices to add to your collections. A tour of dealers may reveal some desirable purchases at prices you won't be able to turn down. You may have to revise your budget for the month.

7. SATURDAY. Good. This day should be much to your liking. You can take things easy or do the things you find most enjoyable and relaxing. There will be very little to tax your energy reserves. You will speed through routine chores or employment activities like clockwork with a light and efficient touch. Time given to reading, writing and study activities will be most rewarding. Your ability to absorb facts and information and to apply concentrated effort for long periods will be at a peak. The study of philosophy and psychology will prove most interesting. Trips to visit friends will be successful. You will enjoy their conversation and company in the evening.

8. SUNDAY. Mixed. This is not the time for a lighthearted or casual approach to affairs and undertakings. In fact, events could take a critical turn, forcing Aquarius to apply themselves with increased diligence. Care and attention must be given to details. Commercial operations that carry a high risk factor must not be left to look after themselves. They will falter if they are not given continued guidance and monitoring. Conditions do not encourage participation in leisure and pleasure pursuits. A more serious mood will prevail. Prospects should be looking brighter. Any anxiety you have about the future will be dispelled.

9. MONDAY. Deceptive. You may devote much time to thrashing out finer philosophical points to little avail. Aquarius can get bogged down in details and abstract ideas and still come to no conclusions. It will be easy to keep your head in the clouds. Dreams and ideals will occupy you even though you have no intention of acting on them. This tendency to fantasize needs to be countered with a practical and concrete approach. Keep your feet on the ground. Attempts to interest others in idealistic plans can fail due to your inability to communicate clearly. Beware of being taken in by attractive seeming people or situations.

10. TUESDAY. Sensitive. Aquarius can move a rung or two up the ladder of success and promotion today. More favorable positions may become available at work. You should be eminently qualified for them as well as for taking on more responsibility. Superiors will do their best to bring out latent talents in you. They may suggest a course that stretches your capacities to the full. Minor disagreements with the people you work with must be kept in perspective. It will be easier to blow such incidents out of proportion. You must not allow your thoughts to wander while you are engaged in intricate work or handling tools and machinery. Accidents are more likely to happen when an operator's attention is diverted. If you have to think over a problem, turn off the power.

11. WEDNESDAY. Difficult. It will be easier to get into trouble while driving vehicles. You will have to keep fully alert if you want to avoid accidents. Leave plenty of time for car journeys. Speeding to destinations is likely to result in heavy fines. Your appreciation of distances and the speed of other vehicles may not be too reliable. While interviews for new jobs may not offer the results you hope for, neither are they likely to be a complete failure. Prospective employers may approve of you sufficiently to suggest that you apply again in the future. Don't become overexhausted today. Energy should be conserved against the time you may have to expend an unusual amount. Concentrate on keeping healthy.

12. THURSDAY. Variable. It would be unwise to push your luck in cooperative ventures or in marital affairs. It won't take much to make partners or spouses see red. Once the dragon has been roused, all hell can break loose. Unwary statements may encourage old grudges to come to the surface. Watch what you say. People you live or work with are best handled with kid gloves. People with whom you have shared a friendship can suddenly become lovers. Happy love affairs can develop with people you have known for a long time. There will be increased chances of Aquarius meeting romantic partners through club and group activities. However, caution is the watchword for today.

13. FRIDAY. Changeable. This is a good day for discussing emotional problems with close friends who have plenty of experience with matrimonial or partnership affairs. Difficulties in a relationship can be solved by airing matters with a third party. It would be wise to choose a confidant who you know has had similar experiences. Relief may come from comparing notes. People who are in a position to offer financial backing or other assistance may be unwilling to do so. Your ideas or situation will not appeal to them. It may be necessary to hammer out legal matters with officials. There should be a carefree atmosphere at work. Enjoy it while you can because it could evaporate in a flash.

14. SATURDAY. Good. Professional and business interests will benefit from background research you can do over the weekend. Obtain books from the library on subjects relevant to your career aspirations. In-depth studies of specific issues will place you at the head of the field. Today is good for negotiating with large commercial organizations. Business conducted on a grand scale can prove extremely lucrative. Smaller transactions may be less profitable proportionately. Aquarius should not be averse to making confidential financial arrangements. Publicity campaigns designed to bring the plight of the underprivileged to the attention of a larger public should meet with success.

15. SUNDAY. Disturbing. Loved ones or spouses may be in a down mood. They may cast the blame for their discontent onto their Aquarius partners. They can make unreasonable demands and complain bitterly when these are not met. Friends are unlikely to provide the happy companionship you are seeking. Parties and group gatherings may depress your spirits rather than give them a lift. Social events may be rather forced and formal. Spending extravagantly in an attempt to buy pleasure and enjoyment will only waste money without bringing the diverting interests you had aimed for. Aquarius can become sad or despondent if they spend time with people who are themselves miserable.

16. MONDAY. Creative. Aquarius should allow the innovation side of their nature to come to the fore today. There will be no shortage of original and creative ideas available to you if you once start giving expression to them. Your love of the new and futuristic will find rich soil in which to take root. Exciting new discoveries can be made. Excellent progress will come from attempts to broaden the mind. This is definitely a day for pushing ahead into uncharted territory. Energetic help can come from people in distant places. Tax and insurance officials may provide some headaches where business finances are concerned. Pay more attention to exercise and a healthy diet if you hope to keep fit.

17. TUESDAY. Good. Avoid taking the most obvious route to obtain your ends in professional and public affairs. The use of subtle and behind-the-scenes methods will be more effective. Employ the approach that competitors least expect. Make full use of inside contacts and people who work away from the public eye. Today is good for background maneuvers. Your grasp of future trends will provide a strong basis on which to make constructive plans. Lay the foundations now for future action. Possible job changes should be kept in mind. It would be wise to start working toward new qualifications. You might enroll in education courses now. Books can provide plenty of inspiration.

18. WEDNESDAY. Mixed. Conditions which affect overseas business interests will be most favorable. Profits can be much greater than expected. Business contacts in other towns or cities may put more clients or commerce your way. At the same time, it may be extremely difficult to get hold of people. It may take some time before you are informed of positive developments. Aquarius can derive great delight from mental and intellectual pursuits. Progress made with study and research work will satisfy your adventurous spirit. Interests can be shared with people who are on your wavelength. It would be unwise to treat elders in a cursory manner. Not only could they have valuable advice to give you but they might help you financially.

19. THURSDAY. Fair. Tact and diplomacy will be more important than usual in professional circles. It is essential to adhere to accepted codes of conduct and practice when dealing with business associates. There is a danger that the unconventional side of the Aquarius nature will take over in the wrong circumstances and make a bad impression on influential people. Do not underestimate the importance of your public image. Large-scale business transactions can prove more profitable than modest deals. Today is good for renewing contact with people who operate in quiet and unobtrusive ways. Aquarius will be pleasantly surprised and gratified by the support of acquaintances with whom they have had little dealing.

20. FRIDAY. Confusing. The more humdrum side of your business operations will start to reward you for all the hard work you have put in. Promises should not be lightly made. It would be foolish to enter into any contracts if you have doubts of your ability to stick to terms of agreement. Ensure that any duties and responsibilities you take on are well within your capacity. Your lovelife is likely to enter a rather disappointing period. However, you will emerge a wiser and more loving person. Your own attitude to loved ones may be the cause of a crisis. Aquarius shoppers will have a successful day. Cast an eye forward to Christmas and start making some basic plans. It is only a few weeks away.

21. SATURDAY. Happy. The balance between investment and earnings in business operations may reach a more satisfactory level. Long-term financial problems can finally be solved through the use of effective publicity campaigns. Aspirations that you hold dear can come closer to fruition. Go all out to realize a dream that has obsessed you for some time. Friends who remember good turns you have done them in the past can come forward with welcome support. Aquarius will meet with success in projects designed to improve living conditions or recreational facilities in your neighborhood. It will be easier to convince people of the validity of your ideas and plans concerning community projects.

22. SUNDAY. Variable. This is a day for Aquarius to be content with what they have and thankful for what they have already achieved. Don't fall into the trap of taking things for granted. It will be easier to set your sights too high and miss what is right under your nose. Let others know that you appreciate the love and kindness they give you. You may have overlooked or neglected loved ones to the point where they seriously doubt your affection and sincerity. Unless you can convince partners of the regard you have for them they may walk out. There is also the chance that new and exciting romances can begin. Don't trade excitement for love that is solid and enduring.

23. MONDAY. Deceptive. It would be unwise to expect others to exhibit the same high standards of honesty and integrity that you yourself display. In fact, people can be purposely dishonest and misleading. Aquarius must beware of being too naive. People will further their own interests through whatever means are most effective. That can include stabbing you in the back. Problems will tend to multiply if you spend too much time mulling them over. It will be easy to distort your view of things by dwelling on difficulties. Later in the day, conditions will be supportive for getting humanitarian projects under way. Official backing may have to be obtained before anything of note can be accomplished.

24. TUESDAY. Uncertain. This is a day for playing your cards close to the chest. It is also good for confidential meetings and secret agreements. Restrict the circle of people who are intimate with your affairs to the minimum. Competitors may steal an idea from you if they get a whiff of your plans and intentions. Aquarius can all too easily adopt an offhand manner with associates. People will not take kindly to being treated in a cursory fashion. Be aware of the effect you are having on others. Be more tactful and considerate. In romance, the slate can be wiped completely clean. Long-established affairs or patterns of relating may come to an end. It is important not to look back.

25. WEDNESDAY. Changeable. Aquarius can be tempted to stick their noses into other people's business or to take unnecessary risks. It would be advisable to act cautiously, especially if it is important for you to maintain an unblemished reputation. The marketplace can become a battlefield today with business competitors vying for contracts and customers. It is important, however, not to shoulder others out of the way in an attempt to secure your bit of the action. People who occupy prominent positions may strike up friendships with Aquarius. It will be easier to obtain loans from bankers to finance new business ventures or expansions of existing ones. This should indicate a good financial climate.

26. THURSDAY. Manageable.. It is important to be more discriminating in choosing the company you keep today. But as it is Thanksgiving, you will probably share part of it with family members. Relatives will be ready to step in and help with babysitting chores, if necessary, or any other assistance you might require. You may receive some valuable information through telephone calls, but will have to keep it to yourself until you return to work. Short trips could be productive, but may involve travel to a friend's house. Listen to what trusted ones have to tell you. Their advice is generally beneficial and is certainly reliable.

27. FRIDAY. Happy. Aquarius will appear more attractive than usual to others today. Prospective romantic partners will be drawn toward you. Exciting new love affairs can spring up. It will be easier to persuade loved ones to go along with your plans. They are unlikely to raise any objections to entertainment or recreational arrangements. Aquarius will have a special gift when it comes to dealing with difficult people. Obstructions can be overcome with your charm and dexterity. Associates who opposed your business plans initially can now be won over to your point of view. However you will be hitting your head against a brick wall if you try to get around obstinate officials.

28. SATURDAY. Disquieting. Go back over your accounts for the last month or two. It is important that income and expenses be brought more into line. This may mean that economy measures have to be introduced. Seek ways of cutting back expenditures. It may be time to consider ways of bringing in additional earnings. Your financial situation can refelct adversely on your hopes for joining new clubs or societies. Annual fees may prove prohibitive. Membership may have to be deferred for the time being. If your duties as a member of a club or group include handling the funds, complications may arise. You may have to shoulder the burden for mistakes whether you are responsible for them or not.

29. SUNDAY. Strenuous. Your finances are probably going through a sensitive period. It will be very difficult to refuse requests for loans from needy friends and acquaintances. It can be also difficult to communicate or draw close to loved ones. They are likely to withdraw into their shells. Attempts to encourage them out of their seclusion are unlikely to succeed. Keep trying. A gentle and understanding approach may win through eventually. People you know only slightly or meet for the first time may be very easily upset. Don't be put off by their reactions. Their troubles may have nothing to do with you. Keep an open mind and don't look for trouble. Try to see their side.

30. MONDAY. Quiet. The month ends on a less hectic note. There will be time to catch up on jobs and letters you have put off. You can save a lot of running around by using the telephone. Business can be conducted just as effectively over the phone as through personal contact. Conserve your energy where possible. You may not have that much to spare. The absence of pressure and demands make this a good day for work requiring long periods of concentration. Studies and intellectual pursuits can yield very satisfactory results. Recently initiated community projects may need an encouraging shove now to help them on their way. Relax and enjoy an evening at home.

DECEMBER

1. TUESDAY. Good. The month gets off to a very lively and positive start for Aquarius. Future prospects are looking bright. You will be very heartened by the enthusiastic response to ideas and plans you have been nurturing for some time. People will be in a receptive mood, and impressed by your outlook on life and your deeply held principles. The more adventurous and experimental side of your nature can come to the fore with good effect in business activities. Unusual methods could gain a significant increase in profit margins. This is a good day for storytellers and writers. Use air travel where possible in preference to surface transport unless your trip is too short. Highways may be unusually busy.

2. WEDNESDAY. Useful. Aquarius should make good use of quiet contemplations. Lessons can be learned by mulling over past experience. Capitalize on previous successes and avoid repeating past mistakes. Don't get locked up inside your own head. You will miss important developments and opportunities in the business world unless you keep one eye on external affairs. Golden chances can come your way. You will have to be ready for action to make the most of them. Aquarius will make good referees and arbitrators today. Your sense of justice and fair play will be commended by associates. The evening will be good for dating romantic partners as well as for meeting possible new ones.

3. THURSDAY. Confusing. Both you and the people around you are likely to be subject to volatile emotions. Rational thinking may not prevail. Decisions based on sentiment should be suspect. Superficial appearances may tend to take you in. You will prefer attractive situations and people for the wrong reasons. Sweethearts may play hard to get or be reticent to make firm commitments. It may prove impossible to get to the bottom of their thoughts and feelings. Aquarius may not know where they stand. Home and family affairs must not be neglected for outside interests. Spouses and family members may need more support and affection then you have had time for recently. Try to make amends.

4. FRIDAY. Variable. Although you may have arrangements in mind for the weekend, it could prove difficult to finalize plans with loved ones. They are likely to be on the move and hard to track down. Risky deals and gambles are more likely to lead to loss than gain. Tip-offs and inside information can be misleading. Don't put money on the wrong horse. It is best invested in enterprises that may be slow in paying returns, but the rewards will be sure and steady. It will be easier now to gain access to influential people who have been reluctant to give interviews or have been tied up with busy schedules. Such meetings should work in your favor even though results may not be immediately apparent.

5. SATURDAY. Uncertain. Unexpected happenings may intervene to upset your plans for outings or entertainment. Recreational activities may have to be canceled. People who are in a position to back commercial operations are unlikely to respond favorably to enterprises which involve a high risk factor. Requests for funding from financiers may be turned down. Children will be in a mischievous mood today. They may get into trouble unless they are guided toward constructive activities. Creative energies and mental concentration will be at the disposal of Aquarius. Good progress can be made with artistic and intellectual pursuits.

6. SUNDAY. Pleasant. Spend the day doing what you most enjoy. Avoid dull and dreary tasks and chores. It is unlikely that there will much of importance to attend to. You can indulge in favorite pastimes or visit friends or places of interest. If you cannot find things to absorb you, boredom is likely to set in. It would then be advisable to work at little jobs or letter writing to fill yawning gaps in the day. Preparations can be made to make the week ahead run more smoothly. Today is good for meetings in secret places or behind closed doors. Secret love affairs can be exciting. Loved ones may be cheerful but difficult to fathom. They could seem preoccupied and prefer to be alone.

7. MONDAY. Mixed. Aquarius are likely to be at the top of the list when promotion chances come up. Your past record will stand you in good stead. Your hard work and loyalty will not have gone unnoticed by employers. Previous and continuing efforts may be well rewarded. Loved ones may not be in the best of health. It is unlikely that symptoms are serious enough to call in the doctor. A restful day may be sufficient to bring about a speedy recovery. However, too casual an attitude to illness can result in a worsening of conditions. It may be necessary to break a date in order to attend to late developments at work. Avoid overworking. Keep your own health in mind.

8. TUESDAY. Easygoing. This can be a humdrum and boring day for Aquarius workers. Regular employment activities may seem endless and tedious. Conditions in general will be rather slow. There is little point in taking time off work for alternative affairs. Efforts to spice up the day will be singularly unsuccessful. Your physical condition can benefit from a little extra care and attention. Eating habits may need changing and more healthy diets substituted for your usual food choices. A visit to the gym or a jog round the park will tone up the system. Friends will notice a marked change for the better in your appearance if you adopt more healthy patterns.

9. WEDNESDAY. Variable. By pooling energy and resources with friends, you will make more effective progress in commercial ventures. A pal can make a trusty partner now. The time may have come to part company with existing business colleagues. They may well be making an unfavorable impression on clients or other business contacts to the detriment of your business interests. Profits can pick up if you change partners, or decide to go it alone for the time being. Any neglect of loved ones for outside interests and ambitions must be curbed. Relationships may be endangered if too much time is given to affairs outside the home which necessarily exclude your family.

10. THURSDAY. Good. You are more likely to raise funding for projects handled on a cooperative basis, than for those carried through on individual initiative. Influential people will have more faith in joint enterprises. Anxiety over legal disputes can turn to relief by the end of the day. Judgments and verdicts are more likely to be given in favor of Aquarius. The day is good for making emotional commitments. Marriages arranged today can develop into very happy partnerships. Existing matrimonial problems can benefit from the advice of older and more experienced people. Talking over problems with parents can help to solve domestic tensions. They may even offer some financial aid.

11. FRIDAY. Disturbing. Aquarius charm will help you to win over people who have been standing in your way. If there has been a temporary holdup in your career plans and aspirations, it will be easier to push past the obstructions and get things moving again. Continue your efforts toward progress in spite of the odds against you. Nothing should be done that might make others doubt your integrity. Avoid the use of unconventional work methods. Aquarius may come across situations or people that corrupt or exploit others. Think twice before you rush in to try to clean up the act. More time and finance than you have at your disposal may be required for such operations.

12. SATURDAY. Fair. Aquarius may receive valuable introductions to influential people through the agency of a friend. Access to authority can be made easier for you. Once interviews with superiors or officials have been arranged, you are likely to get a sympathetic hearing. The help you need will probably be forthcoming. Special requests can be granted. Background research into professional or public activities can place you in an advantageous position. Ensure that you are fully informed before the time for action or decision-making arrives. Although problems concerning shared funds may arise, discussions with partners are unlikely to produce viable solutions.

13. SUNDAY. Disappointing. Aquarius are likely to be blamed for mistakes made by superiors. Once such harm has been done, it may be impossible to undo it. Heavy strains can be placed on shared funds as a result. Hard-earned savings may be threatened. Another facet of someone you have known for a long time can be revealed to you. Your feelings toward a friend may change due to facts that come to light. It may be necessary to withdraw your trust. It can prove very difficult to tie loved ones down to definite decisions. If they acquiesce under pressure, you cannot count on their reliability when it comes to the crunch. Neighbors are best handled with kid gloves to avoid unpleasantness.

14. MONDAY. Challenging. This is likely to be a very busy day. With so much going on, Aquarius may end up chasing their tails. It may be very difficult to keep your thoughts and actions ordered. If your attention and energy is deployed over too wide a field, there is a danger that nothing constructive will be achieved. It would be unwise to place too much trust in people coming from, or residing in, distant places. Factors outside their control may force them to break arrangements or go back on their word. Unexpected events must be taken into account by Aquarius, in spite of the best intentions of others. Your spouse's relatives can be less than charitable and could even be hostile.

15. TUESDAY. Sensitive. Problems concerning distant places can be relieved by airing them to a friend. Acquaintances may see another side of the picture and make constructive suggestions that show you the way out. Your enthusiasm for following training or education courses may be dampened by the pessimism of a loved one. They may have their own reasons for attempting to dissuade you from following a course of action that can lead to change. Your own need to follow such a course will be tested by the obstacles that are placed in your path. There will be no doubt if you can persuade others of your unveering intentions to go through with your plans. Take a strong stand on your beliefs.

16. WEDNESDAY. Special. Aquarius will enjoy keeping on the move and widening their circle of friends and acquaintances. You will have no trouble at all being instantly at ease with people and making new pals. Important new relationships can be formed without effort. People and events will tend to fall into place. It's a good opportunity for teaming up with others in business partnerships and for putting such agreements in writing. Your humanitarian urges can find outlet through involvement in community activities. Club and group gatherings can be quite rewarding. Heavy-handedness in business activities must be avoided. Employ a subtle and diplomatic approach to business affairs.

17. THURSDAY. Disquieting. The pace and thrust of business activities today may prove almost too aggressive and demanding for Aquarius. It may be difficult to summon up the resolve to see commercial operations through to the conclusion. Fierce competition must be met. Don't linger in difficult or dangerous situations longer than you have to. If events prove too much for you, it would be best to retreat. Aquarius may be subject to strong and volatile emotions today. You must struggle to keep the upper hand. If you allow your heart to rule your head, you will say things which you later may come to regret. It will be easier to make wounding or insulting statements to co-workers. Don't let your mouth rule your mind.

18. FRIDAY. Variable. Conditions are unfavorable for business transactions. In fact, important negotiations may have to be called off or postponed to a more positive time. People may try to force you into unacceptable corners. Aquarius must resist the pressure to do things against their will or principles. Don't let others inflict their selfish demands upon you. Be cautious when it comes to making agreements or promises. Commitment should be withheld unless you are pretty sure that you can stand by your word. Loved ones will be delighted to receive flowers or a gift. Little gestures of affection will let other know you care. Attention to family and loved ones is important during the holiday season.

19. SATURDAY. Fair. Prospects are good for undertaking shopping expeditions accompanied by friends. This is the day to finalize the bulk of your Christmas purchasing. Go through your gift list to ensure that nobody has been forgotten. It will be difficult to get a definite answer out of influential people. They will prefer to hedge their bets for the time being. This should not deter you from putting forward new courses of action from those already proposed. Alternative ideas may carry more weight. Joining forces with others in attempts to improve the plight of the needy and underprivileged will bring rich rewards. Humanitarian projects will only gain impetus from the involvement of others.

20. SUNDAY. Changeable. Aquarius may have to step in to fill a gap left by a sick or indisposed friend. Personal plans may have to be dropped in order to help someone out of a tight corner. This may involve having to travel some way from your home. Though extra duties may seem rather irritating, you should attempt to carry them out in a generous spirit. It will be easier to meet influential people in informal surroundings. Parties and social gatherings can provide the perfect context for getting to know people. You should have no difficulty in persuading others of the practicability of your ideas. In fact, people will be impatient to hear what you have to say or offer.

21. MONDAY. Good. It is likely today that you can't see the woods for the trees. Your close involvement in business or employment affairs may mean that you are overlooking essential issues. You need a bird's-eye view to get things back into perspective. Don't home in on details or partial aspects of your work. Keep an overall picture. Past actions can reveal lessons that are pertinent to the present situation. Before making decisions or taking action, cast your mind back to previous episodes that are similar to your current position. This will show you how to make the most of current opportunities. Don't allow willful people to bully you. Let others know what your limits are. Stick to your guns.

22. TUESDAY. Encouraging. Today, feelings should be allowed a greater say than logic and rational thinking. A mental assessment of people or situations is likely to fall far short of the mark. Be prepared to follow your hunches. If rightness is felt in the heart, things are likely to work out well. Beware of suppressing your true feelings and perceptions. Don't put a straitjacket on your sensitivity. Your lovelife can bring much pleasure now. New romances can be begun and existing ones made more fulfilling. Stronger foundations are probably being laid in close relationships even if you are unaware of the fact. The benefits of such developments will be felt in due course.

23. WEDNESDAY. Tricky. Aquarius may find it hard to resist going against rules and regulations. You won't have much interest in acting in ways people have come to expect of you. This can land you in trouble with authority. Unconventional approaches or methods may irk superiors or officials. You must not allow sentiment to influence your actions or decisions in business or employment affairs. It is important to maintain a fully professional attitude. If you act out of your own interests rather than for the greater good, your standing in the eyes of others will diminish. Take the majority view into account. It would be unwise to act in isolation even though you may disagree with others.

24. THURSDAY. Rewarding. The day is good for clearing the decks of loans or impending payments. This will leave you with a clear mind and a freer hand to carry out personal plans. You may be faced with formidable tasks. You will be at your wits end to know just how you are going to manage. Help can come in the nick of time from unlikely people. The Christmas spirit is likely to invade people who have an important say in events that affect you. This can make them more sympathetic to your requests and more openhanded. This may be a good time to ask for a pay raise or a change in working conditions. Later on today, secret meetings or journeys should meet with success.

25. FRIDAY. Merry Christmas. This should be a very gratifying day for Aquarius. The response you receive from friends and family will let you know how much you are loved and appreciated. People will be only too ready to let you take the reins. Your ideas and methods are likely to prevail. Your tolerance and love of mankind will receive full recognition. People may be fascinated to hear your outlook on life. The love and respect that comes your way will increase your self-confidence without giving you a swelled head. Your Christmas stocking may contain something of great value. Today is also good for being in the company of prominent or influential people. Make use of this opportunity.

26. SATURDAY. Disturbing. A heavy strain may be placed on your finances. You may need to find cash in a hurry to cover bills and expenses. Even though you would prefer to put your feet up and enjoy the Christmas holiday, it looks as though you will have to give money-making ventures some attention. You cannot allow existing cash earnings to diminish in any way. Your strivings to bring secret hopes and wishes to fulfillment are likely to come to nought due to lack of finance. Confidential plans may have to be shelved until extra funds can be found. The health of a friend can suddenly deteriorate. Your help or assistance may be needed to bring about recovery.

27. SUNDAY. Variable. This is not a day for staying at home in the armchair. Keep on the move. You will enjoy circulating among your friends and meeting new people. Aquarius will appear attractive and vivacious to others. You may have a block of admirers around you. New romances can start. Your power to exert influence over others can cause trouble with existing partners or spouses. You will appear to be flirting, whether you are or not. If you do make eyes at someone else, you can expect trouble from your mate or sweetheart. They will be in no mood to stand by while you have all the fun. Your mind is likely to be full of creative ideas. It won't be so easy to put them into concrete form.

28. MONDAY. Good. Information that arrives by mail may put a smile on your face. New business ventures should be preceded by some intensive background research. Ensure that you are fully informed before going into action. Get on the phone to business contacts and associates who can put you more fully in the picture. Today is good for arranging meetings and interviews over the phone. Old faces can turn up from the past. People with whom you have lost contact for some time, can come back into your life with very happy consequences. Urges to meet with old friends should be followed up. Business can pick up later on with profitable results. You will have a Midas touch today.

29. TUESDAY. Deceptive. It can be very difficult to fathom just what is going on in the minds of influential people. They are likely to be cagey about their future plans. This can leave Aquarius hanging fire for the time being. Your only course will be to wait patiently for new developments. It would be wise to take anything your employers say or promise with a pinch of salt. Make no new moves as a result of what they propose. A sudden switch of emphasis can occur; or they may simply go back on their word. Planning permission for home changes and improvements can be obtained today. However, things will not be so straightforward in your lovelife. A relationship may be on the rocks.

30. WEDNESDAY. Quiet. It would be a good idea to give more time and care to home affairs and family concerns. Loved ones may need a little more support and encouragement. Do a bit more to ensure that household procedures are running smoothly. Devote any spare time to making the home more comfortable and easy to manage. This is a good day for attending to minor maintenance jobs. You are advised not to allow your mind to focus on anxieties over employment or business affairs. Problems can be blown up to ridiculous size if you dwell on them in excess. Get your thoughts in order, by all means. Do anything practical you can to relieve tension and concern. Avoid unnecessary worry.

31. THURSDAY. Sensitive. The home can be the best of all places in which to celebrate the passing of the old year and the coming of the new. You probably won't be in the mood to mix with lots of people in noisy surroundings. You can drop your defenses at home and be more spontaneous and relaxed. It could be that anxieties are playing on your mind and unsettling your equilibrium. Emotions may be more volatile and unpredictable. It won't take much to hurt your pride or wound you to the quick. Even though you are more emotionally sensitive, loved ones may try to criticize you unfairly. Don't allow it to upset you. Set your sights on the coming year, 1988.

November–December 1986

NOVEMBER

1. SATURDAY. Fair. This is a day for getting out of the rut and using more original thinking. Don't be content with traditional approaches. Your imagination will show you shortcuts and easier ways to handle tasks that you have to undertake in the course of your work. You must beware of eccentric and unusual behavior, though. It will be easy for people to get the wrong idea about you now. They may be only too ready to give you a bad name. Take one step at a time in business dealings. Don't expect too much from colleagues or associates. Aquarians may tend to get a bit ahead of themselves, and take on more than they can handle. Today is good for making a start with Christmas shopping.

2. SUNDAY. Sensitive. This has all the makings of a day spent peacefully at home with the people you are closest to. But it is very unlikely that things turn out in this way. It will be much easier for Aquarians to get into deep emotional water, with sweetheart or spouse, and thoroughly spoil the day. There may be a hairline balance between a delightful and a dreadful time spent with partners. But in the event of the latter, arguments will be difficult to avoid. Recriminations are likely to flow back and forth. All the old resentments can be dragged up once the downward journey has started. Loved ones may seem more like sparring partners than affectionate companions. It will be up to you to call a halt.

3. MONDAY. Variable. This is a good day for laying the foundations of new business ventures. The people you deal with will be on your wavelength. Discussions with prospective customers or business partners will result in favorable terms being agreed on. Today is good for trying to win more business and reach wider markets. Later on, Aquarians may be caused some headaches by the antics of people they thought were friends. Close acquaintances may seem to be doing you a favor, but their real intent will be disguised. They may give with one hand and take with the other. There is likely to be some jealousy or envy of your position or possible successes, and friends may do all they can to prevent you reaching your goal. But they won't want to be seen doing so.

4. TUESDAY. Uncertain. Commercial ventures must not be allowed to encroach on personal funds. Unless these two areas of finances are kept separate, all kinds of confusion will result. And any failures in business activities will leave a large hole in private savings. This is not the best day for Aquarians to handle important business finances, even though they are likely to have some successes, of a sort. It would be much better to leave commercial dealings to partners or associates. The trouble with your own efforts is that while you may at first strike a rich vein, this will soon peter out, leaving you empty-handed. Partners are likely to adopt a less spectacular, but steadier, approach.

5. WEDNESDAY. Deceptive. Follow your nose when dealing with business or public affairs. Your intuitions are likely to be right. Common sense and traditional methods may not provide the best answers now. An inspired guess can produce better results. Aquarians will be very pleased with the outcome of important business meetings or negotiations. This is a good day for handling crucial activities in the world of commerce. Professional life may be brightened by a little mixture of romance. And more than pleasure can come from these liaisons. Someone who turns you on may also show you the way to additional productivity and profit-making. You are more likely to get your way with people who matter through charm and friendliness.

6. THURSDAY. Excellent. Aquarians will enjoy being on their own and getting down to some serious work. You should bring as much order into your affairs as possible. All loose ends should be tied up. Get minor matters completed and out of the way. Clear the decks for what looks like very lucrative commercial operations that are coming up. You will need all channels open to make the most of business that is looming on the horizon. You must be ready to grab whatever opportunities come your way. People in influential positions can make once-in-a-lifetime offers. A missed chance now will be gone forever. But you would do well to keep any good luck strictly confidential.

7. FRIDAY. Good. Get on the phone early to people who can give the most help in your line of work. Those you contact are likely to be receptive, and information you receive will further your interests. If you cannot get hold of people on the phone, go and see them, or write. But don't wait for others to contact you. You must take the initiative now. But in putting forward your problems or requesting help, it is better that you do not act too directly or come to the point immediately. Bide your time in discussions or conversations. Others will be put off if they feel you are being pushy. Some diplomatic meandering is in order. An unobtrusive approach will get the best results.

8. SATURDAY. Disturbing. It may be difficult to avoid quarrels and upsets with loved ones, particularly in the morning. But if Aquarians are especially considerate of the feelings of others, they will go some way to minimizing tensions. Be as kind and loving as you can. Go out of your way to bypass arguments. Don't rise to the challenge of provocation or confrontation. Aquarians may get into troubled waters with people they work for. It is possible that superiors will have different ideas from you as to how certain jobs should be carried out. But you would do better to hold your peace and avoid retaliating. Neither your job or reputation should be imperiled now. Lack of concentration can lead to accidents.

9. SUNDAY. Variable. Don't use words loosely. Be extra careful of what you say. People will very easily form the wrong opinion of you from remarks you make inadvertently. Or misinterpretations can lead to loss of public support. If you are making speeches, check through your text to see that it contains no ambiguities. Some quiet contemplations later on may give rise to lively ideas for making money. If your finances need a boost, this is the time to set about increasing income. Let your imagination take wing when considering new sources of cash. It is not the traditional methods that will come up with the goods. You may even see fit to do a little dealing under the counter.

10. MONDAY. Mixed. Fortune is likely to be with you in money matters. A situation that seemed like impending disaster can suddenly turn out for the better. You may be let off the hook at the last moment. Partners or spouses will be in a cooperative mood. They will be ready to give Aquarians a hand with jobs, or may provide financial assistance. Their words or actions can have the additional effect of enhancing your reputation. But relationships with friends can be stormy. Arguments are likely to break out over money. Misunderstandings can lead to bad feelings. If meetings with friends are desired or unavoidable, it is important that you make your position clear, and that everyone knows where they stand.

11. TUESDAY. Good. Your finances can get a welcome injection from earnings that come through new business agreements. Plans laid in the past may come to fruition now. Conditions are favorable for all forms of action, and Aquarians should take full advantage of them. This is not time for halfhearted attempts. You should muster all your strength and determination, and give everything you've got to the projects you undertake. The more you put in, the more you are likely to take out. If your personal life is fairly clear of problems, you may find time to help others who are suffering or in need. All efforts contributed to charitable or humanitarian causes will be highly appreciated.

12. WEDNESDAY. Sensitive. Get on the move today. You will miss opportunities if you stay in the armchair. Looking up old friends can yield beneficial results for you. Business contracts drawn up now will have profitable results that extend far into the future. Your personal efforts are likely to win you acclaim from the people or company for which you work. Your position within the firm should be more solidly established. But day-to-day business dealings will be jeopardized if you are rigid or heavy-handed with clients. You will lose customers if you employ bulldozer tactics. Don't attempt to get the desired results through means of force. Tact and diplomacy are the order of the day.

13. THURSDAY. Fair. Your friends are likely to have something of prime importance to tell you. Information they pass on can be used to your advantage. Although what you are told may be somewhat surprising, you should waste no time in putting it into operation. Strike while the iron is hot. Don't let valuable opportunities slip past you. Loved ones may get up to some irritating antics. Aquarians may find it difficult to keep their cool. Your patience may be stretched to the limit. If your sweetheart seems to have cooled off a bit recently, don't worry. It is more than likely that partners are feeling more than they are showing. Or someone you are attracted to may be concealing a mutual attraction, at least for the time being.

14. FRIDAY. Changeable. Aquarians are likely to find their minds drifting today. Daydreams and past memories may troop through your mind in endless procession. You may experience a deep hankering for people and places you have previously known. But you must be careful not to drown yourself in sentimentality. Drop old friends a line if you feel the urge. You may also feel like retreating into your shell. Your home will provide a quiet and peaceful environment that allows you to settle down to some serious work. It is possible that you will feel a strong sense of dissatisfaction with yourself in regard to hopes and ambitions. It seems that you have not been making the necessary efforts to reach your own targets.

15. SATURDAY. Variable. This is an excellent day for the buying and selling of property. Profits are likely to be higher than expected. Land and its products will also fetch good prices. Aquarian shoppers may find some welcome bargains on the fruit and vegetable stall in the local market. Today is good for doing some stocking up for the coming festive season. You may be jolted into action by information that comes by letter or phone. It seems that you will have to pick up the loose ends of a job you thought was over and done with. If you have recently applied for a new job, you may have to supply more information about yourself, or attend another interview, even though you have already been more or less assured of a position with the company.

16. SUNDAY. Disturbing. Aquarians are likely to be chasing their own tails for much of the day. You may run into all kinds of confusion if you are attempting to realize ambitious desires. The problems will arise in not knowing which is the best course to follow. You may comb through past experience and try to forecast future trends in an attempt to establish the right move to make. But no action you can conceive will seem to fit the bill or come up to standard. But recent disappointments in your own lack of drive will force you on until you find the right solution. Your difficulties can be further aggravated by important contacts, who insist that you spend more time away from home than you like.

17. MONDAY. Demanding. Friends will not make pleasant companions today. They may turn up in situations where they have not been invited and are really not wanted. Aquarians can be put out and embarrassed by their presence. Unwelcome guests can ruin your enjoyment and prove to be a damper on everybody's spirits. There may be some pull between public activities and romantic hopes. You might have to cancel an outing with a loved one in order to attend to club or group responsibilities. But if sweethearts are given plenty of warning, they should be sympathetic to your predicament. Money matters can provide some headaches later on. Gambling must be avoided like the plague.

18. TUESDAY. Mixed. It seems that your business finances are in turmoil, and will demand a lot of attention to bring them into some sort of balance. You may have to give more time to work than you really want. This can involve the cancellation of pleasure and leisure pursuits. But you will feel much easier in your mind for making the effort to bring some order into commercial affairs. And you will enjoy your spare-time activities all the more when you get to them. Any sacrifices or deprivations should be made up for by special outings. Aquarians will right the balance in their personal lives by treating themselves and loved ones to favorite entertainments or eating places, and perhaps even both.

19. WEDNESDAY. Worrisome. Aquarians may be not feeling up to par. You may not quite know exactly what is making you feel under the weather. But even though you cannot put your finger on an exact symptom, your performance is likely to be under par. It is essential that you do not allow a vague sense of ill health to drag on indefinitely. It would be better to get a checkup and remove any doubts and suspicions about your well-being. Or perhaps you can recognize an emotional cause that is putting you out of balance. You must get to the bottom of the problem one way or another. If you are stuck with a problem stemming from your regular work, the people closest to you will be ready to give a helping hand.

20. THURSDAY. Good. Any overtime or extra sidelines you can take on will bring a welcome boost to your personal finances. By letting your employers see the extent of your skills and abilities, you can place yourself in an advantageous position where future job prospects are concerned. Make sure you undertake your tasks and duties with extra care and completeness. The eyes of superiors are likely to be on you, whether you know it or not. If you can meet the required standards in the time allotted when working on particular projects, financial and other rewards may be forthcoming immediately. Don't rush into business negotiations before doing your homework. Go into discussions armed with all the facts and figures you can collect.

21. FRIDAY. Encouraging. Wait until later in the day to discuss any problems or aspirations you have regarding employment affairs. Those who you work for will be more approachable in the afternoon. This also applies to prospective employers and others whose position can have a bearing on your future career. Make clear to these people what you would like to see happen in the time ahead. You should be able to forge useful agreements if you are requesting changes in working hours or pay rates. State your case clearly, but not overforcefully. This may also be the time to bring out the record books that chronicle past achievements. Presenting previous good work to others will have a beneficial effect.

22. SATURDAY. Mixed. Time spent with sweethearts or spouses will be especially pleasant. Relationships can be put on a firmer footing, and a much better understanding achieved. Friends that you and your partner share can play a big part in this. Longstanding close acquaintances will be in a position to give some objective and affectionate advice on marital or partnership affairs. Some heavy responsibilities may be placed on you by people you work or live with, which means you have to give up ideas of your own. Your plans for the day may have to be distinctly changed. Take pains to see that activities you share with groups of people cannot be used as ammunition by gossipmongers.

23. SUNDAY. Good. This is another day when time spent in the company of loved ones can be particularly rewarding and enjoyable. Let partners know of the extent of your good feelings toward them. Give all the energy and attention you can to family and partnership affairs. You will be wasting a valuable opportunity if you follow your own pursuits at the expense of time spent with mates. Try to arrange outings or activities that you and your partner can share with mutual friends. Such occasions will be a lot of fun and will lift the spirits of all concerned. If Aquarians are undertaking charitable work, you will probably find that the greatest advances come through team work.

24. MONDAY. Variable. Make sure that you are certain of the motives of government officials before getting involved in any financial activities suggested by them. It is possible that such people are acting in a less than honest way. If you do get tied up in shady dealings, you are probably placing yourself at a disadvantage. When underhanded operations come to light, as they are likely to, your reputation will be blown sky-high. People in authority can have their own gain in mind. Today is good for prying into dark corners and traveling unfrequented paths. Any background research you can do in relation to regular business affairs will pay dividends.

25. TUESDAY. Mixed. Don't allow money to trickle through your fingers as you earn it. And money received as prizes or bequests must not be frittered away. This is the time to give some serious consideration to the best way to invest your capital. Get professional advice on how you can make the most of hard-earned cash. Be diligent in keeping records of expenses and any purchases that may help to offset taxation payments. If you are self-employed, it would be as well to find out from an accountant just what you can include in your list of deductions. When dealing with financial matters connected with regular work, don't overlook details and finer points that could make an important difference.

26. WEDNESDAY. Deceptive. It will be easier to handle events that affect you in distant places. If you have been chewing on an insoluble problem, now is the time to seek expert advice. It would be pointless to continue battling on your own with something that is really beyond your grasp. Don't be surprised if people are getting hold of the wrong end of the stick later on. It is then that misunderstandings are likely to occur. Others will all too easily get the wrong idea about you. You should try to offset this by explaining as fully as possible what you are involved in. This is especially so if you are involved in any form of self-development.

27. THURSDAY. Good. If something that is happening far away is giving you cause for concern, it would be best to turn to a trusted friend for advice. The experience of an older acquaintance may provide you with the insight or comfort that you need. Or people you have known for many years may have valuable information to give you regarding advanced training schemes or higher education. Don't allow your expectations of social events to rise too high. They could flop. But such occasions can add to your knowledge and understanding in unforeseen ways. People you meet, or situations that occur, may help you to see that you have been taking an overly narrow view of life.

28. FRIDAY. Successful. Conditions are particularly beneficial to all study and training activities. Any schemes that broaden your mind or improve your skills and abilities are worth a wholehearted involvement. Once you make a start with such endeavors, you will be surprised at the speedy progress you make. This includes more exotic activities such as meditation and yoga. Any training involving sport or physical exercise will be rewarding. If you have examinations coming up, it will be worth burning the midnight oil. Give as much time and energy as you can to research and revision. Relatives of your spouse or partner are likely to give you active support and encouragement with subjects of special interest.

29. SATURDAY. Fair. You may be in for some shocks where regular employment affairs or commercial dealings are concerned. It may be that Aquarians have bitten off more than they can chew. You can suddenly realize the full extent and weight of the responsibilities you have taken on. It seems that more is involved than was at first apparent. But this is not the time to be cowed by the efforts you are required to make. If you can find sufficient strength and determination to rise to the challenge, you can make a resounding success of the ventures you have undertaken. The financial rewards will fully justify your blood, sweat, and tears. And you will derive great satisfaction from winning out against the odds.

30. SUNDAY. Quiet. The more relaxed conditions today will give you a chance to consider the direction your career is taking. Today is good for establishing a clearer picture of your aims and ambitions and for planning the best course of action to achieve them. You may get invaluable help by discussing these issues with the people around you. Your private contemplations will only take you so far. Others will see your situation in broader perspective. If you arrive at any definite plans, there may be opportunities to begin putting them into operation. Any work you can accomplish today will be to your advantage. A visit to a Sunday market may produce items at reasonable prices that will make good Christmas presents for loved ones.

DECEMBER

1. MONDAY. Disquieting. Aquarians should consider broadening the scope of their social activities. Look around to see what clubs or groups you might like to join in your area. You may at first be reluctant to consider spreading your wings in this way. But it seems you may need to counter a certain tendency to pull back into yourself at the moment. In fact, the possibility of mixing with new people may seem quite daunting to you. But it would be better not to allow timidity to influence your decisions. If you can overcome your fears and suspicions, then you will find that new subjects of interest, new pastimes and people will bring another dimension into your life unimagined heretofore.

2. TUESDAY. Variable. It seems that it is time to break with well-tried and traditional methods in handling business finances. The use of a little imagination will show you new ways to deal with monetary problems or procedures. Don't stick with the old out of laziness of habit. The use of initiative and invention will bring its own rewards, and bring more efficiency into commercial affairs. You may be impelled into action by a desire to put personal finances on a firmer footing. But your drive can make you overinsistent and insensitive where others are concerned. Offset your determination with tact and consideration. Contacting people in the background can bring speedy results.

3. WEDNESDAY. Good. Casting your mind back over past experiences can be very instructive now. You can learn valuable lessons from old mistakes and successes. This will also help you to set your targets for the future and plan the best way to achieve them. You may come to see that your present direction is somewhat off course. It is possible that you will want to make changes in your career situation as a result of taking stock of your present position. Your short-term finances are likely to get a boost from closer contacts with background figures. Any money-making schemes you initiate with the object of funding humanitarian projects have a good chance of success.

4. THURSDAY. Uncertain. You may run into problems concerning business and public affairs that you cannot solve on your own. It is likely that older and more experienced people will be able to provide the necessary advice and insight. The best person to approach is someone who has retired from the same line of business that involves you. The information gained from years on the job cannot be substituted by other sources. Your deep-felt urge to help disadvantaged people may run into some substantial obstacles today. People in powerful positions may set standards that seem impossible to meet. But if you set your mind to it, you should find that these heights are easier to scale than you imagined.

5. FRIDAY. Variable. There may be tensions between you and the people you are closest to. It will be difficult to avoid arguments with loved ones. Differences of opinion over money matters may lie behind the prickly atmosphere. And relations won't get any easier until you can come to terms with family members or partners over financial arrangements. Don't wait for difficulties to go away of their own accord. They must be tackled head-on, and as soon as possible. But this is a good day for Aquarians to make moves that can bring them into contact with new companions. Membership in clubs and societies or the services of a dating agency may provide the outlet you are looking for.

6. SATURDAY. Demanding. Don't rely on others to help you with schemes or activities that are designed to help deprived or underprivileged people. You would do well to go as far as you can on your own when handling charitable and humanitarian projects. You will win others over to your side by your single-minded efforts. People in influential positions will be heartened by your determination to succeed. But nothing will be achieved if you wait for encouragement and support. Show others that you can get on without them. But employers or people in high places may attempt to talk

Aquarians into parting with their hard-earned savings. But you must be convinced that your money is being put to good use before consenting to loans.

7. SUNDAY. Sensitive. You must give money the respect it deserves. Don't throw it around or be too open-handed to those who are in need or asking for loans. Keep spending to a minimum. Avoid extravagant outings and entertainments. But if people are very insistent in their financial demands or cries for help, you should not hesitate to tell a white lie in order to preserve your savings. Don't be pressured into parting with your cash, if it really goes against the grain. Money that is handed over too easily now may be sorely needed in the near future. But close relationships will benefit from small gestures of affection, such as flowers or boxes of chocolates. It is not the present, but the thought that counts.

8. MONDAY. Changeable. Current commercial dealings are likely to go off the rails, throwing business finances into turmoil. This will seem to have grave implications for the personal incomes of Aquarians. Your job may appear to be threatened. But don't get too worked up. Things will seem worse than is in fact the case. There is a good chance that the situation will right itself. It is unlikely that your future security will be affected. Regular business will continue to tick, keeping the money flow on the move. Conditions are good for attempts to reach goals you have set yourself. Ambitions can be realized. You will gain by being in the limelight. Today is good for attracting public attention.

9. TUESDAY. Confusing. It will be a day for being on your guard. You should take what others say with a pinch of salt. Neighbors, in particular, are likely to be less than honest. They may twist the facts to their own advantage. Or it is possible that they are not telling the whole truth. Extra caution is needed while driving. Be especially careful at busy crossroads. Watch out for concealed entrances. Make sure you have a full tank if you are driving long distances. You would do well not to put your trust in new associates until you have made a thorough check of their credentials. It could be that people are not as they appear on the surface. You can be badly let down if you invest your confidence prematurely.

10. WEDNESDAY. Fair. This is no time to keep your spouse or partner in the dark where important changes concerning your work are involved. Let loved ones know exactly what is going on. They should be informed of any outside activities that are likely to have an adverse effect on you. No good will come from trying to protect them, or keep things concealed. If you are involved in projects of a humanitarian or philanthropic nature, much good can come from attempts to bring your efforts to the notice of a wider audience. Don't hesitate to use theatrical means of publicity stunts. A great deal of support can be won at this time. Phone calls can be especially helpful to business activities.

11. THURSDAY. Good. Now is the time to tie up the loose ends of long, drawn-out negotiations. Don't allow discussions to go on endlessly. It is unlikely that anything fresh will be contributed at this stage of the game. If you are an avid collector of such things as antiques, pictures, or stamps, conditions are favorable for adding to your collection. On the other hand, if you are selling valuable articles, you are likely to get a very good price. Take this opportunity to dispense with unwanted family silver or antique furniture. The cash may be a greater asset right now. Today is good for planning romantic evenings at home. Sweethearts will love being wined and dined with soft music and candles.

12. FRIDAY. Variable. You may be pressured by loved ones into going at a faster pace than really suits you. They are likely to encourage you to act before you have prepared the ground sufficiently. It could be that others are thinking much more of themselves than of you achieving a successful outcome. You will have to put a stop to partners or spouses projecting their ambitions onto you. You must take your time and act only when you are ready. Conditions are favorable for the buying and selling of houses. If you are looking for a new residence, you should give as much time

13. SATURDAY. Quiet. The day will go by at a very easy pace. The minimum of demands or pressures will be placed upon you. You should be able to relax at home, doing nothing in particular. You will have plenty of time to attend to household jobs and repairs. If you are feeling energetic, you could tidy up the closet or the loft. If you are digging around in dark corners, it is likely that you will come upon old photographs or diaries. These may jolt old memories and prompt some sentimental feelings. You may find yourself hankering for the old times. But time spent with family members can be delightful and can strengthen the links of affection.

14. SUNDAY. Disappointing. You may be better off keeping your plans for leisure or recreation to yourself. Friends, in particular, may try to elbow their way into your arrangements and spoil your enjoyment. Or they may try to dissuade you from visiting places or doing things you have set your heart on. If you end up going along with their plans you are likely to have a miserable day. Your friends and your sweetheart will not make a successful combination either. Nobody will have very much to say. An embarrassed silence can settle on your gathering. If you are involved in group or club affairs, the organizers may ask you to take on some unusual responsibilities in the organization.

15. MONDAY. Disturbing. It is a day for playing it safe in money matters. Any commercial operations that involve a high risk of loss should be avoided. Financial gambles and playing the cards or horses should be left to a time when fortune is running with you. It is unwise to give in to the urge to take even small bets. Once you have started, it will be difficult to call a halt. Give long and careful consideration to any business financial moves before you make them. Hasty actions will lead to mistakes, which can in turn result in heavy losses. Make every attempt to keep your friends and your money apart. If they come together in any way, quarrels are almost certain to break out.

16. TUESDAY. Untroubled. Aquarian lovers are likely to be on a cloud of delight today. Sweethearts can appear to be the center of the universe. With general conditions rather quiet, it should be easier to arrange to spend more time with loved ones. Single Aquarians may have better luck in finding attractive partners. Today is good for making dates with people you have taken a fancy to. Outings with romantic companions will be pleasurable. With pressures off you at work, you may also be able to give more time to creative activities. All work connected with arts and crafts will be satisfying. Working in peaceful surroundings on favorite pastimes or hobbies will be most rewarding.

17. WEDNESDAY. Good. Aquarians may be in a sprightly and efficient frame of mind, but you should not overlook the emotional side of the people you either work with or for. A smile and a friendly gesture will do much to put others at ease. If you keep your nose too close to the grindstone and become a bit machinelike yourself, fellow workers may become rather resentful. Don't be too heavy-handed if asking superiors for favors. A little charm will go a long way. You should try to be more aware of the image you are projecting to the world and the impression you make on others. Don't assume that people know how you are feeling. Today is a good day to put in some overtime. Rewards can be substantial.

18. THURSDAY. Misleading. This could be the time to take a chance with a risky venture. If a project seems to offer the possibility of quick and substantial returns, give it a fling. Nothing is assured, but fortune is likely to be with you. But the element of risk should strike a slight note of caution. You should not stick your neck out too far. There must be a limit to your optimism. And don't neglect your routine business activities. Try to catch up on any work that has been left undone. Don't allow backlogs to increase in size. In your spare time, it would be advisable not to take on strenuous activities. Give your mind and body a rest. Take every opportunity to relax. If there are none, create one.

19. FRIDAY. Disquieting. You will cover more ground in business activities by teaming up with others than by pushing ahead on your own. This is not to say that you should give up your personal drive or cease to strive toward goals you have set yourself. But working with and for others can bring unforeseen benefits that can be greatly to the advantage of your professional aspirations. And these should be kept in the forefront of your mind. Don't allow the hurly-burly of group business affairs to push your real interests into the background. Associates may even go so far as to exert pressure on you to give up your grand ideas. But any coercion must be resisted in all instances.

20. SATURDAY. Variable. It may be difficult to avoid domestic tensions. Partners won't be seeing eye-to-eye with you on family matters. You may try to bridge the communication gap, but the gulf is likely to open wider. A visit to mutual friends may provide a solution to this impasse. If they can avoid taking sides, old acquaintances will provide the ground for a common understanding. But you must keep an eye on expenses if you are planning social activities or visits to places of entertainment. And there may be drains on your pocketbook from other, less obvious quarters. You may, for example, be asked to contribute to a so-called humanitarian project. You must check to see that there is no trickery involved.

21. SUNDAY. Mixed. This is a good time for trying to contact employers or people in powerful positions outside working hours. Meeting them in informal surroundings or entertaining them in your own home can have very beneficial results for you. It will be easier to broach a subject that is on your mind, in this way, than in professional or working circumstances. But before any contact with superiors or influential people, Aquarians should ensure that they are absolutely aware of all the facts pertaining to their case. Do as much background research as possible. Don't take the money-making schemes of your friends too seriously. They won't hold much water and would probably lead to losses.

22. MONDAY. Difficult. This is not the time to beat about the bush in employment affairs. Aquarians may have to move swiftly if they are to make the most of the opportunities offered. Or if your job is threatened, you should not simply wait for the axe to fall. You must take positive steps to try to secure your position. Your actions could well influence the decisions of employers. If pressure is on you to repay money that is owed, you must refrain from dipping into joint funds in order to do the paying back. Those of you who are involved in love affairs can expect some delightful experiences in the company of loved ones. Don't take anything for granted if you are calling on your bank manager.

23. TUESDAY. Confusing. Successes and failures can follow each other in rapid succession in commercial dealings. The swing of the financial pendulum may leave Aquarians in a rather dizzy state. It may be very difficult to know just what is the best move to make. And the confused state of business finances may put you in a quandary where taxation affairs are concerned. Get professional advice on these matters as soon as possible. With events so much up in the air, you may feel it necessary to take out additional insurance policies to cover unforeseen circumstances. If you are hot on the trail of someone or something, you would do better to follow your own nose than listen to the advice of friends.

24. WEDNESDAY. Deceptive. Aquarians need to look facts squarely in the face now. You cannot afford to deceive yourself. Don't take for granted that the course you have chosen is the correct one. Be ready to make some readjustments. If you are involved in self-improvement endeavors, you should step back and examine your motives, or the particular line of activity or discipline you are following. It is possible that you are wasting your time and only kidding yourself into believing in the importance of your pursuits. The dreamy side of the Aquarian nature is likely to come to the forefront. It may be difficult to keep your attention fixed.

25. THURSDAY. Merry Christmas. Needless to say, this is no time for being on your own. Even if you have an urge to be apart from others, you should make the effort to spend a part of the day with family or friends. More can come from attending parties or social gatherings than you would imagine. They may not be the dull family occasions you are expecting. In fact, you are likely to meet people whose ideas are not so far removed from your own. New acquaintances can stimulate you with talk of ideas for social change, and humanitarian principles. Your contact with a kindred spirit may be the start of a blossoming new friendship. This is bound to make the day a special one for you this festive holiday season.

26. FRIDAY. Fair. It will be easier to bring information concerning your work for charity before a wider section of the public. Your efforts are likely to win support and approval. Aquarians will derive a deep sense of personal satisfaction from the recognition they receive. And all the publicity you can earn will make future humanitarian acts that much easier to accomplish. Help can come in professional matters from people in background positions. It can be to your advantage in business affairs to contact people in out-of-the-way places. Today is not the best day for dealing with directors or managers. Older people may have useful information for you.

27. SATURDAY. Satisfactory. Time spent with sweethearts and partners will be trouble-free and happy. It is likely that your financial situation will be healthy, and that you won't feel constricted in money matters. This means you can spend a little more on outings and entertainments shared with loved ones. You can have a good time without having to count the pennies. If you are advertising your products, services, or activities, make sure you use well-designed and attractive publicity. It is worth getting a really good job done, as advertising can have especially profitable results now. You may have trouble in getting answers out of important people.

28. SUNDAY. Easygoing. There won't be a lot going on today. But friends will make good companions. It is possible that you will make new friends through existing ones. This is also a good time to look back over the last year and remember all the new people you have met. You may feel like renewing contact with those you have most liked if you have not seen them for a while. A New Year's card may be sufficient. Or you may want to arrange a get-together. Time given to organized recreational activities will be enjoyable. But you should not put new plans concerning clubs or groups into operation yet. The day does not carry enough momentum to get new schemes off to a good start.

29. MONDAY. Disturbing. You may have to help out a friend who is suffering with a health problem. This can mean giving up spare-time activities and leisure pursuits. If others call on you to return a good deed they have done you in the past, go to their aid, by all means. But don't get drawn into their life and circumstances to an unnecessary degree. Keep your generosity within bounds. There is no need to let others use you as a doormat. It may be difficult to measure good deed against good deed, but you must be alive to the possibility of exploitation. Aquarian shoppers can have a ball today. Today is good for stocking up larders emptied during the festivities. A round of end-of-year sales produces some excellent buys.

30. TUESDAY. Confusing. Today is a day for holding your horses. Don't rush in where angels fear to tread. Give yourself plenty of time to consider all aspects of new ventures before committing yourself to action. You would do well to dig beneath the surface of any new propositions that are put to you. People and situations will be wearing a deceptive face. Be clear and precise in all your communications. Don't leave any room for doubt. People will only too easily misinterpret what you say. Pass on all messages in person. Today is good for contacting long-lost friends, or acquaintances who have been abroad. You visit people today.

31. WEDNESDAY. Good. You should see the year out on a rather secretive note. Don't pass on more information than is strictly necessary. Play your cards close to the vest. You will retain the advantage by keeping others in the dark. Don't allow competitors to steal a march on you because you could not resist spilling the beans. Don't be conned into revealing too much out of misplaced justice. Others will be ready to exploit whatever leads you give them. There won't be much justice once the cat has been let out of the bag. And it is work done away from the public eye that can reel in the profits. Give loved ones the consideration they deserve.

How well do you know yourself?

This horoscope gives you answers to these questions based on your exact time and place of birth...

How do others see you?
What is your greatest strength?
What are your life purposes?
What drives motivate you?
How do you think?
Are you a loving person?
How competitive are you?
What are your ideals?
How religious are you?
Can you take responsibility?
How creative are you?
How do you handle money?
How do you express yourself?
What career is best for you?
How will you be remembered?
Who are your real friends?
What are you hiding?

Many people are out of touch with their real selves. Some can't get ahead professionally because they are doing the wrong kind of work. Others lack self-confidence because they're trying to be someone they're not. Others are unsuccessful in love because they use the wrong approach with the wrong people. Astrology has helped hundreds of people with problems like these by showing them their real strengths, their real opportunities, their real selves.

You are a unique individual. Since the world began, there has never been anyone exactly like you. Sun-sign astrology, the kind you see in newspapers and magazines, is all right as far as it goes. But it treats you as if you were just the same as millions of others who have the same Sun sign because their birthdays are close to yours. A true astrological reading of your character and personality has to be one of a kind, unlike any other. It has to be based on exact date, time, longitude and latitude of your birth. Only a big IBM computer like the one that Para Research uses can handle the trillions of possibilities.

A Unique Document Your Astral Portrait includes your complete chart with planetary positions and house cusps calculated to the nearest minute of arc, all planetary aspects with orbs and intensities, plus text explaining the meaning of:
★ Your particular combination of Sun and Moon signs.
★ Your Ascendant sign and the house position of its ruling planet. (Many computer horoscopes omit this because it requires exact birth data.)
★ The planets influencing all twelve houses in your chart.
★ Your planetary aspects.

Others Tell Us "I found the Astral Portrait to be the best horoscope I've ever read."—E.D., Los Angeles, CA
"I could not put it down until I'd read every word... It is like you've been looking over my shoulder since I arrived in this world!"—B.N.L., Redding, CA
"I recommend the Astral Portrait. It even surpasses many of the readings done by professional astrologers."
—J.B., Bristol, CT

Low Price There is no substitute for a personal conference with an astrologer, but a good astrologer charges $50 and up for a complete chart reading. Some who have rich clients get $200 and more. Your Astral Portrait is an analysis of your character written by some of the world's foremost astrologers, and you can have it not for $200 or $50 but for only $22. This is possible because the text of your Astral Portrait is already written. You pay only for the cost of putting your birth information into the computer, compiling one copy, checking it and sending it to you within two weeks.

Permanence Ordinarily, you leave as astrologer's office with only a memory. Your Astral Portrait is a thirty-five-page, fifteen-thousand-word, permanently bound book that you can read again and again for years.

Money-Back Guarantee Our guarantee is unconditional. That means you can return your Astral Portrait at any time for any reason and get a full refund of the purchase price. That means we take all the risk, not you!

You Hold the Key The secrets of your inner character and personality, your real self, are locked in the memory of the computer. You alone hold the key: your time and place of birth. Fill in the coupon below and send it to the address shown with $22. Don't put it off. Do it now while you're thinking of it. Your Astral Portrait is waiting for you.
© 1980 Para Research, Inc.

Para Research, Dept. MT P.O. Box 61, Gloucester, Massachusetts 01930 I want to read about my real self. Please send me my Astral Portrait. I understand that if I am not completely satisfied, I can return it for a full refund. ☐ I enclose $22 plus 1.50 for shipping and handling. ☐ Charge $23.50 to my Master Card account. ☐ Charge $23.50 to my VISA account.

Card number		Good through Mo.	Day	Yr.
Mr/Ms		*Birthdate Mo.	Day	Yr.
Address		Birthtime (within an hour)		AM/PM
City		Birthplace City		
State	Zip	State	County	

NOTES

NOTES

NOTES

ENRICH YOUR LIFE THROUGH SELF-UNDERSTANDING!
AstroAnalysis — 12 Volumes

AstroAnalysis is a perpetual astrological guide that will provide you with comprehensive, revealing astrological information — *without symbols, calculations, or guesswork!* You can chart your own professional-quality horoscope and open the doors to a fuller, more rewarding life. Easy-to-read Planet Tables, updated from 1910 to 1999, show the positions of all ten planets every day, revealing their influence on *your* destiny. These handsome 8⅛" x 10¾", 256-page paperback volumes hold the key to a richer, more meaningful future.

ONLY $8.95 (plus postage and handling).
Please indicate which sign(s) you would like:

___ 441-03256-7	**Aries**	___ 441-03262-1	**Libra**
___ 441-03257-5	**Taurus**	___ 441-03263-X	**Scorpio**
___ 441-03258-3	**Gemini**	___ 441-03264-8	**Sagittarius**
___ 441-03259-1	**Cancer**	___ 441-03265-6	**Capricorn**
___ 441-03260-5	**Leo**	___ 441-03266-4	**Aquarius**
___ 441-03261-3	**Virgo**	___ 441-03267-2	**Pisces**

(On sale October '86)

Available at your local bookstore or return this form to

BERKLEY
THE BERKLEY PUBLISHING GROUP, Dept. B
390 Murray Hill Parkway, East Rutherford, NJ 07073

Please send me the titles checked above. I enclose _____. Include $1.00 for postage and handling if one book is ordered; add 25¢ per book for two or more not to exceed $1.75. California, Illinois, New Jersey and Tennessee residents please add sales tax. Prices subject to change without notice and may be higher in Canada.

NAME _____
ADDRESS _____
CITY _____ STATE/ZIP _____
(Allow six weeks for delivery.)

NOTES

NOTES

A Startling Record of Prophecies Come True...

MARGUERITE CARTER

...dramatic proof of an ability to bring great help to YOU...

People nationwide have read predictions by this extraordinary woman for over forty years and seen astonishing verifications in the headlines: the **conflicts in India, Vietnam, Israel, Egypt, Haiti;** the **termination of careers of world leaders John Kennedy, Khrushchev, Andropov, Brezhnev;** the **rise, fall and return of Nixon.** In recent years, readers of her special annual **forecast** knew in advance of higher insurance and medical costs, bank failures, the Italian pro-divorce vote, double digit inflation and . . . **no bankruptcy for New York City!** Marguerite Carter's amazing prophecies concerning world affairs date back to the war years when newspapers reported such predictions as: Her marking the end of world War II three years in advance . . . she described Mussolini's downfall . . . Hitler's suicide . . . two and a half years before the events occurred!

Now she says of the year ahead: "In spite of the dire predictions of current 'authorities' we will not suffer a repeat of the '29 stock market crash and its aftermath! . . . I expect an escalation of peace talks and increasing concern over trade agreements in the midst of terrorist activity." **Further, she says we will experience** "a return of student demonstrations as in the 60's, but with the **emphasis on world peace.** These actions will powerfully impact our society in ways totally unexpected and never before experienced."

A lifetime of dedicated study and astrological counseling have culminated in **Miss Carter's Unitology Forecast,** compiled for the individual's birthdate. This guidance, written with warmth and understanding, has proved of great value to the many thousands of clients who have written her, year after year.

The rare qualities of sincerity and dedication to her work have drawn those who seek a better way of life. **Her Forecast with Special Notations** contains the guidance that can open the door to a bright, new future, covering outstanding indications of changes in your home life, associations with others, financial outlook and opportunities.

TEST HER! Send for Marguerite Carter's UNITOLOGY FORECAST with SPECIAL NOTATIONS individually prepared for your birthdate. Print: month, day, year, place, hour of birth (if known) and include $9.95 plus $1.30, toward postage and handling, ($11.25 total) in U.S. funds only. Allow 4 to 6 weeks for careful completion and prompt delivery.
MARGUERITE CARTER, Box 807, Dept. S-7,   Indianapolis, IN 46206